FULLNESS

A MEMOIR

AZURE MOYNA

Published by M & A
moynaassociates.com

ISBN: 978-1-7347460-1-3 (pbk.)
ISBN: 978-1-7347460-4-4 (hc.)
ISBN: 978-1-7347460-0-6 (e-bk)
ISBN: 978-1-7347460-3-7 (aud.)

Cover design: Miladinka Milic, Anastasia MacGillivray
Page design: Catherine Williams, Chapter One Book Production, UK

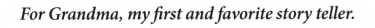

For Grandma, my first and favorite story teller.

FOREWORD

This book contains an accounting based on my memory. Memory, like most things, is not an exact science, but I have captured the events of my life with as much accuracy and specificity as my memory allows. The names of most characters have been changed to protect their privacy. All characters are based on real people and in a couple of cases are blends of two or more real people to avoid reader confusion. Thank you for allowing me to share my memory with you.

Painting by Ashley Claure

1
JALAPEÑO CORN CASSEROLE

Mmmm! I gleefully assembled the ingredients for jalapeño corn casserole on the grey tiled countertop. I was in charge of the side dishes and Sean, the meat. We hadn't been married or in the house that long and I wanted the day to go perfectly. Everyone would arrive pretty soon and I had to get the casserole in the oven and then commence the mad-dash clean—you know, where you're not actually a particularly clean or organized person but you want people to *think* you are, so you throw a bunch of crap into a closet and thrust your body against it like the lid on over-full luggage and pray that no one touches the spring-loaded door handle and gets buried in an avalanche of crap? Well, I was going to do that, then wow our guests with this amazing dish to go with the pulled pork my husband was cooking in the smoker I had gotten him for Christmas.

A coworker of mine had brought jalapeño corn casserole to a holiday potluck a couple of years back. Its sweetness, spiciness, and creaminess, like a carnival treat, had sent me into eye-rolling euphoria and sparked the internal struggle: *I just have to have this recipe... or maybe I shouldn't know how to cook it... oh what the hell!* Of course, I would

3

be the one to ask how to make the most fattening thing there, every bit the fat girl of the office. It was the simplest recipe in the world—a couple cans of corn, a stick of butter, a block of cream cheese, and a few jalapeño slices mixed together and baked at 350° until golden brown spots formed on top. I mixed the ingredients now in my largest casserole dish, sextupled to accommodate the number of guests we were expecting. I exclaimed internally with delight, *So much butter! So much cream cheese!* I practically clapped my jolly hands together. This would certainly be a dish made with love because I *loved* butter and cream cheese. Once I smoothed the surface and resisted the temptation of licking the spoon, I gingerly placed the casserole dish in the pre-heated oven. I loved how when I was with food time slowed for a few moments, life felt less full of stress, and the world was simpler. Once the oven door closed, however, time went back to its standard mortal state and I went back to frantically cleaning.

This was our first house, ideal for entertaining even if the kitchen was in desperate need of remodeling. The house had lots of rooms for guests and maybe one day our own family. I wanted our friends to love it and be impressed with it, to be so happy for us and to feel right at home the way people always felt at my grandma's house. More than them loving it, I wanted *him*, my father, to be impressed with it, to see how much we worked for every one of the six bedrooms. I wanted him to see that the house was surrounded by Ansel-Adams-worthy oak trees and that we had deer that frequented our property, just like he did. Surely if those were things he bragged about his own house, he would find them respectable in mine, I thought, I wondered, I hoped. Sure, Tehachapi wasn't the Bay Area, but it was a charming town and there was something to be said for a quieter pace of life amidst the golden hills, the windmills, and the four seasons—actual snow in the winter, something I had never before experienced, being a native Californian. But none of that would happen today, since there was no way he would ever come to my housewarming party. Our friends would be here any minute and I didn't have time to go down the rabbit hole of thoughts about my father.

Not as clean as I would have liked, but at least the clutter is out of sight. Ready or not, it's time to get dressed unless I want to face everyone in sweatpants.

The single light bulb hanging at the end of the chain only dimly illuminated my clothes. I sighed because I now had to discern what would fit on my body, which seemed to be growing by the day. I grabbed a pair of jeans, a camisole and a brewery shirt to wear over it, my go-to casual outfit. Otherwise, I mostly wore skirts to the office for their comfort and size forgiving nature and wore workout clothes at home. It had been a little while since I had worn my jeans, and even just having my legs in to the calves I could tell by their snugness that I had not been good. *Please don't be too small.* I pulled them up with a little leap. Over the years many a pair of jeans had stopped at my thighs, unwilling and unable to climb the mountain range that were my hips and butt. These didn't refuse to pass but did require jumping up and down to coax them off the peaks. I felt something give way in my grip and saw that I'd snapped a belt loop. *Shit!* The jeans were already cutting into my stomach and crotch but I had a plan to be able to breathe and avoid a urinary tract infection- to not sit down the entire evening. I rigged the remaining belt loops to make the pants ride higher than the skinniest part of my waist. I wanted the pants to cage in my wild gut instead of letting it buck out like it wanted to. *Just don't breathe in too deeply.* Once my belly fat was adequately tucked in, I covered it with a camisole and pulled the tight T-shirt over my head.

When the doorbell rang I didn't feel ready, but I never did. First to arrive were Blair and Jason, friends we would want to show our best foot forward when hosting. Next, Adam and Erin, our best friends, whom Sean and I lived with briefly before getting our first place. Of everyone, they were the ones we needed to clean house for the least. Then Gemma and her tween daughter and a few other friends, their kids, and a couple coworkers. With every arrival, my stomach fluttered as I sucked it in and studied their eyes for visible signs that they were shocked at my weight. I had gained fifty pounds since my wedding several months back. I was sure they must have noticed but they had excellent poker faces while they approached me (but, I imagined, were making concerned, wincing faces over my shoulder when hugging me).

As each couple arrived, the men filed outside to the smoker, Sean, and the beer, and the women stayed in the kitchen with me for girl chat, while the kids ran to one of the rooms to watch TV and play. I put on my best smile and welcomed everyone and declined offers of help in the kitchen. I could hear the muffled laughter and the clinks of glasses outside and could smell the mouthwatering aroma from the smoker every time the back door opened. Blair, Erin, and Gemma sat with me at the bar, while I placed bowls of chips and dips before them. As always, the conversation quickly transitioned from "what can I get you to drink?" to "how's work" to "how are things with fill-in-the-blank boyfriend or husband."

We were spokes on a wheel with Erin at the center, the one who introduced us all. None of us were as good friends with one another as we each were with Erin individually. Erin was a Minnesota blonde, saying things like "uff-da" and "you betcha" in her accent. She was naturally very pretty with light aqua eyes to match her other Nordic features. She was one of the guys though, casual and tomboyish in style, and liked to drink beer and camp and fish. Blair was much more feminine, the girl-iest in our group with me a distant second. She was the type of girl who pulled you onto the dance floor and was simply unembarrassed when in celebration mode. Gemma was a single mom with a slightly raspy voice and though a little hardened on the exterior, was fiercely loyal and tender-hearted. I loved hanging out with the girls. There was an effortless comfort and sense of belonging when I was with them, even though in many ways I was the softest one in the group in terms of life experience, being a college girl and not a recovering addict or single mom or both. What we did all have in common was that we were a bunch of grown kids, trying to prove we had outgrown our pasts in one way or another—that, and dieting.

I had done Weight Watchers with Blair and Erin (their first time, my third). It had been successful for them, they'd both kept off those stubborn twenty and thirty-five pounds, respectively, or at least only regained five pounds of it, but not for me. I had reasoned that my body was just over it and refusing to budge after losing eighty pounds in six months and then regaining every one multiple times on the weight loss roller coaster. I perhaps unfairly believed that they had it easy because they had gained a little weight once in their lives, whereas I had gone up and down forever. I had also done a medically assisted weight loss program with Blair last spring, getting injections in our butts and drinking terrible, dehydrated, gag-inducing shakes. Meanwhile, Gemma was the type of party girl who still looked great, both body and face, even after many late nights.

Blair waved her wine glass dangerously and said, "I've been trying this thing where I don't drink coffee creamer and I eat only vegetables before noon."

"Wait, tell me precisely what you're eating, I wanna try this," I said, mental notepad at the ready as always, excited to try anything, especially if there was a partner involved.

Blair talked in excruciating detail about the wrap she would make herself with one low-point fake tortilla stuffed with so many vegetables it would not stay closed in the Tupperware she brought to work for lunch. Blair flipped her silky dark curls over her shoulder as she spoke. "And then I sprinkle with raw shredded zucchini, which looks a little like cheese—"

I took mental notes along with Erin and swallowed my envy at Blair's discipline down with my beer. *Why can't you be more like that? That is why she looks the way she does and you look the way you do. She is a person in control and you... you are just a hot mess, an Anti-Blair.*

Gemma, a bit bored, meanwhile lifted her shirt and squeezed her stomach around her belly button and said, "I bring a bagel to work." It did kind of look like a bagel, which only made me want to eat one. "It's time to do my chicken and vegetables again," she added. *An everything bagel toasted with extra cream cheese.* Gemma didn't diet and so weight loss wasn't charged and didn't make her crazy, unlike the rest of us, especially me being a food issues girl. When Gemma got to her upper control limit, she simply reined it in until her weight was back to middle of her comfortable range. It was because she was an accountant, I reasoned, that she was able to approach this with such logical sense and, even more annoying, with ease.

Even though I laughed and commiserated with all of them, us all considering ourselves to be fat, they all had something I did not - bodies that were at least considered normal.

When the oven chimed to let me know that the casserole was done, I knelt down over it, pretending to still be engaged in our conversation, but really taking in the ooey-gooey smell and gazing down at the dish like a newborn child. *You look and smell so good and I cannot wait to eat you* I told it silently before setting it on the counter to cool.

The back door swung open. "Hey, Babe?" Sean called tenderly over the blare of the suddenly louder punk rock music. He strolled into the kitchen wafting the smell of barbecue and cigar smoke in that effortless way he always did, not a care in the world. Sean and I moved so differently. He had such ease about him, while I moved in a nervous, self-conscious and urgent pace, as if people were waiting on me.

He was in full celebration mode, pumped and extra happy as always when the guys were over. Friends always brought out the most vibrant side of him. Seeing my husband reminded me just how good looking he was, with his half-Filipino skin, chocolate eyes, square jaw and black hair. He wore a hat with a logo of a rat with cross bones on it, a red shirt with Santa Cruz written on it, and skater shorts. *How the hell did I land such a cute guy?* Had I known him in high school, I would've had the hugest crush on him, as I still did even now. In fact, Sean was the guy who followed through on plans I had originally made with my high school boyfriend - creating a life of our own far away from my father, supported only by our love for one another and our willingness to work harder than everybody else. I loved him for it. I loved him for loving me. Even so, there was something off that Gemma had even pointed out when I first met her, telling me "there is no way a girl like you is Sean Moyna's wife."

"Can you hand me a plate for the pork?" Sean asked.

"Sure," I said, and smiled.

I retrieved the big white platter with a turkey on it—*it'll have to do.* Sean pecked me on the lips as I gave it to him. I could feel the wetness on his goatee and smell the beer, but only minded a little. I knew he loved me and yet I also knew our marriage looked so different than I thought it would. He now worked out of town Monday through Friday, sometimes even Saturday, and we only saw each other on weekends, or what was left of them. I felt lonely, much lonelier than I ever imagined I'd feel when I was married, and it wasn't only because he was gone during the week.

You brought this upon yourself! Indeed, it seemed that my prove-self workaholism had been a relationship transmitted disease that Sean contracted from me big time. He went from being content and comfortable and home every night at his last company to hungry and aspirational and traveling to high profile construction projects at his current company. And it had all been because of my coaching, more like coaxing, as I urged him to stretch himself in his career to rise to his full potential.

The back door swung open again and Sean appeared with a huge slab of meat on the white platter, which he placed on the counter and wrapped with foil to rest.

I created a buffet where the women had been sitting. A stack of plates, napkins, forks, and knives sticking up from a glass, a bowl of Hawaiian sweet rolls, a salad with broccoli, bacon and sunflower seeds, the jalapeño corn casserole, barbecue sauce and the pork butt which we pulled apart with tools that look like bear claws. I peeked my head out the back door and called to the men that dinner was ready. As they filed in to dish up, I asked Sean to turn down the music since the neighbors probably didn't appreciate the volume. He made the endearing "oops" face he always made when I reminded him that he was inadvertently doing something impolite. Sean always meant well, just sometimes he had to be reminded.

"Don't be shy, everyone!" I instructed the group congregating in my kitchen. "Go ahead and dish up!"

"Dude, you are the grill master," Adam told Sean, as he whacked him on the back before turning to me and adding, "Really, good casserole Azure."

"What is it?" asked Gemma.

It had that mysterious look about it that all casseroles do except the familiar Thanksgiving green bean variety. "Cream cheese, butter, corn and jalapeños," I answered trying to keep the nervous giggle out of my voice. "Just smell it, isn't it great?!" My mouth watered at just the thought. I noticed most of the women's eyes fill with anxiety. "Can we get it with more fat please?" Gemma asked. "Perhaps add some bacon or lard?" I laughed along with everyone else, though my face seared red hot with embarrassment. I could always count on the guys, though, to get me when it came to food, enjoying things like greasy burgers and cheese laden casseroles like the one they dished up mounds of now.

"Azure, this corn is so good!" Jason, Blair's husband, complimented.

"Thank you!" I said, and gleamed the way parents do when strangers confirm that their children are beautiful.

The guys quickly made their way into the back yard with their plates.

Erin spooned onto her plate a smaller portion of the jalapeño corn than I could tell she really wanted. She added bread. I noticed her eyes twinkling in a way that was familiar to me as the creamy corn tickled her Midwestern taste buds. Gemma dished up everything too but took even smaller portions. Blair, the most diet adhering of all of us, spooned the salad and pork, no roll, no casserole. I wasn't aware of how fixed my stare was on their plates until Blair surprised me by staring back.

"I'm sure it's amazing, Honey, but I'm low on points," she told me. "I can't get away with it."

"Oh yeah, no worries, I totally understand!" I said, trying to look and feel genuine even with the thoughts that ran through my head: *Well, I see you're still drinking.* I was always baffled whenever anyone would rather drink calories than eat them. *I clearly don't have a body that can "get away with" eating this either, so are you trying to imply that I shouldn't eat like this? Not that I eat like this every day, anyway! And for your information, this casserole is so good that it is worth blowing a diet, as far as I'm concerned.*

I took a deep breath and let it out. *Oh geez, Azure, don't take it out on them!* As usual, I thought one thing and did—nothing. Or at least I tried to do nothing. While actresses try to evoke emotion that they aren't actually feeling in real life, I did the complete opposite- feeling passionately, showing nothing. I always wondered how effective I was at it. Did I have tells the way poker players did and that others picked up on? I assumed the way my eyes darted to avoid contact was my tell, though no one ever seemed to notice.

"Aren't you going to eat?" Erin asked.

"Oh, not now," I responded, "after all that meal prep, I'm not hungry. I'll eat later." The truth was that I was starving but hated eating in front of people in that state. I feared they could read my animalistic hunger by the way I shoveled food into my gullet, even when I deliberately focused on eating slowly and delicately in an attempt to appear normal.

We chatted about annoyances at work, concerts we had been to recently, continued with dieting woes and Erin instilled hope by talking about the Shaun T Insanity workout program, which she had been following.

I watched as one by one, the women brought their plates to the garbage and scraped off any leftovers. I noted Erin ate all of her casserole, but the others had hardly touched their already very small portions. I knew why. I tried my best to not take their self-restraint as a personal offense. I understood that butter and cream cheese were not on most diet plans, but it secretly gnawed at me. What I hated even more than my friends turning down the casserole as too rich were the guys and kids who were dishing up seconds, thirds. *I want some,* I whined like a toddler inside my head. *Will there be enough left for me? I made it after all!*

God, Azure, why do you do this? I made it for people because I wanted them to love it too, but now I'm irritated that they are eating it? You're freaking crazy!

I mingled at the party keenly aware that feeling jealous of those for whom the casserole was intended was like a mistress being jealous of affection her lover gives his wife. It was like an affair, as I stole glances at the casserole throughout the rest of the day, longing for that time alone with it, accompanied by subsequent feelings of shame. In front of the bathroom mirror, I chastised myself. *How disgraceful! What if people knew this is how I actually felt? Then they'll know what a mess you really are.*

When I came back out from the bathroom, Blair and Erin were standing there waiting to hug me goodbye. I hugged them and took in their shampoo and perfume smells. I felt lonely already seeing them go and relieved to be one step closer to being alone so I could eat. Eventually, Sean and I were saying our last thank yous to the compliments on the new house and calling our last drive safelies.

With a click of the door, off into the kitchen I went. I dished myself up a big bowl of the casserole and stuck it in the microwave. I moved about, unable to keep still waiting for it, a potty-dance of sorts. When it was done, I plopped myself onto the couch to shovel a few large spoonfuls into my mouth.

"Ah," I audibly sighed like a smoker taking their first drag after a trans-Atlantic flight. *You know what would make this even better? Sweatpants!* I broke contact with the casserole long enough to go to the bedroom to change. It felt like my stomach and hips exploded out of my jeans when I unzipped them, the way Pillsbury dough pops out of the cylinder. Pulling on sweatpants was like spreading a nice fluffy layer of cream cheese frosting on top. I shuffled back to the living room, switched the light off and the TV on, and settled myself in.

"Hey, Babe?" Sean walked in wearing only boxers.

"Yeah, Babe?" I answered, trying to look natural with my big bowl of casserole.

"I'm gonna head to bed."

"You okay?" I was nervous he was annoyed I was eating, but thought better of explaining that this was the first time I was eating all day. *Don't draw attention to yourself, Azure.*

12

"Yeah," he said, "just tired."

I could tell he was. "Me too," I said, and nodded. "Did you have fun?"

"Yeah." He smiled. "You?"

"Yeah, even though it felt like non-stop work." I laughed.

"You are a great hostess, you take such good care of everyone."

I radiated the pride that I imagined my grandma would have felt to hear me characterized as a good hostess.

He knelt over and gave me a buzzed, sloppy kiss.

"Goodnight, Babe," he said as he turned and shuffled to the bedroom.

"Goodnight."

Alone again. You could ask him to stay. No, what I want right now is food. How is it possible to want someone desperately to stay with you but for them also to hurry up and leave you alone so you can get back to the naughty thing you are doing?

A while later and full, I had at least moved into the bedroom after leaving my unwashed dish in the sink and empty beer bottle on the counter. *I'll deal with that tomorrow.* Though trying to distract myself, all I could think about was the casserole. *I want more. No, just have some tomorrow like a normal person. But it's in there! It needs to be gone so I can get back on track.* Sean's eyes were closed and he was blissfully unaware of the battle going on right beside him. *It needs to go*, I tormented myself. *Maybe I could just throw it in the garbage. Oh yeah, right, you know that the only way for it to go is through you.* I gently placed my hand on Sean' side to gauge how asleep he was. He rustled. *Crap! Azure, just go to sleep and have more tomorrow. No! It's bothering me! Ugh, hurry up, Sean!* Frustrated, I tuned back in to the murder investigation program on TV, trying to drown out the deafening internal struggle.

What felt like hours later, when Sean didn't move when I touched him, I pranced to the kitchen. *Why don't things other than food make me this excited?* This time I didn't even bother with a bowl, I just pulled back the cellophane and started eating straight out of the baking dish while still in the fridge, as if the casserole and I were lovers who couldn't even get inside the door before tearing each other's clothes off. After a few bites, the passion had subsided to the point where I could at least make my way into the living room and plop back into my well-grooved spot. Together at last, Jalapeño Corn Casserole and I cuddled and binged in total rapture. The subtle baked-in heat of the jalapeños, the velvety quality of the cream cheese, the richness of the butter, against the sweet pops of juicy corn, I loved it all.

Of course, with every little creak or knock that houses normally make at night, my reflexes sent the casserole dish beside me between my leg and the back of the couch. *Sean mustn't see.* Then when I was convinced the coast was clear, and Sean was not coming to bust me, I retrieved it and returned to eating. Truthfully, I would have rather had someone walk in on me having sex, masturbating, pooping, all three, than one of my "food things." These were the most vulnerable, raw and primal moments I ever engaged in. This pattern continued: rapture, paranoia, rapture, paranoia, rapture, paranoi-ahhhhhhh so full. So full and so comatose. I nuzzled even more into the couch, completely relaxed. More than fullness, this was the feeling I was truly after and I would float in this numbed state for as long as possible.

Some indeterminate amount of time later, the buzz started to wear off and I decided it was time to get up and get to bed. So full, so very full. My body did something between a hick up and a burp and the thoughts started to creep in. *How did I eat that much? An amount that is meant for multiple people, and* really *meant for multiple people, not those teeny don't-tell-me-that's-really-the-portion-size things, but truly a* lot *of food. Man, I have to start being better tomorrow.* I pulled my knee up toward my torso on the couch and kicked it down to the floor, a fat girl's version of break dancers springing up to their feet from lying on the ground. I set the casserole dish in the sink, on top of the plate I set there previously, filled it with water, and walked away, not considering the irony that I had gone to great lengths to conceal the casserole rendezvous only to leave the proverbial underwear in plain sight for my husband to discover in the morning. Or did I think he was that oblivious to not notice an entire casserole dish missing from the fridge and now sitting in the sink? At least I wasn't contemplating going through the trash unlike that one time. I waddled off to bed and watched more murder investigations while waiting for sleep to come. *God, how did I eat all that?* I wondered. *At least it's gone now. Yeah, at least it's gone. I really can't believe you did that, Azure. I know. But tomorrow I can start fresh, be good, really good this time. Yeah tomorrow, tomorrow I'll be good...* I drifted off into full-bellied slumber.

Suddenly I jolted up chest first as if pulled by a string from my solar plexus, like the girl from *The Exorcist*. It was still dark. *Oh my God, I'm not breathing! Throat burning.* Cough... eternity.... swallow... infinite time... long drawn out gasp that sounded like a croak! *Vomit! It's vomit!* Vomit so hot, spicy, and acidic that it had produced something like ana-phylactic shock. Croaky gasp! *Please stop!* Gasp! Grad-u-al loos-en-ing. Gasp! More loos-en-ing. Breathe—at last breath!

Wheezing rapidly, I hyperventilated as if I had just run a race with an asthma attack. *Oh my God!* I was stunned and terrified. I always knew my eating would kill me but I assumed it would be chronic and over time, the heating-up-a-frog-gradually variety of diabetes, cancer, heart attack in 30 years, but this was going to kill me *tonight*! The thought of dying this way was so... embarrassing. I was always afraid I would choke to death on my food and everyone would know then that my gluttony had killed me, that I succumbed to my devices. It never occurred to me choking to death on my own binge vomit was an option. Death no longer felt far off and theoretical, death was right there in the room, taunting me: *Are you actually going to change this time, or are you coming with me?*

I coughed and felt the burning rawness of my throat as I tried to swallow the saliva my body was now producing in excess. Waves of shame washed over me, with fear as its grinding sand. Tears started streaming down my face as if they had been waiting behind my eyes the whole night and every other night I had binged like this. "This can't be normal!" I sobbed quietly in a whisper. And even though I was no stranger to desperate, pleading whisper cries in the dead of night, my mind could not bear to go back there, back to where I had come from right then. I put my head into my hands and wept. Sean stirred in his sleep and I quieted myself. I didn't want to bother him with this. I was inches away from the person who knew me the very best, loved me the very most, and yet I was completely, utterly, and desperately alone. "This can't be normal," I whispered again into the darkness.

2

PEANUT BUTTER

My cursor blinked in the search bar, a clock measuring the moments I stared blankly, wondering how to word this. I slowly and deliberately began to type "unhealthy relationship with food," the truest statement I could determine. As I scrolled down the search results, a term caught my eye: Compulsive Overeating Disorder.

How could I have never have thought of it this way before? Of course, it was an eating disorder. I had always considered eating disorders as pathological-skinny-people-diseases, but this applied to me as well. I was both sickened and relieved to see such a clear description of my shameful, secret behavior, written in black and white, so objectively:

- ▸ Uncontrollable excessive eating without purging afterwards
- ▸ Eating at night
- ▸ Feeling shame and guilt after eating
- ▸ Feeling no control over eating
- ▸ Eating past the point of satiation
- ▸ Hiding food
- ▸ Retrieving food out of the garbage
- ▸ Turning to food to soothe emotions

Full exposure. I felt the relief you feel when you've been putting off going to the doctor but are sure there is something wrong and then finally just go, deciding that the worst result is still better than the chronic anxiety tugging at your insides. There was relief knowing that there was name and others shared this problem.

I took a sip of black coffee which aggravated my still raw sore throat from the jalapeño vomiting the night before, and read on. Thirty million people in the U.S. have disordered eating, and of those compulsive over eating was more common than anorexia or bulimia. *How, then have I never heard of this before?* Eating disorders have the highest mortality rate of any mental illness at one death per hour. These patients are prone to being obese, anxiety-ridden and depressed. *Yeah, no shit.* Risk factors include genetic predispositions, sexual abuse, rape and emotional abuse.

My mind drifted for a moment to the place I never wanted to return to yet always found myself. It was almost as if I had never left. I quickly shook my head, trying to move my mental cursor to another part of my mind quickly before I got sucked in. I didn't want to go there. As I was breathing more heavily, frightened, a voice that sounded like mine said, "It's time." I nodded. It was scary, but it was also time. I put the cursor up to the search bar and typed in "psychologists that specialize in eating disorders in Bakersfield."

I studied the men's names in blue writing cognizant of the fact that I really would only be comfortable with a female and kept scrolling. I stopped when I saw a description that said "work with therapists online!" underneath the link. I clicked. Bakersfield was out of the way and I most trusted that therapists in Los Angeles would have the state of the art techniques, but that was entirely too far to be feasible to travel on any sort of a regular basis, so an online option would be perfect. Small tile photos of therapists were in a column with their names and a short description. I scrolled until I arrived at a thin woman who appeared to be in her forties. Experienced, but not ancient, someone who might look like an educated and worldly aunt, a teeny bit eccentric but still on the reservation. I clicked her summary which expanded into a blurb.

Behavioral and Cognitive Therapy, blah, blah, blah, I specialize in eating disorders, yeah, yeah, yeah, My personal philosophy is that the tools for wellness are already within us and therapy is about learning how to access those tools. I think I like her. Yeah, let's try her.

I clicked the "Contact Me" button, filled out the small rectangles with my name and email. Then, in the large rectangle where I was meant to list my question for the therapist I typed, "Hi, I am inquiring about setting up a session. I think I have compulsive overeating disorder and I see that is one of your specialties. I'd like to schedule a session. Thanks."

"Babe, you ready to go to the store?" Sean called from the kitchen.

"Yeah!" I closed the laptop and left it on the couch.

The drive in our little black truck was quiet, which happened more and more lately. When Sean first started traveling for work, I didn't give it much thought. After all, the first eight months of our relationship were long distance and not only did our relationship survive but ended in a proposal on Christmas Day. I figured with Sean working away we had the best of both worlds- the independence of single people but the stability of a committed relationship. At first I loved it—not feeling rushed to get home and make dinner, watching whatever I damn well pleased on TV which never included the sports or singing competitions Sean liked to watch, and working late on my laptop guilt free. Plus, Sean often surprised me with flowers at the office during the week or in hand on Fridays when he got home. They were always accompanied by a card written in the nicest man hand writing I had ever seen. We'd have long hugs, passionate kisses and make love from room to room. But this romance seemed to disappear both gradually and all at once, it happened so fast. Now when he came home, it felt like he had just been gone since that morning, when he had actually been gone all week. In fact, our greetings were better suited for roommates who don't care for each other all that much—a mutual exchange of the word "hey."

How have we already run out of things to talk about? Just strike up a conversation!

"How's it going, Babe?" I asked.

"Fine," he responded, sounding distant.

Okay. "Don't elaborate or anything!" I laughed, though I was mostly serious.

He laughed too, but didn't say another word.

Is this about the casserole dish in the sink?

Our first stop was Home Depot. I was annoyed because I had assumed "the store" meant the grocery store, not hardware. As we went inside, I remembered how I loved the freshly cut wood smell reminiscent of my childhood, which perplexed me because my childhood was not exactly pleasant. *I guess even bad childhoods have nice smells.* It was chilly as spring times were in Tehachapi at around forty-five hundred feet above sea level. It had even snowed a few weeks back, which I thought was amazing as a lowlander. I still enjoyed the novelty, even driving in the dirty slush. After Home Depot, we drove to Main Street and hung a right. Downtown Tehachapi was like a town stuck in time: vacuum repair shops, quilting stores, a Christian book store, the Apple Shed diner, boutiques with country women type of clothes, the dive bar, and our next stop, Kohnen's bakery.

I happily went inside to the end of the long glass display of cookies, nougat rings, cinnamon rolls, pretzels, lemon bars, tiramisu, little cheesecakes with fruit or brownie bits on top, and bierocks. Different types of breads were stacked in baskets on displays on the wall behind the case.

"Can I get you anything?" the teenaged boy asked.

"Can I please get a loaf of the sun-dried tomato bread, sliced?" Sean asked.

The slicing machine made a rumbling sound. The boy loaded the bread into a clear plastic bag, twist-tied it closed, and handed it to Sean. "Can I get you anything else?"

"Uh—" I started.

"No, that's it!" Sean told him before stopping and saying, "Were you going to get something?"

"Bierock?" I asked, dreaming of the warm and chewy meat- and onion-filled roll.

"But we just ate breakfast," Sean answered, surprised.

"Yeah, you're right, never mind!" I tried to play it off as if to say *how silly of me, how could I forget we just ate breakfast?* I knew darn well we had just eaten breakfast but that would never stop me from adding a bierock.

"Is that it then?" the teenager asked.

Sean looked at me questioningly.

"Yeah, that's it," I said and smiled even though I was secretly annoyed. *God, Sean, really? You have to call me out in front of the kid? Beirock Blocker!*

Our next stops were the gas station and the car wash. *It's for the best that I didn't get the bierock. After last night, I really need to be good.*

On the mostly quiet car ride home, I checked my email on my phone and saw a reply from Sylvie, the therapist. I anxiously pressed it with my thumb. In her email she asked if we could set an introductory session for fifteen minutes and if we were a good fit, we could continue talking for the rest of the hour. If that sounded good I was to let her know my availability. I hit reply and asked if she happened to be available today. She replied within five minutes that she was and how about one o'clock. I told her yes.

"Babe?" I asked Sean.

"Yeah?"

"I'm going to make a call in a little bit."

"Okay."

You should just tell him what it's for! No, not yet. What am I supposed to say—It's a funny thing about that casserole, good going down, not so good coming back up? Well, you should at least talk to him about something!

"Oh hey, Babe?" Sean asked.

"Yes?" I asked with baited breath, randy for emotional connection and hoping he was initiating.

"Can you transfer to the joint account today? We need to send the mortgage payment."

21

Sad trombone.

At one, I opened my laptop and signed back into the website on which I found Sylvie and fumbled with how to get the video chat going, so I didn't get on until five after. *God, Azure, always pushing it to the last minute!* When my image popped up on the screen, I began adjusting my hair and finding the angle and lighting that minimized my double chin, my rabbit front teeth, the sunken-in-ness beneath my eyes and the flatness of my mousy brown hair. I glanced up to the brick fireplace mantel where our wedding photo caught my eye. How different I looked in a few short months. My airbrushed bride's face was noticeably thinner and oval instead of round, the dimple on my turned cheek more prominent, my double chin not even visible. As I looked back to the screen at my reflection, now a small square at the bottom next to a larger one of Sylvie's image adjusting herself in her chair, I simply felt disgust with myself for being so much more concerned about minimizing how terrible I looked than seeing what *she* looked like or connecting with her.

"Hello, can you hear me?" I asked, shifting my eyes to her.

"Yes, I can hear you fine, can you hear me okay?"

"Yes."

"I'm Sylvie. I'm a licensed psychotherapist."

"Hi," I responded with a nervous laugh, "I'm Azure."

"Azure, like the color?"

"Yes, like the color." I nodded, smiling. It always impressed me when someone knew what my name meant.

"Your questionnaire had a different name," she said.

"That's my first name. I go by my middle name, Azure."

"Okay," she said and nodded.

"It's complicated and always has been. My dad and his side of the family call me my first name, my mom and her family, Azure. At school I went by Azure, but at work I go by the other just because it's easier in the interview process. But people who really know me call me Azure."

She smiled, noticing my nervousness, gauging my behavior, sizing

22

me up, but with kindness. She was a 40-something dancer, presumed by the painting of ballet slippers dangling by ribbons that hung behind her. What I could see of her body was long and lean and toned, and she wore her long auburn hair up in a tight, sleek ponytail. She had a rectangular but warm face and a feminine, almost breathy voice.

"Can you tell me a little about yourself and what you are hoping to get out of therapy?"

"All right. I think I have compulsive overeating disorder. I identify with a lot of the symptoms and I am looking to resolve it, preferably in the next six months because I have a wedding to be in and want to have lost the weight," I said as fast as possible.

She chuckled. "Why do you think you have compulsive overeating disorder?"

The other night I shoveled a family portion of casserole in my mouth with a serving spoon. "Well… because… when it comes to food, I'm…" I sighed, looking down at the floor, "I'm out of *control*… I *really* need to learn to control it better, so I can just lose this weight… by August, and just be done with it. Once and for all! Well, more than once, but for all this time."

"When you say 'out of control with food,' what do you mean?"

I sneak food, I don't stop eating until I am stuffed, I have these weird rituals with food. "Well, I sometimes—" *sometimes?! Who are you kidding? All the time*—"eat a lot… like a lot a lot, until I am really full."

"When is the first time you remember being what you describe as 'out of control' with food?"

As she finished her question, I had an image of my childhood bedroom and my body around aged seven. I was in bed swirling my index finger in an economy-sized jar of peanut butter and bringing a dollop to my mouth so huge that it almost dripped off before it got there. I could almost re-feel the sadness, fear, loneliness and despair melt away into creamy peanut butter bliss that was the closest thing to a giggly hug from my grandma. The closest thing and not even close. Smile. I missed her. Why couldn't I just stay with her forever?

The momentary contentment was interrupted by a sound that started off faintly, then grew stronger and louder—stomps of someone coming down the stairs. I slammed the lid back on the jar, threw it under the bed, lifted the blanket and wiped my gooey finger on my nightgown. I quickly rolled so my head would be facing away from the door. *Breathe slowly so you look asleep*, I told myself. The door swung open, the light turned on abruptly, blinding me. "Get your fucking ass upstairs and do the goddamn dishes!" he bellowed. Dad.

~

I squeezed my eyes really hard, back in my adult living room. "Don't remember," I told Sylvie, staring off into the distance, "very young, it honestly feels like I was born with it. I can't remember a time when I didn't do it."

"If you had to guess."

"Maybe five, seven."

"Okay." Sylvie nodded in a reassuring way. "Our introductory fifteen minutes is up. If you would like to keep going, I'd like you to tell me about what it was like before then."

"Sure, we can continue." I was surprised at how quickly she got me to access the place I avoided at all costs. "I really mean it, though I cannot remember when I didn't do this. Food has always been a thing for me."

"Okay. Can you tell me a little bit about your family?"

"Well, to be honest, I grew up in a pretty abusive household."

"In what way?"

I sighed. "Emotional, verbal, physical, financial."

"Can you take me through what a typical day was like growing up?"

I felt the sudden urge to create a diversion, to back-peddle, to pretend this entire conversation was one giant prank call.

"What do you mean?" I managed.

"Just an example," Sylvie coaxed.

Every muscle in my body clenched, like some isometric exercise.

I didn't want to go back there. Dealing with the painful snippets of memory that came to me like lightning bolts were one thing, but to linger and spend time there in my memory was something else entirely. Playing that movie in my mind gave that time, that place, gave *him* life again, making the past present and the monster manifest.

"What's going on in your body? I can tell you're tense," Sylvie asked.

"It sounds silly, because I know I don't live there anymore," I said as my eyes darted around the room embarrassed, "but it makes me scared to even think about it."

"That doesn't sound silly at all. Just ease into it. I am right here."

Like you're any match for him!

I closed my eyes and took a deep anticipatory breath in, then released it, letting my words ride the wave of the exhale so they wouldn't chicken out. "Well, typically my mom would inadvertently do something that would make my dad mad…"

And just like that, my couch was no longer my couch, but a mustard wing back chair. My suddenly smaller feet were no longer resting on the hard wood floor, but dangling above the faded pea green and carrot colored carpet. In place of my laptop, the thick, heavy, stagnant table of my childhood home sat in front of me with my mom to my left, my brother, Jake, to my right and my dad at 11 o'clock.

"Stupid shit!" Dad hissed through his gritted teeth. My mom, brother and I kept our eyes down so as to not to claim his words by way of eye contact. Suddenly, he slammed the serving spoon into the white bowl with the green floral border so loudly it sounded as though it were breaking. My mom, brother, and I flinched.

I slowly looked up at him, at how the softness of his sandy hair contrasted against his furious, rabid grey eyes, weathered skin and black gummed mouth. It was almost as if these finer features of his- his fine hair, loose belly, slim arms and legs were the sheep's clothing he used to conceal his true nature.

"Don't call me stupid," my mom answered, leaning forward so her long dark hair spilled in front of her shoulder.

He laughed in a sinister way and holding her gaze as if to say *watch this* and said, "Kids, tell your mother how stupid she is."

"Don't do it!" she instructed in a deep voice of authority.

"Shut the hell up!" he yelled as he kicked her in the shin.

"Don't!" she screamed in pain, clenching her leg, which already had bruises from other nights.

"Tell your mother what a real bird brain she is," he said.

Reflexively, my brother and I laughed at *bird brain* and looked at one another. Jake only had a vague resemblance to my dad, having the same beauty mark on his upper lip, but Jake was always the parrot on my dad's shoulder, repeating practically everything my dad said. I couldn't blame him—my dad seemed as powerful as Superman, even if his persona was more Lex Luthor. Dad had even built our house himself. But seeing any of my dad in Jake, physical or character, made me immediately regret laughing and wish I could take it back.

"If I am a bird brain, then you are Hitler!" my mom yelled.

He laughed, then looked at me. "Go on, tell her how stupid she is."

"Don't call her stupid!" I commanded in my young voice, looking him dead in the eye.

A look of shock came over him. How dare I defy him that way!

We had just started dinner and he leaped up and yanked the plate from my place at the table.

"Get your fucking ass downstairs!" he yelled.

I got up and started heading for my room, which was downstairs instead of upstairs like in most houses. I was partly anxiety-ridden for having the food taken away—again—and partly grateful for a temporary reprieve from the yelling and screaming.

He called my name and I froze mid-step on the stairs. "Take your brother with you and watch TV."

I knew what this meant and felt sorry for my mom. I was probably the youngest person in the world to have a TV in their room. I wondered why he had the foresight to put it there in an attempt to drown out the sound of him hurting her instead of just not hurting her anymore.

Jake joined me and grabbed the railing behind me as best as he could with his six-year-old hands. As we continued down the stairs, Dad exclaimed "You are turning them against me and it's going to cost you!"

"Come on," my mom attempted to reason with him.

"That'll cost you five hundred dollars."

"No!"

"You want to make it a thousand?"

I turned at the bottom of the stairs and saw him standing over my petite mom and poking her in the flesh where the chest and shoulder meet, moving her chair back each time as he repeated "Stupid shit! Stupid shit! Stupid shit!" spit flying though his clamped, snarling fangs. She sat there but began looking vacant, looking slightly down, and not at him. Once her chair was against the opposite wall, he pinched Mom's thumb as hard as he could, while she buckled in mercy.

Sensing he could look downstairs any second, I hurried Jake into my room, closed the door, turned the TV on and the light off. Then, pressing my ear back against the door, I turned the door handle ever so slowly until I heard the faint click. I swung it open fast so it wouldn't creak. Making eye contact with my brother, I knew I didn't have to raise my finger to my lips to tell him to be quiet. He and I did this so often that we knew the routine. We crawled on our hands and knees, first hugging the wall away from the stairs so as not to be seen, then crossing the hall and positioning ourselves against the side of the staircase. We poked our heads around and looked up. He was out of sight and yelling at her the whole time but I couldn't make out the particulars, his voice was muffled like bombs in a WWII movie, though somehow deafeningly loud at the same time.

We must have caught Mom's eye because she looked down at me. Our eyes remained locked except when she flinched as he lunged towards her, and Jake and I recoiled behind the wall. We watched as he shoved her, snatched her glasses off her head, snapped them in half and threw them to the floor with a flick of his wrist. He grabbed her by the forearm as she moaned half in pain, half pleading. He then proceeded to stomp on the glasses to make sure they were good and broken. Then he twisted her arm and shoved her into the stone fireplace. As she tried to get up, he shoved her down to the floor and stomped on her body just as he did to her glasses to make sure she was good and broken too. Then he turned away, done with her as she lay there on the floor like a wrapper. But he quickly decided that her presence spoiled his appetite, and he went back over and pulled her up.

"Stop it! Stop it!" she pleaded as he led her to the front door, opened it and bodily threw her onto the deck in the cold damp night before slamming and locking the door.

As prey animals who need to survive are keenly aware of the signs of the predator, my brother and I hurried back to the room quickly and silently so as not to be found out. We heard the thundering sound of him coming down the stairs and held our breaths. The thuds continued past the room and on down the hallway. My brother and I sighed in relief although I could see in the glow from the TV that he was still looking at me wide-eyed. "It'll be okay," I whispered to him, lying, I didn't know it would be okay. In fact, I was pretty sure it wasn't going to be. In fact, I was pretty sure we were going to end up like that family where the dad killed the wife and kids before maybe turning the gun on himself.

A few minutes later, Dad's footsteps went back up the stairs, and I heard the telltale clinking sounds of him pouring himself another gin and tonic and turning the TV on.

Knowing the coast was clear, at least for a little while, I told Jake that I had to go to the bathroom. I went down the hall, locked the door behind me and turned on the faucet. I then unlocked and opened the door to the side yard, elongating sticky spider webs like taffy before they finally broke. It was raining and the waxy oak leaves of the trees that surrounded our house accumulated it before sending fat droplets to splat symphonically onto the deck and ground.

I stepped out to the dark unlit deck covered by leaves in various stages of rot, and then onto the earth. I made my way up the very dark and steep side of the house to the railing of the entry deck. My mom was sitting on the step and hunched over, holding herself crying. I sighed with relief that she was alive, conscious and not being eaten by wild animals.

"Mom!" I whisper-shouted several times before she heard me. She mouthed, "Go back! Go back!" and waved her uninjured arm desperately. I knew she didn't want to get in even more trouble with him. So, I retreated and went back to my room defeated. Why hadn't she asked me to find her keys and sneak my brother out so we all could get away together, somewhere where he could never find us?

I reached under my bed and retrieved some pastries I had taken from the garage freezer a couple days previously. I offered one to Jake, but he declined. We were different in pretty much every way possible: He was extremely introverted, I was more outgoing. He was skinny, I was fat. He had a photographic memory, I was artistic. He internalized his feelings, I ate them.

I carefully picked off hair and lint and other under the bed nasties and gobbled in three bites what should have taken ten. I loved these forbidden goodies for the respite they provided of course, but also as the trophies I had gone to great lengths to obtain. I instinctively touched my hip which was still a little bruised and sore.

My food adventures always began with the sharp pinch on my hips from the counter's edge as I leaned forward like a gymnast on the double bars, reaching for the keys that sat on the windowsill. Holding by the key and not the key ring to keep jingling to a minimum, I would slip out the front door and cross the long, dark, slick, moss-covered brick pathway that separated the house from the garage. As I traveled, the Snow White oak trees peered down at me, watching my every move. The greatest hazards; however, weren't actually outside, but rather inside the garage, which required I play the part of Indiana Jones to avoid the poisonous spiders in the wood pile, the jagged wood edges of the door that our old dog destroyed and even holes in the floor from where my dad hadn't finished it. Once I passed the tests of valor; however, the garage was always complicit in my food raids.

"What kind of house has freezers with locks for the sole purpose of keeping one of the kids from eating?" the garage would ask me disapprovingly like some kind of fairy godmother. "Here, take this step ladder and carefully get the key off of the nail on the beam up there and help yourself."

I did, carefully, since I knew hitting the cement floor would really hurt. When the freezer door opened, the yellow light illuminated the tasty things that were meant for everyone in my house but me as if it were a welcoming Parisian bakery display. I retrieved several pies and unwrapped them right there in the garage, since the wrappers made a crinkle sound, and shoved them way down into the trash can underneath other garbage. Then, I'd put the pies themselves between my stretchy pants and my stomach and pull my shirt down over them. Luckily my parents preferred I wear large shirts to conceal my weight. They told me it was slimming. Little did they know that my loose clothes also concealed little pies filled with cherry, blackberry or apple flavored goo.

I traveled by Hansel and Gretel path of imaginary breadcrumbs back to the house. When I went inside, I had to act natural, as if I weren't in pain from being freezer burned because frozen pie crust had fused with my skin. To my amazement, it always seemed to work with my parents. Jake, though, could always tell and always gave me a knowing look. But he hardly ever told on me. I knew he felt sorry for me that I was never allowed to have anything he was, that everything I ate was monitored, counted, logged, trended and scrutinized.

When finally back to my room, I would peel the pies off my skin and my belly with a "ssst!" and my belly would be glowing pink. I would eat at least one the pastries frozen, impatient, unable to wait until it was thawed. The flaky buttery crust exhaled steam as though it were warming up at a camp-fire because the pies were so cold. I stored the ones I wanted to save under my bed since my mom had found the sticky gooey bits shellacked in the white wood cubby of my headboard behind the children's books I never read (as if we were one of those families where the parents read the kids a bedtime story). "Pig!" Mom had shouted through gritted teeth while vigorously scrubbing the goo with Ajax.

30

Still, I relished my world in my room without food rules, where I was allowed to have seconds—thirds if I wanted—I could eat it *all* if I wanted to. Food was my imaginary friend but real and physical and sweet and comforting and playful. The only catch was that it had to be secret and any dinner conversation was inside my own tortured head: *I wonder what's worse—living here where he could kill us or living in Bosnia with a loving family in the middle of a war? What if I never knew my dad? Which would be worse—not knowing him and wondering what he's like, or knowing him and him being evil? What if he were only mean at nighttime and was nice during the day? What if he said "sorry" sometimes for being mean the night before? What if he promised to change? Even if he didn't change, it would be nice to hear that he knows it's something that should be changed. Why aren't I more like a Disney princess and a little less like Cookie Monster? If I were, maybe things would be different.*

Once full, falling asleep was a little easier. Jake and I often did so holding each other's hands, though he always flinched and his body went stiff when touched. My parents said it was because Jake had been born premature, but I thought it was from something else. Unlike most kids, I didn't have nightmares. I suppose when you're living in one, sleep becomes a welcomed chance to escape for a few hours. But like all peaceful times at our house, they were fleeting and interrupted to a rude dose of reality. I awoke to the sounds of quiet sobs and found my mom sitting on the end of the bed. My mom transformed what would be moans and wails into long, drawn out whispering exhales that he couldn't hear or else. I sat up and put my hand on her shoulder. "It'll be okay, Mom," I whispered to her as she cried, again lying. She continued unfazed as if I weren't even there. "Don't be sad, Mom," I continued. Again, she did not respond. I leaned forward and hugged her and although her arms didn't reciprocate, I did feel her hot tears on my neck begin seeping through my night gown. "It'll be okay," I repeated over and over, trying to convince the both of us. When she did reply it was in a whisper, "Azure, it's important for you to know this—never let a man treat you this way. Kill him first."

31

~

There Sylvie was, looking all serene and concerned, while I was salt-water-logged, snotty, and exhausted. I suddenly felt a little embarrassed. I hadn't intended to get that emotional.

"But I don't live there anymore and I just need to get over it," I said.

"Hold on," Sylvie said abruptly. I stopped as though the teacher caught me passing notes.

She remained silent for a moment, I suppose to give gravity to what she was about to say.

"You know statistically, Azure, you should be a heroin addict."

I looked down and not at the computer. At first, I thought that was kind of an extreme statement, but I knew it made sense. I had surmised that my childhood was not the run-of-the-mill abuse, but was more of the twisted mind-fuck variety, at least that's how I felt. And heroin isn't exactly accessible to a seven-year-old, but food is. Maybe there was a reason, *a good reason*, I was like this.

"You're actually really lucky to have found food," she continued.

Oh yeah, I feel really lucky, let me tell you. I rolled my eyes like the teenager I still felt like. *It's only taken over my entire life, dominates all my thoughts, almost killed me yesterday, and is definitely killing me slowly.*

"I see your point," I said a little embarrassed for having rolled my eyes that way. "Otherwise, I might have a needle hanging out of my arm right now."

"I want to work with you weekly; does same time next week work?"

"Yeah, sure."

"This week I want you to be gentle with yourself."

I snorted.

"Really, though, gentle."

"Okay, okay." I smiled, again like a teenager. "Talk to you next week."

Closing my laptop, in the same comfortable nook of the couch in which I had curled up with the casserole mere hours ago, I felt completely wiped out and yet strangely cleansed. Not clean, just slightly less dirty, until I was filled with a sudden urge to go to the kitchen and microwave the brie in the fridge.

3

FOLGERS INSTANT

I t was a sad house, a hidden house, just like he wanted it. It was down the hill so you couldn't see the house from the street. It was surrounded by Valley oaks, buckeyes, pine, wild plums, bay trees, and poison oak. There was a particular worm-rich, earthy smell in the ground there, as if something dead was fertilizing the soil. The deck railings gave splinters, and discolored tears dripped down from the shingles on the house's exterior.

The hidden house concealed much pain. It was a private world for abuser and abused alike, all suffering, with an enchanted Sleeping Beauty's-castle type of dilapidation. The front door was a stable door, where the bottom half could be closed with the top half remaining open, giving the illusion of an open-door policy. But no one just dropped by our house. There was no "make yourself right at home." Few were welcome and those only came with ample notice and after a rare cleaning and staging to make the visitors believe we were what we were not —normal. In this house love was only expressed in the dark, in secret, in fearful moments where he couldn't hear and when the air was thick with the possibility that he would really do something crazy. The laughs that took place were usually his wheezy smoker's laughs and were always at someone else's expense.

The house had a dusty, stale smell and thick energy people usually use to describe haunted houses. This wasn't helped by the dim lighting or the bathroom mirrors facing one another, giving the illusion of a million selves standing in a never-ending corridor. Though it was the nineties, the house was a seventies time capsule. A basket with dried fuzzy burma reeds sat beside the front door on the faded pea-green carpet. The couch had vertical brown and tan lines like a Mexican blanket. The chandeliers had long dangly strings of capiz-shells, which jingled if doors were open or you passed on the stairs beneath them too quickly. The kitchen floor of cold, white hexagonal tiles was framed by carrot orange counter-tops. The walls were decorated with abstract paintings and driftwood art that looked like grey corpses.

Because the house was down the hill from the street, the living rooms were upstairs and the bedrooms downstairs. My room was just to the left at the foot of the stairs. The walls were bone white, so were my curtains, so were my dressers, and so was my bedspread with blue squiggles. My brother's room was down the eternally long hallway and across from the bathroom.

The dining room was upstairs next to the living room which had dark brown beams shining out from a single point in the stone fireplace and large koa slab shelves displaying collections from my parent's travels to Europe and South America, slides of their scuba diving trips in the Carribbean and South Pacific, books on history and science and stacks of *Newsweek* magazines and unread *National Geographics.* The western side of the house faced a county park of oak trees, whose waxy leaves glistened in the sun. The view was gorgeous and transporting. Of all of the living things around our house including the deer, raccoons, and birds that frequented our property, my favorite were the oak trees. The more deformed they were, the more beautiful they were. It was as if they reflected our pain in the angst-filled positions of their limbs.

If the house was a medieval kingdom, the dining room table was the stocks at the center, where family members would receive our humiliating, debasing, and cruel punishments for hours on end. Like everything wood in our house, the dining room table was made of koa. The table, made of a two-inch-thick slab, was thick and heavy and unmoving, just how we were not allowed to move from it until he was done with us. The table's legs resembled something like boomerangs, which was fitting because no matter how far away I have been from that table it feels like my experience brings me right back there every time. In Hawaii, where my parents were married, koa represents integrity, strength, prosperity and health of a marriage, everything that my parent's marriage didn't have at all or only had an illusion of. His place at the table was his throne where he was dictator, but still always an engineer. He always kept graph paper, mechanical pencils and a coffee mug with an engineer-themed design with gears, rulers, and such. I don't think he ever washed it. The inside was permanently stained with concentric brown rings, like the age rings in a tree. The outside of the mug had brown marks where his bottom lip would go. The reek of stale Folgers instant permeated from his place at the table as did the jingling sound of his perpetual stirring with the short spoon that he always used.

He was six-feet tall but seemed so much taller. He was around 185 pounds but seemed so much bigger. He was a dead ringer for Robert Redford, if Robert Redford perpetually wore a hardened, furious scowl on his face with hate radiating from his black-pitted grey eyes that held you in a fixed glare. He had an eagle's beak nose and white capped teeth surrounded by gums that were grey and black from decades of smoking. His face had that wrinkled, weathered look from years of fishing in the sun. He always wore a Tom Selleck mustache which underlined the permanent scowl he wore. He wore the same clothes for decades. Not the same style of clothes, the same clothes. He was incredibly intelligent having earned a double PhD. He never wore a wedding ring because rings were "for girls and faggots." Belief in God was no different than believing in Santa Claus or the Easter Bunny and faith, to him, was a sign of mental inferiority. He didn't smile, not even for pictures. He had the ability to size people up, to see into their soul and determine their biggest fears and insecurities. If he sensed non-compliance, he was at the ready with the most below-the-belt criticisms ever spoken. Your heart was the bull's eye, his words were his arrows, and he was a sure shot.

Some would call him draconian, cantankerous, cunning, tenacious, opinionated, intense and brilliant. My grandma called him a rascal, my mom a dictator, a tyrant and Hitler. To me He was a blend of a deity, animal and human, something like Calibos in the old school claymation *Clash of the Titans* we watched on VHS, dangerous like a snarling animal, powerful as a god and well camouflaged to those outside our family in the body of a human. He seemed to delight in hurting other people or at least getting under their skin. He enjoyed pulling right into a parking space or gas pump someone else had been patiently waiting for. He would conveniently disappear to the bathroom when the bill came at the restaurant. Life was a chess game that required manipulating, controlling, and strong-arming others to achieve his objectives. If ever anyone reminded him that what he did was wrong, he not only didn't care, but he found it funny as hell. If you had something he wanted, he was entitled to it. And if he saw you as standing in his way, you would experience a wrath unlike you have ever experienced before. If you were in relationship with him, one reality was clear: he was winning, and you were losing.

His only love was power, and being able to control another's emotions was his biggest turn on next to hoarding his money. He favored his version of the golden rule: "the man with the gold makes all the rules." He was ruler and we were his subjects and there were only two ways out: death or escape.

4

DAY-OLD HOSTESS

The following morning when I woke up, Sean was already gone. I sighed. How could it be that I was already lonely, I had just woken up. I vaguely remembered waking up at three thirty and seeing the piercing light from the bathroom break through the darkness when he was getting ready. I was recalling the shushing sounds of the shower and the sink, the clunking of his work boots on the hard wood, his "be a good dog" whisper to Trixie, Ruby and Crane, and the kiss he gave me before he left, but I had immediately fallen back into slumber. Sean was so traditional that way, going off to provide for his family. And there was something so attractive about him in jeans and work boots even though he walked the tight rope between the upper management suits and the construction workers whose safety he oversaw. I just wished I had known that my talking him into jumping to a bigger bond, where he was no longer one of the biggest fish, would mean seeing each other so little. More than that, I wished that my urging had not been rooted in the desire to impress my dad, and that that desire didn't seem to eclipse the desire to see my husband on a daily basis.

After a couple of minutes looking at the ceiling and the walls of my room, I mustered up the courage to get up. It was the beginning of a deceivingly sunny day where it looks much warmer than it actually is. I touched the window and quickly pulled away, the glass feeling only slightly warmer than an ice cube. I noticed a deer peeking out from behind one of the oaks on the side of the house. I watched for a few moments as it majestically nibbled and carefully stepped. We were so very different in our solitude, the doe tranquil in hers and me depressed in mine. I sighed and started getting ready for work. I grabbed a long skirt and a shirt and threw them on in a couple minutes, and carried my shoes in my hand. The dogs' collars jingled and their nails clicked on the hard wood as they followed me into the game room to let them out in the back yard. I turned and went into the kitchen to pour what was left in the coffee pot from four in the morning into a mug. Of course, some of it spilled over the side. I didn't bother wiping it or the counter. When the metal dog bowl clattered with falling kibble, the dogs bounded back inside, Ruby leading as always, food obsessed like me. With all their noses in the bowl, I knelt over and gave them each a pat. "Be good guys!" I called as I grabbed my bag, a reusable fabric grocery bag that had my laptop inside along with the crumpled mail I needed to deal with floating somewhere at the bottom. I walked out to the little black truck barefoot, the path cold and punchy every time I stepped on a little pebble. It was just my way of rebelling against having to wear my work shoes as long as possible.

On the way to work, I sipped my coffee and spilled a drop the size of a pencil eraser on my shirt. *Freaking hot mess! That's what you are! You're lucky you're good at your job, Slob!*

I was already running late for my still relatively new management job in Quality Assurance at a biomedical device company, my big break, and second to last step towards making Director by the time I was 30 to prove myself to my dad. *No time to turn back.* I flipped my hair from behind my shoulder to the front. *Hopefully that will cover it! Oh crap! I forgot my healthy lunch at home! Oh well, I guess I'll just have to grab a sandwich or Mexican.* I wasn't all that disappointed.

As usual, since I had to go out to lunch, I decided I had to eat badly for dinner too. It just didn't feel right to me to have a substantive lunch and then eat kale, even if it was cooked. When I walked into the house with the plastic bag of takeout, the dogs tried to scale my legs like a sheer cliff.

It always takes me three days to get over a binge I told myself as I devoured my food. I took an accounting. *The jalapeño corn casserole incident was Saturday, an entire round of microwaved brie Sunday, Mexican food today. That means tomorrow it'll be better!* I thought of the greens I planned to eat. *I should go get some Reese's since I won't be able to have any of that after tonight.* Just about then, the phone rang. It was Sean for his nightly check in. After confirming that we were both still alive, I slid right on into the soap opera that was my job as if Sean were tuning in. "Freaking Nancy and her insubordination!" I whined. "Her and her miniskirts and her thigh high boots that she must have to get at a sex shop or something." Sean just mmm-hmmmed me.

"I wouldn't even care what that Erin Brocovich look alike does if she were just willing to get with the current century like I am being paid to implement there. She just refuses." *More like Erin Broco-bitch.*

"Why can't you just get rid of her?" Sean asked.

"I can't. I haven't been there long enough to learn all of it. Plus I'm on a deadline to overhaul Quality Assurance there." *And my life.* "But anyway," I went on and on and on. "Hello? Are you still there?"

"Yeah I'm here."

"Why aren't you saying anything?"

"I'm just listening." I heard him exhale loudly and I stopped my story. "What are you up to?" I asked.

"Just here in the room."

"Where are you this time?"

"The Microtel."

"Is everything micro?"

"Yes."

"Is the TV even a baby TV? That would be so cute!"

"It's pretty small," Sean answered, unamused. I went quiet and so did he. Our conversation became more about being silently with one another as we separately lived our separate lives, each hearing the faint and muffled sounds of what the other was watching on TV. I knew my complaining had bothered him, but I didn't apologize, just wished that he would confide in me the same way. But, nothing ever seemed to bother him the way everything seemed to bother me.

Sean said "Well, Babe, I better go, I have to wake up early."

After saying our goodbyes, I loaded the dogs in the car and drove to the gas station to buy a pack of Reese's, and since I was already there a pack of Peanut M&Ms and Peanut Butter M&Ms.

The next day, I did pack kale for lunch as planned. Before work I also followed along the hundreds of burpees and high knees and jumping jacks in the Shaun T Insanity exercise program in my sports bra and underwear in my living room. After work, I did the Wii dance program to break a sweat. For dinner I had a bowl of spinach with hummus in place of dressing with a sprinkling of sunflower seeds and dried cranberries.

When I talked to Sean that night, I enthusiastically told him about my new diet plan. I would be fifty pounds lighter in two months. And even though it is bitter and barely edible, I was really starting to like kale and I felt so good and energetic that I imagined that I wouldn't mind the taste so much. Sean was supportively encouraging. "That's great, Babe!" His voice had more life in it than other conversations we had had lately. I was slightly melancholy when I got off the phone. The next day, I bitched more to Sean about such and such at work and the woes of dieting. The following day, day three of kale and spinach, I decided to tell Sean about working with Sylvie. "I've decided to see a therapist," I blurted out.

"Really?" Sean asked, clearly surprised and maybe even a little disturbed.

"I actually just learned I have an eating disorder."

"Then you should."

"Yeah."

"Yeah."

That's it? No other questions? Nothing else to say? What is he sup-posed to say? I don't know, but something!

Whatever his thoughts or feelings were, he kept them locked away in his own private world. And asking him to share them with me felt absolutely and totally out of the question, so instead, after hanging up I used my finger to lick out the rest of the hummus in the container.

The following day, Thursday, we told each other we missed each other and how much we were looking forward to seeing one another the following day. When I got home on Friday, he was already home and had had a couple beers. We went to Slicks, our favorite restaurant in town, and after sharing the southwest egg rolls, I ate part of Sean's salad dripping with blue cheese dressing, then my cheeseburger. I ate my sweet potato fries too and was secretly annoyed each time Sean grabbed some which I presumed was in exchange for having some of his pre-dinner salad.

Guilt ridden from my diet slip, I opened my laptop for my call with Sylvie Sunday morning. *I wonder if Sylvie will be able to tell what I did just by looking at me. She is a therapist, not a psychic! But still.*

"How has the week been since we last spoke?" Sylvie asked. She wore her hair up in a bun today. The lighting was different this time than last and I noticed how pale her skin was and how her auburn hair contrasted against it.

I adjusted the laptop on the brown pillow which sat on top of my folded leg. "Fine, I guess. I mean… I haven't lost any weight."

"Patience. Trust this process. Listen, Azure," she said, "there is something I want to explain: when you have trauma, it's like swallowing a whole steak and it just sits there inside you, unable to digest. With therapy, what we do is take that steak back out and cut it up into small, bite-sized pieces that you can digest."

Steak! I thought involuntarily. *Oh my God Azure, how can you be thinking of food even in therapy? No wonder you are the way you are! Medium rare with a side of sour cream and horse radish. Azure, stop!*

I nodded. "Okay."

"Today, I think it would be helpful to go over some family history with you," she continued, "so I can know who you are talking about when you mention family members. Are you comfortable doing that?"

God look at those shadows underneath her cheek bones without even having to fake them with blush like I do! It would probably be inappropriate for me to ask her about her diet and exercise regimen.

"Sure," I finally responded.

"Your parents aren't still married, I presume?"

"Not anymore."

"How old were you when they were divorced?"

"Twelve."

"How was that for you?"

"Well, they should have gotten divorced *way* before that, so I certainly wasn't one of those kids who were devastated and wanted their parents to get back together."

"How about siblings? You mentioned a brother?"

"Yeah, Jake."

"Is he older or younger?"

"A year and a half younger."

"What's he like?"

"Very introverted, bookish, history buff, naturally fit, not many friends."

"What about extended family?"

"My grandma and my dad's side of the family lived in Seattle."

"Were you and your grandma close?"

I smiled sadly and instinctively looked up at my mantel where a little picture of her hung in a teal iridescent frame beside my wedding photo. It was from her ninetieth birthday and she looked so radiant. The corsage of pink and white flowers she wore brought out a rosiness in her cheeks and lips. *I miss you!* I called out to her in my mind. "She was my most special person in the world. We really got each other, you know?" By the time I finished my voice was crackling and breathy.

"She's passed away?"

"Last year, before I got married."

"I'm so sorry to hear that. She sounds like she was very special." Sylvie's voice was genuine and kind.

"It's okay," I said, even though I hadn't been since she died.

Sylvie smiled understandingly. "And you're married, but no kids yet, right?"

"Yeah, Sean, and no kids yet. I kinda wanna figure this food and weight stuff out first."

"What scares you?"

"About having kids?"

"Yes."

"I am already so overweight and pregnancy isn't going to help." I shrugged my shoulders and looked out the window, thinking of an even more blown out body.

"It sounds like you are very concerned about that."

"I am."

"And your parents had a very unhappy marriage, it sounded like from the last session."

"That's an understatement," I laughed.

"And how does that compare to your marriage now?"

Oh it's going to be like that, Sylvie!

"There's no comparison!" I answered quickly.

"So you would characterize your marriage as a healthy and loving one?"

I laughed nervously while I raced from the couch to a spare bedroom with my laptop outstretched in front of me. Once convinced I was out of ear shot, I gave the most diplomatic response I could, "Well, we've been together a while now."

"What do you mean by that?"

"Well, there isn't as much passion as when we first met, but that's normal, I think."

Even though you are still newlyweds?

Sylvie nodded and notated something. The silence and whatever

44

conclusion she was writing made me uncomfortable and so I offered "But there's never any doubt about whether he's The One."

That part was true. In fact, even though we knew it sounded cheesy, Sean and I were pretty unapologetic about the fact that we felt our love was fated. We started our marriage vows with "You are the one" and we believed in celebrating the anniversary of the day the universe brought us together much more than the day we were married.

"Oh?" Sylvie asked.

Here I am spilling my guts and Sylvie barely responds. Psychology training must mostly consist of learning how to contribute the fewest words possible to a conversation. You win again, Sylvie.

"I always knew that I was looking for a very particular type of person," I started. "Someone who was driven, aspirational, educated, had a good career trajectory, but also someone who was street smart, had gone through a thing or two... and most importantly someone who would be understanding toward my crazy assed family. Basically, a successful and compassionate reformed bad-boy."

I laughed at the absurdity of it, and felt somewhere in me that although I had hit most of the criteria, that I hadn't been careful enough when assessing the most important one: compassion.

"And which of these qualities would you say are like your father?" Sylvie asked.

I felt like the childlike part of me had been outed, as if Sylvie had spotted a collection of teddy bears in my adult bedroom.

"Well, they are all basically like my dad: the educated, successful, street smart except for the kindness I was looking for, obviously."

Sensing Sylvie wanted me to elaborate, I continued.

"You see, I wanted my dad to respect whoever I ended up with, which was a tall order because my dad doesn't respect anyone. No matter how amazing a person is, my dad always has something negative to say. Like if a person were educated, he'd say they were too soft or gentile. If a person were street smart, he'd say they were low class. And my dad's no-win attitude shaped my own criteria. Like, for example, I have had lots of guy friends whose families were all 'Leave It to Beaver' and I just knew it would never work. I knew that the right person would need to have a rough past in one way or another to ever fully 'get me.' It took a long time, but I eventually just became resolved to the fact that I'd never meet someone who met both opposing criteria. Of course, Murphy's Law: once I decided this, I met Sean."

My eyes twinkled at the memory and the magical way in which the universe works.

Who would have thought that me, the weird girl, would meet her husband in the most cliché way possible: at club in Hollywood.

I went on to tell Sylvie how going on five years ago, by broken plans and happenstance, I winded up clubbing with my best guy friend Alex. I had just lost a bunch of weight and wore a short white dress with a black rod-iron looking French design, which sort of glowed in the strobe lit, black lighting of the club. Alex and I had agreed to point out people we thought the other would find attractive and as we were dancing and sweating, he yelled to me as best he could over the thumping base, "I think you'd like that guy behind you!"

It was then that I saw Sean for the first time. He gave me a little smile from underneath his hat. I could tell by his clothes that he was a grown-up skater boy with punk influence and I found that so irresistibly hot in a Bender from *Breakfast Club* kind of way. Confident from alcohol and Alex's presence, I turned and started dancing with Sean. I was shocked when he not only didn't walk away but actually started trying to talk to me, which was difficult over the music. I heard that his name was Juan and I told him my name was Azure, which I had to repeat several times. We left the dance floor, got drinks and talked more. He pulled me by the hand upstairs and downstairs and somehow tracked down the four other friends he was with that night to introduce me, and I learned later, to hear me pronounce my name over and over. He's so clever that way.

"Sean! Not Juan!" he laughed when we exchanged numbers at the end of the night.

Normally I would have died of embarrassment, but I just laughed it off.

Less than an hour later, Alex and I were in a Del Taco drive-through with other three-a.m.-ers when my phone rang.

"I think it's him!" I exclaimed to Alex. "What do I do?"

"Answer it! Wait, first tell me what you want."

"Quesadilla, side of sour cream, chips, and nacho cheese. Hello?" I must have picked up on the last ring.

"Azure?"

He said it right!

"Yeah?" I answered in a questioning way even though I knew it was him.

"Hey, it's Sean. I just wanted to call and let you know that I'm not going to play games and wait a few days to call. I really like you and I want to see you again."

My face flushed. No one had ever been so assertive with me before.

"I'd like that," I responded as neutrally as possible.

An eruption of crinkles approached my face as Alex handed me the bag with our food.

"Okay, maybe this weekend?" he asked.

"Here's the thing—I actually live in San Diego."

"I go to San Diego all the time for work. I'll be down there this Friday. Maybe we could get together then?"

We agreed and said our goodbyes.

"So?" Alex asked expectantly.

I handed him his burrito and filled him in.

"Azure, no offense," Alex started between mouthfuls, "but this guy sounds a little eager. Are you sure it's not one of those lose-that-number situations?"

I hesitated and thought about it. *Cool guys statistically don't tend to be psychos, right?*

"I hear what you are saying, Alex. I don't know what it is about this guy, but there is just something about him. I have to see him again."

I tried to put my finger on it—that something. It was as if a voice from somewhere within me wanted to blurt out "Where the hell have you been? I've been looking all over for you!" As if we were friends who got separated at a concert that lasted my entire life so far.

The following day we were on the phone again, talking about everything and nothing- his job in safety, my plans to go into biomedical after graduating. His being from Santa Clarita, my being from Redwood City. His parents were divorced, he had an older brother. My parents were divorced, I had a younger brother. I liked to scuba dive, he had always wanted to try it. His favorite color was blue. My name meant blue.

"I know," he answered in a voice so sexy, I felt my life had become a movie.

God I like him! I thought as I flung myself backward onto my bed like a school girl.

I knew he really liked me too, but selling people on my personality, as in only the upbeat, enthusiastic part of my personality I showed other people, was never a problem for me.

Making it to Friday was excruciating. As the professors droned on, all I could think about was Sean. The only class that made any sense was my neurobiology class in which we were studying the cocaine like high of falling for someone, which was really from a surge of the neurotransmitter phenyl ethyl amine. And all I knew was that I needed to get my hands on some more of that.

When Friday afternoon finally came around, I paced around the house, compulsively checking my hair, makeup and placement of my shirt to maximize the illusion of a flat stomach. I wondered if it would be enough. *Will he wonder just how much he had been drinking when he fell for this fat, ugly troll?* My phone chimed and when I picked it up, I saw "just parked" on the screen. My heart pounded fast and hard as I went out front, trying to keep a cool look on my face.

"Hi!" I smiled as he walked up. He smiled back. *Oh my God, he's so much cuter than I remembered! There's no way a guy like that would be into me.* When he let himself into the green chain-linked fenced yard, Trixie ran up to him and climbed on his leg, whining excitedly as though she missed him.

"That's weird!" I said, "She always barks at new people."

He bent over and rubbed her black haired pink belly as if she were already his.

We walked the couple blocks to the main drag and to my favorite rooftop bar and ordered Cadillac margaritas. *If everyone could see me now, although I am eating Mexican food. I'll have to run an extra hour tomorrow.*

"There is something I wanted to tell you in person," Sean said.

Oh god, he's married! Or moving to the east coast. Or maybe he only has a few months to live and thought he should tell me before we get too involved.

"I have a bit of a past and it's only fair that I be up front with you about it."

Married, definitely married.

"I used to have a drug problem, but have been clean for a few years now."

He said it without hesitation. He continued. "I am super motivated to make up for lost time, career wise. I just want you to know, especially since I know it's so different from your background being a college girl and all."

Oh, I see what's happening. I am being friend zoned. Why do guys always feel like they can open up to me, but then conclude that all we can ever be is friends? Oh well.

"What do you think?" he asked.

I looked at him in the eye.

"I don't judge you. And I hope you wouldn't judge me either," I answered with more sincerity than I think I even understood at the time. "I actually think it's amazing. Quitting drugs? A hell of a lot fewer people successfully do that than graduate from college."

Sean smiled in a friendly way and asked "Wanna get outta here?"

"Sure," I answered.

I need to study anyway, so maybe just friends is better.

We walked toward the beach and at the end of the block instead of turning toward my house, Sean headed towards the pier. I was puzzled but decided to go with it. We walked past the hippie kids and Sean dropped a couple bucks in their open guitar case.

"It's my way of paying it forward," Sean explained. "Or paying it back, I should say. You should see me with the Girl Scouts," he chuckled.

I told him I had been a Girl Scout and that I was impressed by his generosity.

When we got to the top of the pier, the breeze whipped my hair. *At least I've been doing so much cardio I'm not out of breath like I usually am*, I told myself.

With the Pacific Ocean to our front, we made our way down the thick creaky boards.

"So, finals are next week?" he asked.

"Yep, and I'm not even close to being ready."

And then I felt his broad hand take mine gently but assertively.

Oh my god! He's actually holding my hand!

I tried to continue calmly as if my feet hadn't just left the ground.

"Yeah and bio-chem is just killer, no matter how much I study."

"You'll do amazing," he said and when I looked over at him I could tell his faith in me was genuine.

Warm fuzzies!

I thanked him and asked about the work that brought him to San Diego.

He told me more about his job overseeing safety for a roofing contractor and how his region was from San Luis Obispo, south. As he talked about the nuances of fall protection and the challenges of convincing construction guys to wear the lifesaving harnesses, I studied him nonchalantly. I loved how his eyes were the same hue as the brown gravy Grandma made at Christmas. I thought it was so cute how they squinted into little crescent-moons when he laughed. I practically drooled over his smile, which was straight out of a dental commercial and seemed to stretch over his entire face. He must have picked up on my gazing at his mouth because suddenly the world was spinning for a brief moment before I landed against his body and his lips were pressed against mine. And for perhaps the first time in my entire life without food, I was whisked off to a place of timeless, experiential bliss.

Maybe not just friends.

I smiled wider than I probably ever had before in my whole life and laughed in disbelief.

He's cute, actually likes me, is career driven, and *has a rough past? Check mate!*

Sean gave me a confused smile and asked flirtatiously "What?"

"Nothing," I answered with a coy smile.

5

FAMILY SIZED

Of course, therapy isn't exactly known for re-experiencing all of one's happy times. Sylvie and I quickly settled into a routine of re-hashing other stories of evenings at my house growing up, all basically the same as the first. This time my mom made him mad over this, that time she made him mad over that, this time it was about me gaining weight, that time it was also about me gaining weight, but all the same violence, all the same terror, all the same trapped anguish.

So far, therapy left me feeling completely exhausted and totally ravenous. It seemed like whenever I went back *there* in my mind, I got hungry, starving in fact. Accessing my emotions took the lid off the haunted well and released insatiable hunger, turning me into a bottomless pit. *Ugh! Isn't this therapy stuff supposed to be doing the opposite?* I was disgruntled with Sylvie, therapy in general, and myself, my weak self who could not control this. I knew it wasn't fair to blame Sylvie or therapy, and chastised myself for being such a bitch as to try to put this on her. *But seriously, if this is something that should be expected, shouldn't she have warned me?*

And I hated the artificial ending of therapy. I'd be crying hysterically and then have to button it up, put the lid back on because we were at the 55-minute mark. I wished it could just feel organic and we could go on for a while longer until there was a more natural ending. But perhaps my biggest annoyance had been the homework assignment I was given every week—to do everything lovingly. When she followed up with me the following session, I laughed, embarrassed. "I am not even sure what that means." She repeated to do everything lovingly and I took this to mean I was supposed to figure this out for myself, just like everything else in my life.

Frustrated again, I shut the laptop and put it beside me on the couch where Trixie, Ruby, and Crane sat up, hopeful it was time for a walk. Trixie, a long-haired Black and Tan Doxie, was sleek, graceful, delicate, and quiet. Ruby, who was the short red-haired variety, was round, sassy, food-obsessed, determined, and loud, like me. Crane was good looking and easy going, like all Golden Retrievers, and like Sean.

During the week, the dogs were my only company when I wasn't at work, not that I felt particularly connected to anyone at work. My new company turned out to manufacture just as much stress as they did medical devices and I was both the production manager and the main consumer of that stress. It was my first real position in management and I spent most waking moments working, anxiety ridden that I would fail in the job that would have finally earned my dad's respect, if I didn't fuck it up, of course, which he was always sure to remind me was my only great talent.

Sometimes I would find myself in what might look like a catatonic state but to me it felt like everything was spinning, that I was sitting in my new house, new job, new zip code, new marriage, old 80 pounds to lose, gaping hole from my dead Grandma and not-dead father. Then a million little insects would break free from an egg sack inside my gut and begin crawling all over me from the inside as if my body were hollow and they were swarming the walls. *I need something*, I thought. Much as I imagine a drug addict needs a hit, or an alcoholic needs a drink, I *needed* food. If I fed the insects, then they would stop feeding on me.

Sylvie and I talked about expanding my coping repertoire, but all I knew was that when I was in this state, a glass of wine, a hot bath, a call to a friend would just not cut it. I needed carbs and saturated fat and I needed them stat.

As I put my groceries on the belt, I looked down, avoiding eye contact with the checker and those behind me in line. My goods were separated on the belt in two sections—in front honey mustard kettle chips, spinach dip, frozen macaroni and cheese with "family size" splashed in italics across the front, and Ben & Jerry's New York Super Fudge Chunk, followed by kale, spinach, tofu, apples, soy milk, "super food powder," hummus, grapes, flax seeds, broccoli, and cauliflower. As the checker scanned items, I kept my head down, scrolling through the already read emails on my phone, as if it would camouflage me.

Half way through, he paused. "Ma'am, is this yours too?"

I looked up. He was asking about the healthy food that he expected to see the plastic bar separating. "Yeah," I answered abruptly. *Oh my god, he knows what I am doing. It was so obvious. Why didn't I mix the food so healthy and naughty were more evenly distributed? Azure, you hate it when the good food touches the bad food! I wonder what he thinks. Does he think I have a husband who eats super healthy and I eat exclusively junk food? Or did he think I was picking food up for a neighbor —perhaps a health-conscious old lady? Or was it as clearly distinguishable for him as it was for me—tonight's food vs. (start) tomorrow's food?*

When I got home, I put all the tomorrow food in the refrigerator as quickly as possible, not even taking it out of the bags. *I'll deal with that tomorrow.* Tonight, I would have a smorgasbord just for me. The dogs serenaded me as I poured the contents of canned dog food into their dishes. I laid tonight's food on the coffee table—along with one of my husband's 22-ounce bottles of beer. *This is going to be so good. Only one more thing to do.* I unzipped my pants, peeled them off and threw them on the love seat. This was no place for waistbands. Just as I was about to start, I heard *Do everything lovingly* echo in my mind in Sylvie's breathy voice. "Oh yeah? Watch me." I said out loud, taking a deep smell of the food.

54

I started with the spinach dip, scooping huge gobs of it on the honey mustard chips. I loved the tang, the crunch of the water chestnuts, the liquidy mayonnaise base, the contrast of the sweet and salty chips that both complemented and tasted weird with the dip. Two-thirds of the way into the container of dip, I moved to the mac and cheese. Although there was more than enough time after inserting it into the microwave to walk the wrapper to the garbage can, I did not, instead throwing it haphazardly *at* the counter. When I missed and the wrapper fluttered to the floor like a butterfly, I thought *I'll deal with that tomorrow too. I'll eat cleanly and pick up after myself, and be super organized and get all my work done in an orderly fashion and be clean and put together looking, and be that other, better version of myself.* The beeps of the microwave marked the end of the three minute eternity.

Waves of steam rose from the black plastic container I burned my fingers on, as I carried it to the living room. Trixie, Ruby and Crane let out a whimper "please can we have some?"

"Oh, okay" I conceded, bringing a forkful to my mouth to blow before letting it fall to the floor. I shoveled some mac and cheese into my mouth, chewed, swallowed, shoveled, chewed, swallowed, repeat, took a swig of beer, repeat, repeat until I was so full that I felt an almost tingling sensation on my body. Life was now bearable. But I still had one more thing to go: ice cream. I opened the container and saw the partially melted chocolate magic. I spooned some into my mouth. Smooth, velvety, just how I wished my life was, with delightful surprises of crunchy pieces.

Once I was a dash above comatose, I figured it was time to go to bed. *What to do with the food I didn't finish? I could and should throw it away but it always bothers me to have uneaten food in the trash. I could try to power through and finish it. No, too full, actually too full.* I was a little pleased with myself that there was a point where I was genuinely too full. Normally I stopped eating and pretended to agree with dinner companions who said they were full and put their forks down. But I rarely felt so genuinely full myself that I could not fathom another bite. I placed the spinach dip and mac and cheese in the fridge, and ice cream in the freezer.

I headed to bed, but I was wide awake. *I can't believe I ate so much. I am such a failure. I really have to stop doing this. I am going to stop tomorrow. Tomorrow. Starting at midnight, I am a new person. Okay, Azure? Okay. It's the last chance before none of that stuff is allowed anymore… Well, it's been a little while and I suppose I have made some room in my stomach.* I threw back the covers and crept to the kitchen, grabbed the spinach dip, chips, mac and cheese, and ice cream. I put it all on the nightstand beside me and painfully forced myself to eat as much of it as possible until I actually reached absolute fullness, where it felt like the top of my stomach was at my tonsils and just breathing too hard would make it bow out of my mouth like a frog. In a state of delirium, I drifted off.

After a slumber as deep as Sleeping Beauty, minus the beauty, I woke to the evidence of my recklessness. The remaining spinach dip was discolored on top, the surface of the mac and cheese had developed skin, the ice cream was soupy and dripping. The nightstand, which was on Sean's side of the bed, was now ringed with chocolate and solvent bonded with macaroni and cheese noodles and globs of spinach dip. But it was the morning, a new day, a day I vowed to be healthy and organized and clean and put together. *A new day! A new me!* I got up and started to get ready for work. But after a few minutes, those creepy crawly feelings started to come back. *I should just throw the rest away. But, I mean, I won't be able to have those things any more. And I didn't really get to say a proper goodbye.* I stood for a moment, thoughtless, before this one crept: *Maybe "today" didn't start at midnight, I mean a day is any 24-hour period, right? Right! So today, I do declare, starts as soon as I get to work.*

As I drove to work, I scooped the now liquidy and extra-tangy spinach dip with left-over chips, slurped frothy chocolate used-to-be-ice-cream from the container as if it were a Starbucks and spooned film-covered mac and cheese into my mouth. I parked near the trash can at work and threw the containers away. I then grabbed my plastic lunch container with kale, spinach, hummus and dried cranberries inside along with the bottle of undrinkable super food drink. As I turned toward the building I thought, *Today. Today I'll be good.*

6

BOLOGNA SANDWICHES

Being good never lasted long, usually several days to be exact when
some real or imagined offense would send me running from spinach
straight to Fettuccini Alfredo's arms. And more than food choices, a type
of paralysis descended over me, stripping away my abilities more and
more with each passing week. Dragging myself to work and then home
again felt like asking the terminally ill to run a marathon. Even sitting
felt like an incredible energy expenditure so I mostly just laid around
thinking *maybe if I eat a little something, I'll feel better.* And for those
fleeting moments while I was wide-mouthed and chewing, slurping,
licking, I *did* feel better. But immediately afterwards I felt terrible, which
only made me want to eat again. I cried more and more, not just in my
sessions with Sylvie and on the phone with Sean, but on the couch by
myself during the week, much of the weekend when Sean was home, on
phone calls with Tiff and Erin, and even sometimes at work, after quickly
closing the door to my office.

How could I be crying this much? I wondered. *What do I have to be
so freaking sad about? Nothing!* part of me would answer, while simultaneously another side of me would say, *Everything. God, Dad's right*

about you! Just a bitch looking for something to bitch about. What do you have to be so goddamn sad about? You're married, have new house, a six-figure-job, everything you have ever wanted! Your life is finally good. And yet you still find a reason to be sad. But still there was an emptiness in me and around me so palpable that I could not will it away. In fact, I could not imagine *anything* making it better. I thought the road to healing was going to be glistening with smaller pants sizes and increased self-confidence but so far therapy didn't seem to make anything better.

Sean knew that something was up. He said it every time he came home, not with words but with the extra loud clanging he'd make doing the dishes I had let pile up all week long and the exasperated sighs he'd make while crumpling paper or plastic food containers into the trash can from the nightstand, the coffee table, and the car.

As I lay on the couch, I called to Sean. "Just leave it! I'll do it."

After a moment of silence, he'd sigh, "It's okay," in as monotone a voice as he could muster. I could smell his dissatisfaction.

"Really, just leave it, I'll take care of it."

He continued without responding to me and I, giving up, continued to lounge and watch TV. I thought – no, *knew* – that I was a useless pile of crap but I also knew that I just simply didn't have any energy to get up, that if there was an activity that required even less energy than lying down, I would be doing that instead.

"I'm already doing it," he said flatly. I could hear the irritation in his voice. I rolled over and got up, with great difficulty, went to the mouth of the kitchen and leaned against the doorway.

"Babe?" I asked, a yawn–stretch catching me at that very moment. It seemed like a particularly inopportune time for Sean to glance up at me, arms outstretched stiffly in the sweatshirt I had stolen from him, double chin amplified, white unattractive legs exposed from underneath the shorts I had no business wearing. He just looked back to the sink.

"Please let me do it," I said, even though I stood where I was.

"I said I'm already doing it. I'm almost done."

"Are you mad?"

"No."

"I can tell you're mad."

He threw down the silverware into the sink with a clash that made me wince.

"I'm not mad," he started, even though he obviously was. "I've just been gone working all week and come home to this. But it's no big thing to me. I just take care of it. I'm someone who just does it and doesn't feel the need to bitch about it."

My face shifted. "What are you trying to say?"

"Just that."

"So, you think all I do is bitch about it?"

"Well?"

"Really?" I said sarcastically as I crossed my arms, any guilt about the dishes and the filth disappearing in an instant.

He turned to face me quickly and explosively. "Every freaking day when we talk on the phone it's work this, work that, my dad this, my dad that, this person pissed me off, that person pissed me off. Ev-er-y sin-gle frea-king day."

I hated the way his face looked, which surprised me. I could not have imagined hating anything about Sean.

"I don't think you understand! My job is so stressful and I don't have the right resources or tools right now! And I need this job. And you have your issues with your dad, yes, but not like my issues with mine. You have no idea what it's like! And I don't understand why you don't under-stand—you've spent time with him, you know what he's like!"

"You think my job isn't stressful?"

My eyes fell down and to the right. I knew it was, even though I also maintained that he didn't understand.

"And I somehow find a way to take care of myself and not put it on other people!"

My eyes flared back up to his. "You think I *want* to be like this? Who would *want* to be like this?"

"Then be how you want to be!" he shouted.

"If only it could work that way for me. Life a
Wouldn't that be easy!"

"It is easy, you're the one who's making it hard!"

"I'm not you!" I shouted. I was crying now
sensitive! Maybe I'm *too* sensitive! Maybe I'm fu
know what's wrong with me, but this is just how I a...
give a shit."

I wanted him to be concerned for me, to say things like "Let's get you
some help, I'm here to support you." But he didn't, and I simply couldn't
bring myself to ask.

I began sobbing, shaking, and bobbing weak-kneed. "Why won't
anyone help me?" I wailed. I wasn't looking at Sean, because I didn't
mean him in particular. This was so much bigger than him. But still,
I couldn't help but notice him as an underwater shadow in my peri-
pheral vision, just standing there. I didn't care. I was too consumed and
had lost it. "No one ever helps me! I'm always alone! My whole life, I'm
always alone!"

I heard Sean's footsteps and felt his hands on my arms. I squirmed,
but he held me harder and pulled me in and hugged me so tightly it
almost felt forceful. Although I stood there with my arms limp to my side
for a moment, I eventually wrapped them around him and breathed in
his familiar manly smell.

After a long moment, he started swaying us, humming our song and
telling me that I wasn't alone.

∼

The next day, I was crying before my session with Sylvie even started.
I didn't even find it funny that her dog, Amelia Earheart, a Doxie like
Trixie and Ruby was climbing on the love seat behind Sylvie, trying to
lick her face while she was trying to be professional. Sylvie was alarmed
and asked me what was wrong. I told her that Sean and I had fought and
explained the fight from my perspective and emphasized that no one, not
even my husband, the person who was supposed to love me the most in

hole world, seemed to really understand me, let alone help me. Sylvie ked me to elaborate on the type of help I was looking for him to give me. I explained that I just wanted him to understand my pain, to be concerned about me, to help me. She asked if I ever told him that's what I needed.

"No, of course not!" I answered, almost disgusted at the notion.

"Why not?"

"I don't know."

Sylvie looked at me. I wasn't going to get away with this one.

"I don't like asking people for things!" I whined.

"Why not?"

"Because... then they'll know what they are."

Sylvie sat back. "Wow. Azure, I want you to repeat that whole thing back to me."

I sniffled. "I don't like asking people for things because then they'll know what my needs are."

"Wow. Do you hear it? That is profound, Azure, bravo!"

I laughed, embarrassed. I hated it when people said things like bravo to me.

"Expressing your needs growing up was not safe; even having your dad *know* your needs was not safe."

I nodded, "Because they would be used against me."

Sylvie nodded understandingly and continued, "But if Sean or anyone is going to help you meet your needs, you have to share them."

I nodded. She was right even though it felt so impossible.

"I also wanted to talk to you about something. This isn't a clinical diagnosis because I haven't met your father, but based on everything you have told me, I believe he is what is called a malignant narcissist bordering on sociopathy."

I gulped at 'sociopathy' and yet was filled with the same relief I felt when I had seen "Compulsive Over Eating Disorder" displayed on my computer for the first time.

"I don't want you to focus too much on the title," Sylvie continued. "The behavior and most importantly, your reaction to the behavior is what I want us to focus on. Specifically, when people grow up with a parent like this, their thinking tends to be absolute, black or white, all or nothing. And it can blind them to seeing things that were there."

I nodded.

"Is it true that no one has ever tried to help you, ever?"

"No, bu —"

"Wait, hold the but."

"Okay."

"It may not have been the exact help you needed, or the amount of help you needed, but there were attempts at help?"

"Yeah."

"Can you tell me about one of those times?"

I nodded. "There was this time in fourth grade."

~

The day started out the usual way, with my dad telling me to get my ass onto the pea-green enamel scale that had "Hey Fatso!" diagonally scrawled across the face. I remember holding my breath as the scale's finger wagged back and forth already scolding me and how I leaned back a little thinking it would register lighter. When it arrived at the number, still too much, of course, I heard the click-click followed by the circling sound of his mechanical pencil on the key lime graph paper he held. When I tried to slink out of the bathroom he bellowed "Commere!" as he tilted the paper so I would see as he moved his pencil up and to the right to connect yesterday's dot to today's with angered purpose.

"I've never met a kid who could who could just stick their finger into butter and eat it." He made sure to look me right in the eye. "It's enough to make a person vomit."

My eyes dropped from his face and down his body, dressed in his short sleeve button up shirt with the engineering pocket on the left breast, brown work slacks and office shoes. I did not recognize my body in his, with his skinny legs and mostly flat stomach, perhaps only inheriting the wideness of his hips.

The drive to school was quiet, the sky morose and grey. I turned away from Dad as much as I could in part because Jake's legs were on my side of the seat since the gear shift was in front of him. After getting out of the truck, Jake and I silently walked in our own respective directions. I was equally self-conscious at school as I was at home since I was the husky kid with huge feet my mom insisted on covering with Velcro shoes and the worst clothes the nineties had to offer.

Miss Schinzinger, my teacher, was a feisty woman, though Dad preferred to describe her as a "total bitch." One thing was for sure, she was focused on not tolerating any nonsense from any of the fourth graders, which is why she made her annoyance with me no secret when my name was called during reading time and I didn't even know what page we were on.

At lunch, I sat with Heather, my friend from Girl Scouts, on the metal picnic tables. I pulled my lunch out of the rolled up bag the bread came in. It consisted of a sandwich made of one piece of cheap, expired white bread made soggy by the single slice of bologna folded between it. No mustard, no mayo, no lettuce or tomato. You know how when food is made with love, you can just taste it? Well, it was as if my mom's misery seeped from her psyche into the wretched food I was about to (not) enjoy. My likes and dislikes did not factor in at all for lunch… or dinner or any other time for that matter. Only what I was *allowed* to have mattered. When I wasn't given this sandwich for lunch, I was encouraged not to eat at all. Maybe then I would lose weight, my mom would tell me. Of course, I ate the unappetizing sandwich anyway. I never went hungry on purpose. My favorite days at school were when someone's mom would bring cupcakes for the class for a birthday and the last day at school because that is when our emergency kits were returned to us and I would eat the canned Vienna sausages and granola bars my mom packed in there. Still, I looked longingly at Heather's brown bag lunch—a sandwich made with nice fresh bread, salami, cheddar cheese and mustard, a bag of chips, two chocolate chip cookies, and a note from her mom written on the napkin. You could really tell her mom loved her.

Heather offered me a couple Cheetos when she was done with them. I knew she could tell that food was different for me. She probably saw my eyes move back and forth between the snack table and my mom's watchful eye at Girl Scout meetings. Or perhaps it was the time Heather's mom bought me a Happy Meal when she drove me home one day. Heather had a puzzled look on her face when she had to show me how to open the golden arched red box and told me it was "no big deal" when I profusely thanked them over and over.

After eating lunch, Heather and I played four square and a boy in our class commented on the way my boobs jiggled. I was among the first in my class to get boobs, but that was probably just because I was fat. Then as if telepathically reading my mind, I suddenly heard Bianca Garcia call out across the yard, "Asher, basher, fo-fasher the big fat thrasher, Asher." *My name is Azure, not Asher*, I thought. I didn't dare say it out loud to her though, because that would just let her know that it bothered me and she would do it even more. I learned at least that much from my dad. The bell ringing didn't mean the end of having to deal with Bianca because she sat next to me in class. During the afternoon, she did her usual—ripping paper from my trapper keeper, scribbling all over my class assignment when I went to sharpen my pencil, scratching my arm with her fingernails, and pulling my hair when Miss Schinzinger's back was turned. I wondered why Bianca was so mean to me, but the answer was so clear—the victim in me brought out the victimizer in her. I wondered if my dad knew Bianca and told her to treat me this way since he couldn't be there with me at school. Sensing movement near our desks, Miss Schinzinger turned and snapped, "Stop messing around, you two." *I'm not messing around*, I thought, *it's her!*

I imagined going home and telling my fictional, other dad about Bianca, how she was mean to me, and him saying, "don't listen to the kids that call you names. To me, you're the most beautiful and fun girl in the world." But that was fantasy, and in reality, I would have to do what I always did—endure.

The only person I fanaticized about as much as my other dad was John O'Sullivan, swoon! John was gorgeous with chestnut brown hair and light eyes. He had a bowl haircut and looked a bit like Matthew Lawrence whose Teen Beat pics were way cuter than cookie cutter Jonathan Taylor Thomas, as far as I was concerned. I could stare at John all day, and I did, which is probably why it was very public knowledge that I was in love with him. Even Miss Schinzinger knew. The boys would tease him for it too, and he'd punch them on their arms and tell them to "shut up." But it always seemed like he was saying "shut up for teasing me" not "shut up for reminding me the hideous gargantuan troll is in love with me." He always looked at me with kindness, even though I knew it was embarrassing for both of us.

I did always wonder if I was that obvious, if my feelings were that transparent. If it were so obvious that I loved John O'Sullivan, was it also obvious that I was distracted in class because something was wrong at home? That I was worried about my dad killing my mom one day? Or the other way around? If my love for John O'Sullivan were so obvious, why couldn't Miss Schinzinger see the pleading in my eyes?

Just then, the school secretary's voice came over the loudspeaker to the entire school, calling me by my first and last name, not Azure, and adding, "To the office, please." My eyes got wide. Suddenly the entire class erupted in unison in another "Ooh!" I must have been in trouble but what did I do? I was both humiliated and terrified.

Heart pounding fast, I left the classroom and walked down the long outdoor corridor under the awning that stretched the length of ten to twelve classrooms to the office. When I got there, the secretary looked at me both sympathetically and awkwardly. "We are going to one of the portables," she explained. "I will walk you there."

I followed her down the long corridor. We came to a portable nestled between two wings of classrooms. We climbed its noisy metallic stairs and she swung open the flimsy door with more force than she intended. Inside, there was a table with two men in suits sitting on the opposite side. It was dimly lit. The school secretary told me to have a seat and explained that I was going to be talking to these men and I would go back to class when I was done. She left.

They made some casual introductions, told me they could be trusted, and that I should tell them the truth. I nodded. I don't recall them saying what agency they were from, but they didn't have to. It was very clear they were in the "police" category. I could tell they were trying to be kind and understanding and nonthreatening, talking more softly than my dad ever did.

"We're here to talk to you about your parents and your brother."

"Okay?"

"How is everything at home?"

"Fine."

"Really?"

I looked at the corner of the room. "Yeah," I answered.

"It's really important you tell us the truth." They too called me by my first name, which made me distrust them because it showed me they hadn't even gotten to know anything about me. "Is your mommy or daddy ever mean to you?"

Mommy or Daddy? What did they think, my life was a Disney movie? He had never been Daddy. And he had never wanted to be, since that was for sissies. And my mom? She sure as hell was no mommy either. It was suddenly clear what they were up to. I thought, *if they are trying to manipulate me, they should have sent a woman, and not called me by the name he does.*

The men looked at each other before one asked, "Does your dad ever pull your hair, for example?"

He had warned us that this would happen. That night earlier this year when the police came to the house, he warned us with his eyes that if we told the truth, he would kill us, literally. The police had told us that it was okay to tell the truth, that nothing bad would happen, but cops didn't know shit, bad stuff happened every single day. After they left, Dad kept us at the table for hours yelling, asking us if we wanted to live in foster care and never see Grandma again and instructing us that if we were ever approached again we were to say we were never hit, never yelled at, our hair was never pulled, we loved our family.

I faced these two men in suits who sat at the table that was too high for me. The one on the right had a mustache which reminded me of my dad, but I could tell the other one was the one in charge. "No, he doesn't," I answered.

"Your brother said that he did."

"No, he's wrong," I answered while knowing this was my chance to escape. But an equal part of me knew this escape would never be safe because my father would still be out there. Plus, what if this foster care place was even worse? "My brother must have seen it on TV and made it up."

"And your parents don't hit you?"

"No." That part was pretty true. The physical things weren't *exactly* hitting.

"But your dad hits your mom?"

"No," I said firmly, trying to look them in the eye and not down, since my dad always seemed to know I was lying when I did this, but the force in which I said it clearly had a charge. My heart was pounding hard but I focused on breathing slowly in an attempt to look relaxed.

"Your dad never hurts your brother? Or you?"

"No."

What will I say when he asks if he is ever mean to me, calls me names, tells me not to eat? The men never asked, and so I never told them. They knew I was lying, holding back, and I knew that they knew. And we all knew that if I didn't say anything, they couldn't do anything. When it was clear I wasn't going to crack, they told me that if I ever wanted to share anything with them to tell the office and they would call them.

Back at class, I thought about whether to tell Dad. I imagined that he would have been proud of my performance, and that imagined pride and my hunger for it made me feel dirty. More than that, I just wished my dad could be transformed into my other dad, that my love, like Belle's could transform a Beast into a Prince. *My other dad would hold my hand and laugh with me. He would come to my swim meets and tell me "good job." He would cradle my face in his hands and wipe away tears with his thumbs and tell me, "it'll be okay" if I were sad. He would tell me he loves me when he drops me off for school. Or he would at least tell me he loves me sometimes… Even just one time…*

The bell rang and I made my way to the front of the school where mom would pick us up and take us to the YMCA for swim team practice. I hoped that today my mom wouldn't make comments about how I was "already this size" at aged ten while I was wearing my swimsuit.

When Mom's grey Mercury Sable wagon pulled up, the first thing my brother did was lean way over the seat with his butt in the air to rummage through coats and boxes with papers for my mom to grade for her third grade class in search of Girl Scout cookies, Pop Tarts, or other goodies she kept in there. He resurfaced with a silver packet of strawberry Pop Tarts. I wasn't allowed to have these things but my brother felt sorry for me and he had become pretty good at sneaking them over to me. And I loved him for it.

I shoved the Pop Tart into my shirt sleeve like an oversized poker card. My plan was to go to one of the bathroom stalls in the locker room and eat it quickly before changing into my suit. But in the parking lot, my mom spotted my suspicious looking shirt.

"Hand it over," she demanded.

"No!" I started to walk briskly to the door of the building.

She hurried after me and grabbed my arm. "Stupid child!" she called loudly, as she smashed the pop-tart inside the cloth.

Some of the blood red gooey Pop-Tart innards fell to the asphalt, some remained uncomfortably sticky inside my shirt. I furled my brow in anger, though my eyes also welled up with tears I struggled to not let break free, devastated as much for the loss of my treat as for her treatment of me.

By chance, Audrey, the head of the Y, approached and asked my mom, "May I ask just what it is you are doing?"

Flustered and embarrassed my mom started explaining. "Hi Audrey, you see, Azure is not allowed to have Pop Tarts; they are for Jake for when he has a good day at school. My husband has Azure on a really strict diet and if he finds out she's had one and if she gains any weight, we will all be—" she searched for words and finally finished "— in big trouble."

Audrey looked at me sympathetically and then back at my mom. "What does Azure get when she has a good day at school?"

I never heard the answer to that question; my mom motioned for me to go on inside. When I got to the puke pink locker room, I went to the bench in the far corner and cried facing the open metallic door as I undressed and very quickly put the swimsuit on, already so conscious of my body. I looked down at my shirt in a wad on the bench and then picked it up and peeled the sleeve back and picked off the big chunks of pop tart and ate them. Then I put the inside of the shirt sleeve in my mouth to suck off the berry insides like a starving kid's lollipop. When one of my teammates came in to change, I quickly threw the shirt into my bag and discreetly picked the cotton fibers off of my tongue. *Stupid child.*

In my all-grown-up-now house, I wiped my eyes still feeling every bit the stupid child. I looked down at the floor in shame. And even though I could tell part of her wanted to just let me feel sorry for myself for as long as I needed, Sylvie's job was to help me grow and sometimes that requires gently challenging.

"So, is it true that no one has ever tried to help you?" she asked.

"There were times," I admitted, "but it was rare and didn't work anyway."

"And now? Does anyone try to help you now?"

"Sometimes. Sometimes, there's friends and Sean."

7
FRENCH AND ITALIAN CHEESES

It had been several weeks since our dishes fight, and Sean acted like everything was normal as usual. He and I fought so differently. I was the type of person who needed to hash it out, go over everything that was said in detail until the feeling of resolution arrived. Sean, on the other hand, was the type of person, man, who strongly believed in saying something once then dropping it, never speaking of it again, and certainly never being reminded of it ever again. He despised it when I would bring fights up again. He would stop talking and his voice would audibly tense and slow to a careful and deliberate pace when he would begin speaking. I would in turn pick up on his irritation and say something indignant, offended that he would be so clearly irritated when he could have, and I thought should have, been compassionate towards me. That would inevitably lead to a second fight. So, I was trying my best to drop it as well and be mindful to not complain about work or life frustrations.

It had been several weeks and while I was still not a perfect house cleaner, I was at least making an attempt to throw away my food wrappers, load a few dishes and purge some crap. It seemed like we were making progress. Sean returned to surprising me with Starbucks in bed

71

on Sunday mornings and resuming our dream house hunting driving adventures, which we used to do when we were dating. Sean, ever the practical one always liked single story houses with well-constructed roofs. I liked houses with large lots, stunning views and elements of character like a stone face or diamond grid windows.

Soon it was our first date anniversary, five years. Sean surprised me with a trip to the Madonna Inn, a flamboyant boutique hotel in San Luis Obispo. I was beyond thrilled, mostly because he knew there was perhaps no better way to show his love for me than indulging my obsession with surprises, since they were one of the only things even better than food to me.

We left the house early and winded down the hill from Tehachapi on Highway 58, down into Bakersfield and on toward the coast. We pinched our noses at the stinky section of road and drove extra slowly by the large, idyllic, white plantation house with the beautiful white fence that we admired every time we drove by. We stopped at fruit stands with old-time trucks outside with crates for decoration and bought nuts for the road. We marveled at the desolation west of Bakersfield and the beauty of the rolling golden hills that start east of San Luis that gently rounded into each other like scoops of caramel ice cream, speckled with beautiful and lonely looking black-barked oak trees.

I remembered how my dad, my brother, and I used to go down to San Luis fairly regularly to go hiking at Montaña del Oro state park. It was a rare time when my dad mostly left me alone, just driving and listening to Neil Diamond, the Beatles, and the Doors. It was so peaceful to not hear his yelling. Still I hated being in the car with him, so I sat, forehead pressed against the window, and stared at these same hills and oak trees and imagined I had been born to a different life.

Sean and I pulled up to large, white and majestic Victorian style Madonna Inn. We didn't get the famed Caveman Room, which required a reservation at least six months in advance, but instead we got the Old Fashioned Honeymoon suite. It was so cute and fitting for us given that we were still newlyweds, even if we had been having a rough go of it so far. The room had green carpeting, yellow and green floral wallpaper, and antique furniture—fancy seating chairs and a step-up bedroom with ornate carved wood framing separating it from the living room. The toilet even had a pull cord flush from the ceiling. The suite made me feel like I was Gigi and Sean was Gaston. I felt like I had finally made it, since I had always dreamed of staying at the Madonna Inn all those times growing up when we passed it on the way to the Motel 6.

Being with Sean in San Luis Obispo was easy. We sipped beer at local breweries and talked about our careers like we were best friends again. We bought twenty-two ounce bottles of barrel-aged beer to enjoy back at the suite and told each other that when we retired and moved to San Luis, we'd be regulars at the breweries and have steins engraved with our names hanging on the wall. We ducked into little side streets in town and spent way too much money on the most decadent French and Italian cheeses you have ever tasted from a real fromagerie. We purchased hand-made chocolates, with pistachio, salted caramel and chili filling. We walked hand-in-hand and kissed waiting for the crosswalk signal to turn.

Back at the Madonna Inn, we sipped beer from the Madonna rose-design stemware at the waterfall overlooking the pool area. I loved time with Sean when we were both in this state, both of us savoring life and food and drink, and being, adventuring, and most of all dreaming with one another. He held my hand across the table. We laughed a lot. We made plans for the future—travel and entrepreneurship.

"Maybe we could try to make a baby while we're here," Sean suggested playfully.

"Don't go getting carried away!" I corrected kidding, but not really kidding.

Baby aside, it seemed like anything was possible while in Sean's company and on vacation. Driving to Hearst Castle the following day, Sean did so with his hand on my knee. Hearst Castle was like visiting another planet, more opulent than I could have even imagined in a dream home. The gold leafed tile of the indoor pool was too much as was the dripping filigree on the interior of the main house. But when we came to the guest cottages, now those were dream homes that were actually within reach.

"One day we'll have a house just like this," I told Sean as he stood with his arm around me while we waited for the docent to open the door.

"Yeah," he agreed as we marveled at the curved red Spanish tiles on the roof, detailing on the carved wood doors, and the fuchsia bougainvillea confetti over the green ivy tablecloth that crawled up the sides of the house. Once inside, we made our way to the window. The ocean view was simply spectacular. The windowsill blended with the golden mashed potato hills that expanded all the way down to the ocean without a single visible manmade structure in between.

"Yeah," Sean repeated again in astonishment at the view.

"We're going to work hard, harder than people who have super supportive parents."

"You and me against the world," he told me, just as he had when I first confided in him just how imperfect my family was years before.

"One day?" I asked him.

"One day. Right here in San Luis Obispo, we'll have a house just like it."

I breathed in the fresh air that was both country and ocean and looked at the most spectacular coastline in the world as if nothing was going on with me, food, my body, my mental health, my dad, and with our life back in Tehachapi. We were perfect, life was perfect, and dreams really would come true.

8

MR. GOODBAR

"**H**ello?" I answered.

"Yeah," a familiar voice stated authoritatively, as if I had asked a yes or no question.

"Hi," I said tentatively, shocked and trying to process. I had only spoken to my dad several times in about as many years. The last time was when Sean and I were buying our house and my dad, disapproving, drained an account of twelve thousand dollars I had earned working, grinding our escrow to a standstill. The time before that was my wedding. The time before that was after Grandma died and he demanded that I transfer him the money she had left me and I declined.

I was suddenly aware of my stomach dropping a story or two. I had been folding clothes, but felt the need to sit down on the edge of my bed. It was always a gamble with my dad. Would he be an asshole straight off the bat or would he behave relatively normal for a little while? He told me about mail that had arrived for me but he had just thrown away. *Okay, I guess the answer is normal, for now.* He complained about the latest woes of his rental properties and how "pig headed" my brother was being, and what a bitch my mom was for refusing to let him continue to dump his trash into her garbage cans since he had canceled his garbage service to save the inconsequential dollar amount per month.

"So how is your job going?"

I told him: "It is a ton of work and there are countless gaps that need to be plugged yesterday, so I have been working around the clock."

"You need to leave work at work," he said as though this was new, fresh wisdom. "Before I retired, I was known as The Teflon Manager because nothing ever stuck to me."

He was proud and I rolled my eyes. *He actually thinks that was a compliment.* Even if he knew what his coworkers had meant, he thought they were suckers for doing his work for him.

He asked, "How are things other than that?"

Tell him! Tell him! Maybe this will be the moment when he finally understands! "Fine," I said, "but there is actually something I wanted to talk to you about."

He didn't respond, but I knew he was listening.

"I've been seeing a clinical psychologist. It turns out all those years, with food and my weight going up and down, it turns out that I have an eating disorder."

"Oh bullshit!"

"It's not bullshit, Dad, it's real! It's called Compulsive Overeating Disorder."

He laughed. "Look chickie, you're fat because you like to eat!" He laughed some more and gave himself a high five.

"Dad, it is real, look it up! It's called Compulsive Overeating Disorder!"

"Fat people make up fancy terms all the time."

"Look it up! If it's not real, why would there be clinical psychologists who specialize in it, then?"

"To take advantage of dumb shits like you!"

I clenched my fists at the sound of his wheezy laugh.

"Like I always told you," he continued, "a fool and their money are soon parted."

I pursed my lips and exhaled loudly through my nose and into the phone, prodded one too many times.

"You and Mom gave this to me!" I exclaimed with a raised voice. "All that putting me on diets, counting my carbs from the age of seven, weighing me every day, graphing my weight, giving Jake one thing to eat and me another, sending me to school and bed hungry, encouraging me to not eat, all of that! Not to mention the other abuse. It was clinically predictable—no scratch that, a god damn *clinical certainty* that I would end up with this! You did this to me! *You* got that?"

"You and your quack shrink are the only ones dumb enough to buy your bullshit!" I could hear the jingle of him stirring his coffee in the background. I shuddered. He chuckled. "You think what *you* went through is abuse? You don't know the first thing about what abuse even is, you pansy assed—"

I hung up on him. The hot burning anger from my cheeks turned into hot burning eyes that stung from crying, again. Sean had heard me shouting and came from the other room to hug me.

"He's just an asshole," Sean murmured as he stroked my hair.

I sobbed. "Why can't he at least acknowledge me?"

"Because that would mean admitting he was wrong. He will never do that."

I looked up at him, noticing the sincere, compassionate way his eyebrows curled up at the center. I knew he wanted to be able to fix this for me, to instill this insight so clearly that I would be indifferent to my dad's hurt. And that maybe then Sean and I could get on with our happily ever after. Instead I asked, "You don't think ever?"

"No," Sean answered in his blunt way.

No, Sean, maybe you're wrong. Agreeing with Sean meant agreeing that my dad and I would never figure it out. But there was a twinge in my stomach that told me that at least my body agreed with Sean.

Sean's opinion was an informed one. When Sean drove with me to the Bay Area to meet my family for the first time, I thought very seriously about asking him to turn around in the middle of our six hour drive.

"I'm with you, not your dad. It'll be fine. He can't intimidate me," Sean had told me.

He had no idea what he was getting himself into. True to form, Dad let Sean's hand remain outstretched for some time before he determined the delay was enough to establish dominance. Only then, he got up and shook Sean's hand. I was surprised and impressed how well Sean did communicating with my dad, assertively, strong, not intimidated and not backing down, but politely. My dad of course debated everything Sean said, and pointed out that Sean was less of an outdoorsman than men in our Pacific Northwest family. I was so proud of Sean for holding his own, for biting his tongue when my dad made little comments to him and to me (even though they were so far from the usual I got from my dad that they were practically compliments), and for keeping a straight face when my dad said for us to let him know when we wanted to take a shower so he could turn on the hot water.

Sean always had an amazing talent for sizing people up, undoubtedly one of the positive skills garnered from his past. Dad was certainly not the first man to try to puff his chest to Sean and Sean had been in situations with more immediate danger a hundred times at least. Sean was surely right, I would never get the acknowledgement I was looking for from my dad.

～

The following week, Sean was gone again, and as much as I tried to convince myself I was going to start being "good," the run in with my dad made me seek the comfort of Ben and Jerry and their junky friends.

By the time the weekend rolled around and it was time for my session with Sylvie, I had gained the better part of ten pounds. I began crying practically as soon as the session began and I started in with my usual: my dad this, my dad that.

Sylvie stopped me.

"You talk about your dad as if he's almost godlike," Sylvie started, "but I know through our work that you have learned he just has a profoundly wounded inner child."

"Yeah, I suppose."

"I am not buying it. You seem like you are holding back. What is it?"

I considered. "It's hard for me to think of him as a wounded child because it feels like a justification, like saying he had a good reason for treating me that way, and that is like saying it was okay on some level." I made a disgusted look. "I just have a really hard time with that."

"I understand," Sylvie said.

I highly doubt that.

"I want to take this a different direction, and it will probably be uncomfortable for you at first. Are you willing to do that?"

I shrugged. "I guess."

"I want to explore ways in which you and your father are actually similar."

"I'm nothing like my dad," I answered, offended.

"There is nothing you have in common? There are no good qualities? Even the most heinous people have *some* good qualities."

"True," I conceded, "like Hitler's gift of persuasion."

Sylvie laughed. "Right. So, can you tell me some of your father's good qualities?"

I thought for what seemed like minutes.

"Well," I paused, "I grew up in a family that values education… and travel."

"That's a great start. What about paths? In many ways I bet you walked similar paths?"

"As in, we were both abused?" It was something I vaguely knew always, but only mentioned to Sylvie last week. Even though she hadn't been surprised, of course, she glommed on to it. Suddenly it was our Leading Theory of My Father's Behavior that she wanted to discuss more than I did.

"Yes. You know what they say, 'hurt people hurt people.'"

"I mean, his father beat the crap out of him all the time and teased him for his weight and what he would eat."

I thought of the black and white photo of three boys that sat on my grandma's dresser. The husky boy in the Boy Scout uniform on the left out-massing his older and younger brother combined. My dad. I remember being so shocked that the slender father I knew, who hiked every day and ate nonfat cottage cheese and graphed my weight and counted my carbs, used to be fat himself, used to be like me. Why wasn't he more understanding, then that this was just how my body was? The answer was clear: he hated me for being his walking before picture, so much so that he tasked me with overcoming my genetics, being an alchemist of sorts, reinventing my biology into something different. I knew that was just as impossible as willing myself to have thick auburn curly hair instead of his fine golden straight hair.

"He just doesn't want you to end up like Aunt Toots," Grandma would tell me. Aunt Toots, my great aunt, was not a small lady and loved to eat and her visits would be focused on food rather than sight-seeing. The family told stories about Toots planning the menu for lunch during breakfast, planning where they would go out to dinner over lunch and stopping for ice cream on the way there. I knew that I was basically the same way, a food-centric person and this was clearly shameful in my family. My mom loved food too, but she was thin so it was okay, in fact it was considered cute. As family lore would have it, my mom took the "see you tomorrow" at Baskin Robbins literally and she went so often that when she moved, the store threw her a going away party. These stories were always told in a clear tone of 'isn't that darling, the thin woman eats fattening food.' I always knew my family's stories about Toots would have had the same cute overtones had she been thin, that my dad and I came from a long line of husky people who were shamed about their bodies even as food was their most constant source of love and affection. And maybe we did also just love food—and what's so wrong with that?

What happened to him? I wondered. What happened to the boy who liked the Mickey Mouse Club, Howdy Doody, and Bugs Bunny? Who used to write science fiction? Who raised mischief with his friends?

Who liked chocolate bars? How had we been so similar and grown up to be so different? What had his father done to him to transform him so profoundly?

"My biggest regret in life is that I didn't kick my dad's ass," my dad would say, "for making me stand in the bathtub with my hands at my sides and get hit, for making me go to school with a hand print on my face." I understood, but never really felt that way, myself. I never wanted violent revenge except in the heat of the moment. All I ever really wanted was acknowledgement—for him to say, "I know I hurt you and I'm sorry," even if it was accompanied by a true but diluting statement like, "So I wasn't perfect," or "I did the best I could," or "I didn't know any different." Was there anything I could ever do or say to get through to him, to talk to that inner kid in there, to make him understand my pain the way that the boy I imagined him being would? Nothing I had ever tried had been effective.

"Oh honey," Grandma would say in that soothing See's Candies kind of voice, "your dad *does* love you, he just has a funny way of showing it."

I wondered if it was possible for that to be true.

"What else did you come up with?" Sylvie asked.

"Hmmmm," I thought, "well, this one thought keeps popping in my mind." I laughed in an embarrassed way. "We both stole candy."

Sylvie smiled approvingly.

Awe, father daughter bonding, I imagined her thinking.

"My dad used to tell this story about when he was a kid and he went to the dime store and slipped a bag of jelly beans under his shirt and headed toward the door. He hadn't anticipated that every step the bag would make a very loud crinkle sound. When he would tell this story, he'd squeak his voice to imitate the crinkle, which was so out of character for him, since he was usually so serious and pissed off. He described how kid him started walking faster and faster toward the door 'crinkle, crinkle, crinkle.' And when the shop owner looked up 'crinkle, crinkle,

crinkle, crinkle, *crash!*' as the jelly beans cascaded all over the floor and my dad took off running. He loved that story." I mused, thinking of how I didn't mind his smokers laugh when he told it.

"And you had a similar experience?" Sylvie asked.

"Well, sort of, but it wasn't as funny.

I was eleven and we were visiting my mom's family—her mom, brother and his kids, who lived near Sacramento. Grandmother was equally controlling to my dad, but not abusive. She was southern by birth but British in her formality. She always wore dresses the same well-tailored straight-lined style of Jackie-O and meals at her house were served with a salad fork, a dinner fork, a soup spoon, a tea spoon, a regular spoon, a butter knife, and a regular knife. Even chips were served with a spoon. She was absolutely completely and totally against profanity or vulgarity of any kind, no matter how slight, consumption of alcohol, my father and all things that reminded her of him. The feeling was mutual. In fact, I never once saw my dad in the same place as any members of my mom's family. He referred to Grandmother as Grandmother Troll and most of the time we were forbidden from visiting her, which is why my mom always had Jake and me sleep in our clothes the night before and leave as soon as Dad left in the morning.

Unlike Grandma, Grandmother was not warm, she didn't give hugs or make up stories or have a playful bone in her body. I remember when we arrived for that trip, my mom turned to give me a final warning: "Remember, if you gain a single pound, we won't be able to come here anymore." She shook her head and added "It's so unfair to Grandmother."

Unfair to Grandmother? I thought.

Once inside, my brother aimed straight for the massive display of jars on the mantel filled with different types of candy. When I heard the glass-on-glass scraping sound of a lid rising from a jar, I headed over there. My cousins, Krissy and Kevin ran over to join him. When

I approached the mantel, Grandmother stopped me. "Now, now! The candy is for your brother and cousins. Not you."

"The last thing that girl needs is a trip to the candy jars," my uncle Ronnie chimed in.

Butt out, I thought.

"Awe! How come?" I pleaded to Grandmother, even though I knew she'd give me the answer she always gave.

"You don't take after this side of the family where you can eat what you want without gaining weight," Grandmother answered, "but your brother does."

"But it's not fair!" I exclaimed.

"Life isn't always fair," she told me.

This is the way trips to Grandmother's always started—that candy is for them not you, the donuts are for them not you, the chips are for them not you, stop complaining and enjoy your half a grapefruit.

Not a single pound, I reminded myself as I watched which candy jingled from the jar and into their hands.

Grandmother was right, I did take after my dad's side of the family which put on weight easily. And Jake did take after my mom's side of the family. But how could Grandmother judge me—cheat me!—for something I was born with? I didn't choose to look like my dad's side of the family, no more than she chose to be petite. Being petite wasn't something she worked hard for, or earned. She was just born that way, she won the genetic lottery. How could she take credit for it?

She must have felt a little badly because she offered, "It's such a shame. You have such a pretty face."

I had been hearing that line my entire life and hated it every single time I heard it. It was unmistakably *not* a message of "you're pretty with a round body" it was "you *would* be pretty if you *didn't have* that round body." And I wished how I looked wasn't always a topic of discussion.

"She looks just like her dad," Ronnie added.

My mom and Grandmother agreed. I knew that they hated my father and everything that reminded them of him. And I was the kid who looked like him.

Uncle Ronnie bragged about how well Krissy and Kevin were doing in school.

"Maybe your cousins can give you a few pointers," my mom rubbed in.

"Uh-huh," I responded, unamused.

When it was time for lunch, we made our way to Sizzlers. While at the table, Uncle Ronnie, Krissy, and Kevin started snickering. "Rotund P.B.E.," I heard one of them say as they chuckled and pointed at a morbidly obese woman walking by on the way to her table with a full plate in her hands.

"What's P.B.E?" I asked. I knew what *rotund* meant, so I braced myself.

"Professional Buffet Eater," Uncle Ronnie responded in a low voice though he was giggling. My cousins snorted with laughter.

How mean! They had no idea what it was like to be overweight.

"That's why you should watch what you eat," he continued, "otherwise you'll grow up to be one of them."

At least I won't be mean! I thought.

Uncle Ronnie went on to tell my mom about diet pills available for sale in Mexico that expand in the stomach like a sponge to make a person feel full. My mom jotted it down on her memo pad using the pencil she kept tucked behind her ear.

Can we please just have one meal where we aren't talking about my weight or unsolicited diet tips? I wondered. I looked down at my plate, full of unlikely combinations of buffet food and now a heaping helping of shame. *I'm going to show them!* I thought. *I am not a P.B.E.-in-training!* After waiting for the rest of them to make a couple more trips to the salad bar, my mom asked if I was finished. I looked down at the table. "I'm not hungry" I lied. My mom reminded me how much it cost and that it was important to get our money's worth. *Nothing I do is ever right!*

After lunch we went to the Dollar Store nearby. I hated them all. And more than that I hated that I always had to pretend it was okay and just take it. I looked through the aisles of cheap toys, neon clackers, snap bracelets, kitten puzzles. I was not going to ask them to buy anything for me, I didn't want anything from them. I kept walking and came to the candy aisle.

The yellow wrapper of a Mr. Goodbar caught my eye. *I deserve it*, I thought. *They are so mean to me!* I looked left and right to make sure no one was near me before I stuffed the candy bar into the floral stretch pants I was wearing. I covered it with my oversized pale pink shirt. I made my way to the front of the store slowly to conceal the crinkle of the package. "I didn't find anything," I told my mom with obvious obstinacy and less obvious rebellious satisfaction.

When we got back into Grandmother's Chrysler, I could feel the chocolate bar snap in half at the seam of my hip as I sat down. The break had ripped the package. *Oh no!* On the drive back to the house, I slowly and carefully reached into the space between my shirt and pants and broke off little pieces. Turning my head to the window so I couldn't be seen in the rearview mirror, I slipped them into my mouth. I let the chocolate melt around the peanut bits and then slowly chewed so they wouldn't hear. As we drove, I could feel the bar getting softer and softer against the heat of my body. *I can smell it. Oh no, can they smell it?* I became paranoid.

When we got back to Grandmother's house, throughout the afternoon I continued to sneak my hand into my shirt, returning with a finger-full of melted chocolate with peanuts. When the wrapper was nothing more than a corpse, I went to the baby blue and pink 1950s style bathroom and carefully coiled the wrapper in toilet paper and buried it in the trash underneath other booger soiled wads. *Phew!* I sighed audibly. I had gotten away with it!

Or so I thought until my mom used the bathroom after me. She came out with an angry, determined look on her face. "Let me see your clothes!" she demanded.

Oh no! "What?" I asked innocently, the lie surely showing on my face.

"Let me see your clothes!" she said with precise pronunciation. "Stand up."

I did. She raised my shirt in search of pockets where she assumed I had put the candy. It revealed brown smears on the inside of my shirt and the skin of my stomach above my stretchy pants. "I knew it!" She revealed the wrapper in her hand, freed from its toilet paper disguise. "Where did you get this?" she demanded to know.

"I don't know," I lied.

Uncle Ronnie and Grandmother joined in the interrogation. Somewhere between the fifteenth and twentieth inquiry, I broke. "Fine! Dollar Store!" I yelled, exasperated.

"So, you are a liar *and* a thief," Uncle Ronnie said in front of everyone. *Butt the hell out!* I thought. *You're not my dad!* My cousins snickered.

"You know which side of the family this comes from," my mom said to Uncle Ronnie and Grandmother. I was now the fat, average student who looked like my dad and stole too. Their judgment and disgust were palpable.

My mom shook her head. "We are going to march your butt over there right now and you are going to apologize and pay for this," my mom said.

The entire car ride, she asked "Why would you steal?" on repeat and I met the question each time with silence. I knew she didn't really want an answer, only to pound the shame into me. *Really? Why would I steal it? I am never allowed to have any of it! I have to sit there and watch my cousins and brother help themselves to candy jars and donuts and chips and be told I would be able to have some too if it weren't for my unfortunate, 'rotund' genetics. I was told I would become a Professional Buffet Eater if I wasn't careful. Of course I stole it, you assholes!*

My mom stood close beside me in the store as the checker finished with another customer.

"My daughter has something to say to you." She looked at me expectantly.

I looked down at the ground and not the envy green apron of the employee. I started, "I'm sorry—" but was interrupted by my mom.

"Look at him in the eye and stop mumbling."

I looked up, tears building in my angry, embarrassed and ashamed, bloodshot eyes. "I'm sorry I stole a candy bar," I blurted as adolescents do. "I'd like to pay for it now." I held out the dollar my mom had given me in the car before we went in. I was mortified as the checker lectured me about stealing and that I could go to jail next time. What was more mortifying than stealing or the accumulating line of people spectating my apology was *what* I had stolen. Why couldn't I have stolen a toy? Of course, I was the fat girl apologizing for stealing a candy bar! I was sure the checker was probably thinking, "Clearly you get enough candy bars at home." I was sorry. I couldn't help but wonder, though, if I was the only one who understood all that had led me to do it.

"I'm going to have to stop you there. We are out of time," Sylvie interjected.

Of course, I thought, *open up but be sure to keep it to fifty-five minutes or less.*

"Today's homework will be for you to practice thinking of your father as a profoundly wounded inner child. I think this is the key to get you to a place of forgiveness."

"Okay."

But I don't want to forgive, I thought, but did not say. I would save that for another time.

9

CURRIED CHICKEN SALAD

When Tiffany's wedding was a few weeks away, I could no longer avoid the sports jersey yellow bridesmaids dress wrapped in plastic that hung in my closet. I unwrapped the dress and let the plastic cover flutter to the floor. Although I knew I had gained and not lost weight, I was crossing my fingers that somehow it had redistributed in a way that would make the dress fit, even though it wouldn't have fit when I ordered it. I could tell even holding it up that it was not good. *Why did I have to buy this in a smaller size? Why was I so optimistic that this would be good motivation to lose weight? Why was I so foolish to think that motivation is treatment for a legitimate eating disorder?* Dread prickled from inside my stomach and rippled out like pebble circles in a lake.

After staring at the dress for a number of seconds, I unzipped it, weaved my arms through the butt and into the arm holes, ducked my head under the fabric which I could feel was already tight, and pulled. *Thank God my upper body is smaller than my lower body!* The dress successfully made it, albeit snugly, over my bust, my waist, but then—*Oh crap!* The floor length material stayed bunched up at the small of my back, the base of Butt Mountain. I tugged, and it budged a little, but I also knew the A-line skirt was not meant to look like a tight mermaid gown and was also not intended to be a cannot-sit-down-seams-popping hazard, and even that would only take place if it was possible to get it over my butt which it was not. *I expected for it to maybe not be the most flattering but to not fit at all? You're so stupid, Azure! Why would you purposefully order an expensive dress that was too small to force you to lose weight? What am I going to do? I'm going to fix it and not stress Tiffany out before her wedding.*

I peeled the dress back off me the way it had gone on but it was much harder and the dreaded stuck-midway occurred. *Will it come off? Will I have to Incredible Hulk this off my body?* I kept pulling and wiggling. And after a few pops it finally broke free from the wide part of my shoulder blades. Sweaty faced and flush, I tossed it on the end of the bed. I power walked around the house with my smartphone in hand, the dogs' collars jingling as they followed me. I picked up the top of the dress to reveal the tag and completed my Google search: "boutiques that carry SH4287." Nothing discernible came up. I went to the designer's website, heart beating fast. *Tiffany is going to kill me!* I clicked on the "find a retailer" link and typed in my zip code. No results found. I changed the drop down to 200 mile radius, one in Los Angeles. Then I moved the drop down to 500 miles. One in L.A., one in Orange County, one in San Jose, one in San Francisco, one in Vegas. I took a breath. *Okay, Azure. It'll be okay. One of these places will have it.* L.A. was closest, so I pressed that location first and then the phone number. As the rings sounded in my ear, I scolded myself. *I can't believe I'm going to have to spend another $175 on a second dress!*

"I was wondering if you happen to have dress SH4287 in size 16?" I asked. "I accidentally ordered a 12 and just realized it."

"What's the dress number?" The woman on the other end asked unenthusiastically.

"SH4287," I repeated.

I heard the clicking of her keyboard.

"That dress has been discontinued."

My stomach did a back flip.

"And you don't have any more in stock?"

"No."

"Do you have a suggestion for what I could do? I'm in a wedding and don't have the right size."

My pleading tone didn't faze her at all.

"You can call other boutiques and see if they happen to have it in your size or larger."

Or larger, great. "Thank you, I appreciate your help."

She hung up without a goodbye or a good luck.

I was already mad at myself, but apparently, I was also annoying middle-aged former beauty-queen-sounding boutique workers.

Okay Azure, don't freak out, just call the next one. Orange County? None in stock. Vegas? None in stock. San Francisco? None in stock. I was practicing my *Hey Tiff, I was thinking, what if I had a special dress? After all I am matron of honor!* when a kind woman from San Jose confirmed that they also didn't have any in stock but asked, "Have you tried getting extra fabric, so it could be altered?"

Oh thank God! "No I haven't! How do I go about that?"

"We would contact the designer and see if they have any that could be sent."

"Is that something I would call about directly?"

"We would need to, since we are the retailer."

"I cannot tell you how much I would appreciate that. Thank you so much!"

She took my name and number and said she would call me back in a little while.

Overcome with relief, I decided to celebrate with the rest of the box of Sean's Cheese-It's. My phone rang.

It was the nice San Jose lady. "I have some bad news," she said apologetically, "since the dress is discontinued, the designer is no longer sending out extra material."

Maid of dishonor. "I don't know what I am going to do. I have a medical condition that makes me gain weight easily," *not a complete lie,* "and the size I ordered no longer fits and I am in my friend's wedding in three weeks!" *You lying sack of shit!*

"You poor thing! I am so sorry to hear that!"

You are a total asshole and are collecting karma. Like a cigarette, every carb, every gram of fat is taking seven minutes off your life. You are going to catch a rare disease and die for lying like this!

"Let me make one more call and give you a call back," nice San Jose lady said.

"I really appreciate your help and if it doesn't work, that's okay, too."

My head dropped. I hated taking responsibility for the places I put myself, even if it was true that I had an eating disorder that felt beyond my control. I would just have to admit to Tiff what happened and take her disappointment and anger.

My phone rang again.

"Good news!" nice San Jose lady exclaimed. "In this case they are making an exception, and we are sending it to you at no additional cost, just shipping and handling fees."

Nice, real nice. Dad would be proud of you and this con of yours. "I can pay for the fabric too," I said.

"No, no! We insist. We are just so happy we can help you during your difficult situation."

"Thank you, thank you so much!" was all I could manage.

We made arrangements and I thanked her again for her above-and-beyond kindness and generosity, hung up the phone, and burst into tears.

The rectangular box arrived a week later, now two weeks until the wedding. It was like Christmas morning as I peeled back the white tissue paper top, then bottom revealing the shiny satin fabric. I never thought I would be so relieved to see Laker jersey yellow. I immediately called to find a seamstress and finally got a hold of Margaret, an older-sounding lady who said she could help me.

Margaret worked out of her house, which was a small rambler with old blue carpeting. She wasn't a smoker, but there was the same stale greyness about the inside of her house. She led me into a room which was best described as a hoarder's sewing room. Materials of all kinds and colors draped from curtain rods, even corduroy. *Do they even make that anymore?* There were three visible sewing machines, one on the desk and two in different places on the floor beside piles of clothing, measuring tapes, a large plastic board with one inch square grid printed on it and plastic sandwich bags full of spools of different colored thread. Margaret plopped down in her chair. "Now what are we doing here?" she asked. I explained that the dress was a size twelve and needed to be a sixteen. She pursed her lips disapprovingly. "It will be difficult, if it is even possible. Go ahead and try to get yourself in it."

Right here? I sat my bag down in the corner of the room with the most open space. With my back to Margaret, I removed my top. I pulled the dress over my head. I didn't bother taking off my pants because the dress didn't go down that far.

I turned to Margaret.

"Wow, isn't that dress a wonder!"

I nodded, not sure if she was commenting on the see-in-the-dark color or how it in no way fit on my body.

Margaret got up, placed her hands on my shoulders and twirled me. She looked at me clinically as if I were a very unappetizing dish she were being made to ingest.

"You got yourself into a pickle, dear, didn't you?"

"Yes."

My back was to her now. She pulled the tag from behind the strap.

I could hear the plasticky creak of her glasses. "Size twelve!" she exclaimed. "Honey, you are much, much too big for this."

"I know, that's why I am here."

"Whatever made you order such a small dress?"

You're right, Margaret, I haven't already been thinking of these questions myself, punishing myself enough about it. Thanks for the reminder. "I have a medical issue that caused me to gain lots of weight very quickly."

"Hmm. You know, I have been seeing a lot more girls like you. Back in my day, girls were size five, maybe seven, but now they are twelve, sixteen!"

I wonder if I can find another seamstress at this late date. Remembering the calls I made, I just answered, "Mmm-hmm," with my lips turned in and pressed between my teeth.

"Go on and get out of it if you can and we'll get started."

I removed the dress and put my shirt back on.

I handed Margaret my dress and she took it to her desk. Looking at the fabric under the light of her ancient desk lamp and through her glasses that sat halfway down her nose, she said, "You're really lucky to have found me. No one else in town would be able to help you."

I heard the sound of ripping seams as she used this tool that looked like it might trim nose hairs to pull the dress sections apart.

She glanced over at me. "Honey, don't get comfortable, I'm going to need you to put this back on."

"Okay." I removed my shirt again and put the dress back on. The sides of fabric fell to the floor.

"Honey, you need to remove your pants and get on the stool."

I unbuttoned my pants and stepped out of them while beneath the dress and became aware of the wind tunnel on my butt from complete lack of coverage.

Margaret asked for the spare material. I made sure to bend at the knees to pick it up, so as to minimize ass-stick-outage and handed it to her.

I stood on the block and Margaret stood at my back. *Please God, let there not be stains on my undies!*

Margaret began pinning new material between the separated panels.

"Wow, honey, you weren't even close to a twelve."

"Yep, Margaret, I know. I get it."

"Lucky for you I can help you."

"So lucky, thank you." *Even though I am paying you for a service and this is not you doing me a favor.*

Margaret was finally done pinning, after complaining about how quickly I needed it and reminding me again how lucky I was to have found her to help me with this major predicament.

I thanked her, left, and headed straight to P-Dubs and got myself a curried chicken salad to go. *Stupid Margaret!* I thought as I shoveled forkful after forkful into my mouth.

10

MELBA TOAST AND WEDDING CAKE

Tiffany looked gorgeous on her big day, as brides always do. Her makeup dramatic, her dark hair perfectly styled in a loose up do. We bridesmaids all wore matching robes and pranced around the hotel room as Tiff was being primped. I, being the token big girl, was the only one in Spanx, I noticed, which I had to fight from rolling up my thighs and down my stomach and accept cutting off my circulation. *If I didn't need these to fit into that damn dress, I would take them off right now and never ever wear them again. In fact, I vow to never ever wear them again after today. I am done with this! My body is fat, oh well. I don't think I need to be in physical pain too.*

When Tiff was perfect, we all ventured out to the lawn with the bay at our backs to take photos. The photographer got some of Tiff and Brett, and then instructed the bridal party to get in. "Oh no, it's okay" I called.

"Azure, get in, we need the whole bridal party!" Tiff insisted.

I begrudgingly stood there and gave my best smiles, feeling so guilty for taking up the space and looking the way I did.

I felt Tiff was disappointed. I had known what she meant when leading up to the day she made comments like, "Everyone loses weight in preparation for a wedding." And since she still lived in the Bay Area, an airplane ride away, she must have been even more surprised to see how much bigger I had gotten. As I stood there holding my bouquet with a smile plastered on my airbrushed face, I thought, *Believe me, Tiff, I wish I could lose weight. I am not doing this to you, I am doing this to me. There will be no redo of your wedding. I know I can't say in six months, "Okay I am ready now, let's redo those pictures!" I know and I am so sorry. I wish I knew the switch that flips me from gaining to losing.*

After photos, we made our way to the ceremony site, where people were already seated. The coordinator lined us up and started us down the aisle. *Don't you dare be the big girl who falls, Azure!* Sean was seated on the edge of the aisle and smiled at me as I approached. I smiled back. *I wonder if this is reminding him of our wedding.* The ceremony seemed long, but maybe that was because I kept shifting my weight back and forth, the shoes being killer. *If you weren't so big, maybe the shoes wouldn't hurt so badly. Oh shut up! Just don't pass out. The big girl passing out during the ceremony would be major mission failure.*

When the ceremony was over, we walked back down the aisle two by two as we had come in. After we went to the end, the photographer announced he wanted to get more photos. *More photos! How?* Suddenly, I felt extremely hot and sweaty as if I were in a sauna. I began fanning myself but realized that perspiration was dripping down my face.

"Azure! You're sweating!" Tiffany exclaimed.

I was fanning myself. "I know, I am so sorry, I'm having a hot flash or something!"

"Aren't we like thirty years too young for that?" she asked, laughing.

"Yeah!" I laughed, though I wanted to cry. *She's just talking about your sweat, not that you are fat. But you're sweating because you're fat, duh! Just forget it! It's her wedding and she wants it to be perfect. Just overlook.*

When we were done with the fifty-millionth picture, we finally joined the reception of white linen table cloths, yellow flowers with grey accents and candles. Dinner was already waiting at our places. I was starving and quickly downed three pieces of bread with butter, devoured the vinaigrette tossed salad and stuffed the rice pilaf, vegetable medley and beef with gravy before even taking a sip from my champagne. When I finished eating, I let out an audible "ah." I looked for Sean who was seated separately since I was at the bridal party table and we smiled at one another. I missed him. I wanted to sit next to him, to feel his strong hand rest on my thigh under the table.

Realizing that my speech was coming up, I downed my champagne and then another two. Brett's best man made an ill-prepared, booze-fueled speech. I poorly delivered my otherwise decently written speech with jokes, sentimentality, and a clever gift that tied it all together. *Why am I so sucky at public speaking?* And then Tiff's dad made a beautiful speech about how Tiffany was such a smiley wonderful baby that he and her mother decided to have two more. And now his little girl was all grown up and he was giving her away at her wedding. He was so proud of her and her accomplishments, and the wedding was her vision realized. He never could have imagined when she was a little girl what an accomplished and beautiful young woman she would grow into. He welcomed Brett and wished them every happiness in their life together and offered a toast and everyone clapped, not in an obligatory way but because it was truly moving. I think I clapped hardest of all, even though I was also wiping away tears.

Thank God it was one of those weddings with surprise snacks— beef sliders and fries in little baby containers. Sean and I partook enthusiastically, albeit for very different reasons. We washed it down with whisky sodas and danced. My hair whipped from side to side as I danced in rare form, rare more for the fact that I was happy and carefree than drunk. I threw my head back and laughed more exuberantly than it felt like I had in years. I noticed a sparkle come into Sean's eye as he looked at me. It was as if he recognized someone he hadn't seen in a long time. He leaned forward to whisper something into my ear over the music.

"You know we could try to make a baby tonight," Sean said.

His breath tickled my neck and made me scrunch my shoulder up reflexively.

"Yeah right!" I exclaimed recoiling back and hitting him playfully.

"It would make a great story!"

He gave me a coaxing face, a guys' version of batting his eye lashes.

"No, babe!" I shot him a serious look.

"Fine, fine."

Sean took a sip from his glass and looked around the room, seeming to look anywhere but at me.

You should say sorry, explain more about why you're not ready. No, I can't get into that right now, especially not when I've been drinking. Maybe being buzzed is a good thing, you might actually share more, open up. NO, I answered myself firmly to shut down the thought.

It was another song or two at most before Sean leaned forward and said "I'm tired, let's call it."

I nodded and followed him off the dance floor and toward the hotel elevator. When I stumbled a bit, he put his arm around me to stabilize me.

There you go, you tease. Forcing him to touch your drunk ass even though he won't be getting any after mentioning the b-word.

I was too out of it and exhausted to even answer myself, but was with it enough to find the elevator ride extra awkward when the couple in there with us was clearly heading to their room to finish what they were starting with their making out and wandering hands.

I wished Sean and I were older, that we were in our fifties already, where we could just shrug at each other and grumpily say "damn kids." But we were peers with the couple, young and supposed to be having the time of our lives, screwing each other's brains out with abandon, not caring if the neighbors heard us, not caring if a baby became of it because we were married after all and had our ducks in a row.

Instead, after a couple of false starts inserting the key card into the door, we passed out on top of the covers with most of our clothes still on.

~

That week, I told Sylvie that the wedding had been great, but that I'd been feeling sad and I hated myself for feeling like a hater.

"They have nice families and you don't! Just get over it!" I scolded myself aloud.

"I'm going to stop you there. Do you hear yourself? How hard you are being on yourself?"

Sylvie had a concerned and pained expression on her face.

I nodded slightly.

"You know what that is, right? Your inner critic?"

I nodded.

"And you know whose voice that is, right?"

I nodded again. "My dad."

"Yes, your dad. And would you call your dad's voice a fair and reasonable one?"

I snort-laughed.

"Okay!" Sylvie smiled, glad she had gotten through to me. "I want to work on silencing that voice a bit."

I smiled. "Okay."

"But isn't it interesting that in our first session you mentioned that part of what led you to this psychological work was proximity to your own wedding? Why do you think that is?"

I adjusted myself on my couch and repositioned the laptop. This one was easy. "I always had this idea of how life would be when I was married, you know? I had this image of what I'd be like, what life would be like."

"Describe that more, and remember, focus on the emotions that come up for you."

"Back in high school and college my plan was so clear: get away from my dad, lose weight, get a degree, meet husband, land a six-figure job, buy a house, have kids, build an empire, have a perfect life. It was like I had this fantasy version of myself that I thought I would become when I got married."

"Can you describe her for me, that other version of yourself?"

"I know it sounds silly but I have long thick hair, I'm slim but curvy still, and look like me, just enhanced. I am super organized which is helping me manage my weight, my career and being a mom. I have a happy, glowing disposition because I *am* happy. And even though I'm not a millionaire yet, I have accomplished a lot of what was on my list, but"—the tears started welling up—"it's like after I got married, got the job I wanted, and got the house, I was stuck with the rude realization that I wasn't different at all. Just the same shitty me!" I sobbed. "I know it's crazy but I *really* thought I would become... a different person." I cried more. "After I tried so hard!"

"Tell me about that, trying hard."

As my breathing slowed from hyperventilating, I remembered an apartment less than two years ago in Santa Clarita, where I stumbled bed-headed into the kitchen. I recalled that Sean and I were happy to have our own place at last, but missed our old roommates Adam and Erin, who were so kind to let me couch surf while I job hunted after my dad cut me off, telling me that I had "made my choice" by pursuing a relationship with Sean.

I opened the freezer and grabbed a small baggie filled with ice, lifted up my shirt and placed it on my stomach. From the drawer where we kept the silverware, I retrieved a syringe from where the steak knives should go. I opened the fridge and pulled out the medicine vial from beside the jars of mustard and hot sauces. I jammed the point into the rubber cap and held the bottle upside down and carefully pulled the clear liquid until it reached the 2 ml mark.

I winced aloud as I peeled the bag of ice off my red skin. I was always a baby about needles and even though I was injecting myself daily at this point, I was by no means ready to just take a needle. I pinched my pink cold fat. *I can't believe I am doing this*, yet I quickly jabbed the needle in. In slight horror, with the needle dangling out of my skin, I pushed the plunger slowly before pulling it out and recapping it. I smiled, a little proud of myself for doing it right that time and not like the other day when I had given myself a stinging bruise from pressing the plunger too quickly. This hormone was reportedly convincing my body that I was pregnant, which, combined with restricting food to two Melba toast crackers a day, meant that my body would metabolize my own fat.

With the syringe in the biohazard bag for safe disposal later, the adrenaline rush began to dissipate, allowing familiar thoughts of shame to rise to the surface. I had done crazy things to lose weight before, including a couple of the medically assisted programs where you get injections multiple times per week and eat exorbitantly priced processed cardboard, but I had never injected *myself* before. *I can't believe I've sunk to this level. I'm officially a diet junkie. But it's not like I have a choice!* I pleaded with myself. *My wedding is only fifty-three days away.* Indeed, it was too late to "do it the right way" for the most important wedding detail: to squeeze into my wedding dress.

I was already running late to work but prioritized another seven minutes of undulating the Shake Weight barbell in different positions, all of which looked pornographic. I would have to do these exercises twice a day to tone my arms, in addition to crunches, squats, and leg lifts, which I would also do at least two more times in the bathroom at work during the work day, before attending a kickboxing or spin class after work and then maybe doing an exercise video after that at home.

My transformation was nearly complete. Get married: 53 days away. Transform body: 53 days away. Six figure job: well that depended on how things went with this company I was interviewing with near Tehachapi. If I got it, it would be my big break from analyst to management.

My analyst job mostly consisted of chasing people down to complete their assignments. In fact, my boss actually called me her flunky once. Although she later apologized, there was some validity. I presented myself as smart when I knew full well that I was mostly just tenacious. I wore Desperado Eau de Perfum to work with not so subtle notes of urgently-trying-to-prove-myself. I was clamoring to get to the next rung of the ladder, to be in the next tax bracket, to earn respect from people, most of all my dad. In the meantime, I saved for the wedding and house that our parents weren't helping us with, by tutoring after the gym on weeknights and on the weekends, often not getting home until nine or ten. The stress of that combined with also squeezing in classes for my Master's degree had not been good for the waistline.

Neither had been grieving the death of the one person who loved me unconditionally—Grandma. I last saw her the Christmas before when I showed her my wedding dress. We both cried and she told me that she would find a way to be there one way or another. I assumed I would have someone FaceTime her during the ceremony. But soon she was gasping every other word on our calls, even with oxygen. At her funeral she looked like herself but deflated, wearing one of her everyday outfits and a very obviously handmade necklace my brother had given her. I tried to erase the image of her in the coffin and instead imprint the memory of her at her 90th birthday, rosy cheeked and spry, only gently clutching her walker.

I had been planning a big wedding but after Grandma died, I decided it was too much to handle and that we'd elope to Hawaii. A smaller wedding would be better, I reasoned, just in case Dad made a scene. My cousin Connie's wedding had been so lovely and her dad, my dad's brother, played the part well. I clung to the hope that my father would do the same for me, or better yet, be magically transformed into my other dad by tuxedoed magic. I wanted him to be like Steve Martin in *Father of the Bride*, sure, neurotic over cost (which he would have helped us with) and overwhelmed with the nuances of wedding planning, but wanting his daughter to be happy, remembering her as a little girl, talking her off the ledge when she has the inevitable fiancé drama before the big day.

I knew all that was too much to realistically hope for. I would settle for him making it through the day without an outburst, if he could even give that to me. I tried so hard to make my wedding perfect, to make me perfect, to make our life perfect so Dad would not have any logical reason to not be proud of me. And my wedding *was* perfect. Though I didn't weigh the lowest of my adult life, the injections had gotten me down to a size nine, very good for wide-hipped me. There were only eight of us total including Sean and myself: my immediate family, Sean's mom, Tiffany and another friend.

We were married in the late afternoon on the lawn of a small house overlooking a private beach of blond sand, ebony lava, and aqua ocean. I had never felt more beautiful—airbrushed and big-haired like a Texas beauty queen. My cream dress had the perfect shape of an upside down calla-lily. A locket with my Grandma's picture hung from my bouquet of teal orchids and coral roses. It was appropriate for Grandma to figuratively walk me down the aisle, not just because my father wouldn't, but because if there was anyone who loved me so much as to give me away, it was Grandma.

Sean met me with his hands outstretched. We read our vows that started with "You are the one." When we turned after being pronounced husband and wife, I was surprised to see Jake wiping away a tear. Of course, nothing from my dad, but I was too happy to care in that otherwise perfect moment.

After the ceremony, we enjoyed a piece of chocolate macadamia nut wedding cake: in retrospect, the inflection point - from losing weight to gaining. I'm not sure if it was the months of injections and Melba toast, or if it was just that good, but the moist cream filled sponge was so much more than a cake to me. It was the food equivalent of "making it," the pinnacle of a mountain I had spent my whole life climbing. Sweet success.

There was no father–daughter dance, no toast, no gift even. My dad's favorite gift was always the promise of a gift, which he would not deliver on, even joking "it's the thought that counts." Shockingly, he did pick up the tab for dinner at the restaurant where bungalows hovered over shallow fish-filled water. Sean and I smiled at each other telepathically agreeing that Dad had felt pressured to do so, and probably would not have if Sean's mom and Tiff hadn't been there. Still, something miraculous did happen: my family acted normally for an entire day, no outbursts, no embarrassment.

~

"It sounds like you had an absolutely lovely wedding," Sylvie said.

"It was the most beautiful wedding I've ever been to. But I would think so," I said with a laugh.

Sylvie chuckled. "I know we all go into milestone events and have an idea of what our life will be like, and reality rarely measures up to fantasy. But you did something that shows your healing even then, before we even started our work—you were able to lower your expectations to meet your dad where he was. That's big!"

"Thanks," I answered, surprising myself that I may have actually agreed.

"Now we just have to work on you loving yourself, just as you are."

11

GOING TO BED HUNGRY

"**W**hat the hell is wrong with me?" I pleaded to Sylvie as I found myself crying yet again. This time I didn't even feel I had a good excuse, but was crying due to the general darkness that had grown since I started therapy. "Will I ever stop crying? Will this pain ever stop?"

"Azure, this is a grieving process. You are grieving the father you never had and the childhood you never had. And that takes time. So, be *gentle* with yourself."

I nodded. "That makes sense."

"So. I've been meaning to ask you..." she began.

I gulped.

"I was consulting our session notes and wanted to touch on something I have written several times. You seem so focused on your dad. It just begs the question—what about your mom? I have to say, it seems like you let her off the hook."

I wonder if Sylvie is a mom. If she is I need to find out how her body looks like that after giving birth.

"Yeah," I answered tentatively. "I mean, my mom was a part of it—the dieting, the weighing, having me console her after my dad abused her..."

I took a breath and started to tell Sylvie the part of the story I had left out so far.

~

It was January and my mom had been acting strangely when she pulled up to the YMCA to drop off Jake and me for swim team practice. She was uncharacteristically nice, touching both of us, and being well, happy.

"See you at home," I told her in a flat pre-teen tone, suspicious of why she was acting oddly.

She gave me a look, half smug, half pity, and answered, "See you later."

I tried to put it out of my mind during swim team practice, focusing on trying to keep up with Jake, who had a natural swimmer's body and whose talent was always complimented by strangers even.

Dad picked us up as usual in the rickety silver truck with the hole in the floor near the gear shift and the greyed index card with his gas mileage calculations covering the speedometer. I noticed a red Geo Metro pull out behind us. Miles later, when the red car had gone straight at the stop sign everyone but us turned left or right, had turned left at the light as we did, taken the weird right that's more of a straight, made a left at the preschool, and followed us to the base of the hill, I turned to my dad and told him, "That red car is following us."

"Bullshit, he's just headed the same direction we are."

It is following us, I thought, certain as I continued to watch it in the side view mirror. The city streets gave way to the one lane road that headed up the hill to our neighborhood. As we passed fork after fork going up the hill and the car was still on our tail, I told my dad again, "It's still following us."

"Lots of people live up here, dip-shit."

I quieted, even though I knew I was right. When we got all the way to the house, the car passed by. *Is it possible that the car is going to one of the two houses at the end of the dead end street?* Our house was dark and the lights weren't on outside. *Hmmm, that's weird. Mom's car isn't here.* My dad muttered angrily to himself as we walked the dark path to the front door, something about "Selfish bitch" and "What the goddamn hell is she up to?" My dad unlocked the door, swung it open and turned on the light. The three of us gasped in unison and froze mid-step.

She was gone.

"Sir?" a man's voice said from behind us. Startled, we all turned. I saw the red Geo Metro idling at the top of the driveway.

"Yeah?" my dad said, with his signature what-the-hell-do-you-want tone.

"You are being served." He handed my dad a large envelope and asked him to sign something. My dad did, tilting the clipboard toward the glow of the light fixture in the entry. I had never seen Dad genuinely stunned like that. I expected him to be mad and slam the door but he was in such a stupor that the door barely clicked shut.

Mouth still agape and full of nauseous dread, I made my way into the house. I could see that many of the travel treasures on the living room shelves were gone. Jake followed me as if we were doing a walk-through of a rental property. Little art pieces and the dreaded "hey fatso" scale were missing from the upstairs bathroom. We went downstairs and saw blank spaces in the shelves where photo albums tagged with my name and my brother's were kept. Boxes that were in the crawl space were gone, as were her clothes, of course. The hide-a-bed was gone. The photos that hung along the wall in the hallway and in the stairwell were gone, leaving only dust rectangles and paint discoloration as evidence that they had once existed. Jake and I separated to survey what was missing from our rooms. The painting of the girl reading that I was afraid of was gone, as were a lot of my photos and drawings and memorabilia from my closet. My Girl Scout uniform was gone. *She helped herself to a bunch of it?* It was so violating. When Jake came out of his room, I could tell that he had found the same state in his room.

We went upstairs. My dad sat at his place at the table with the cassette tape my mom had left him tossed to the side. I strained to read it sideways so that he couldn't tell I was doing it. In my mom's cursive, it read "You Don't Bring Me Flowers Anymore." There was a manila envelope at Jake's and my place at the table. We both opened ours. Mine was a book she'd read to us as kids, called "I'll Love You Forever." Like everything else, leaving the book had been deliberate and planned. This was not something she decided to do today. This was something she had carefully planned over a period of time.

Our stupefied silence was broken by the sharp ring of the phone. Being in middle school, it was undoubtedly for me, a friend wanting to talk.

"No one answers the phone! Got that?! You are not to tell *anyone* until I say so."

I didn't respond. I looked over at my brother who was rocking himself and staring off into space as if catatonic. He was always skinny but there was something about his hunched over position, with his arms crossed in front of himself that made him look fragile.

I looked to her empty chair, a chair I would never see her sit in again. *I'm going to throw up*, I thought. The house was so full of the void of her. I remembered us ice skating with my Girl Scout troop and making blue corn tortillas at the Children's Discovery Museum. My eyes welled up with tears that broke free and streamed down my face.

"No, no, no, get that crying shit the hell out of my sight!" Dad commanded. He looked like he was busy trying to solve a complex math problem.

I went downstairs to my room and reflexively lay in a fetal position on my bed.

I just can't do it anymore! I remembered Mom pleading quietly to Aunt Barb the last Christmas we were in Seattle. And Aunt Barb's answer: *If it's that bad, I think you need to leave.*

Never let a man treat you this way, kill him first.

I became aware of a profound emptiness in my stomach. It's hollow, *all of me is hollow.*

She is gone. She escaped. She left us here.

12

BOILED BRUSSELS SPROUTS AND NON-FAT COTTAGE CHEESE

My phone vibrated and when I looked down, "Mom" displayed on the screen. When I answered, she immediately dived into her usual monologue delivered in her signature over-enthusiastic tone. Conversations with her always felt as if I were tuning into her personal news feed that ran constantly in the background, as if I had just switched on CNN. She told me about her retirement and her volunteer job, her other volunteer job, the latest with her longtime boyfriend, his kids, my brother, people I didn't know, asked for my advice that she would end up not taking, and so on. When an hour and a half later she finally asked how I was doing in the obligatory way she did, I decided to say more than my usual one word answer of "okay."

"Well, Mom, it turns out that I have an eating disorder. I've been seeing a psychologist about it."

"Oh!" She sounded insincere but trying to be polite.

I didn't say anything, curious what she would say next.

"Do you think you may be finding yourself a little down because you've put on some weight? It always seemed to me that was the case when you put on weight before."

I sighed, frustrated. "Maybe I gained weight because I struggled with food, not struggled with food because I gained weight."

"Uh-huh."

I could tell by the tone of her voice that she didn't agree. *Typical Mom, she thinks she knows more about me and what I'm going through than I do.*

"What?" I asked. "Just say it," I said.

"I just think you are happier when you're smaller."

I grunted. *She doesn't get it.* "It's a real thing. You can look it up."

"What's the name of it again?"

"Compulsive overeating disorder."

"Com-pul-sive o-ver-eat-ing dis-or-der," she parroted as she wrote it down in the spiral notebook she kept near the phone.

This annoyed me. *It's not like she's going to do anything with this information anyway.*

"And by the way, it's caused by trauma," I added.

"Oh no, Azure, not this again."

"I should be able to bring it up every time I talk to you for the rest of your life if I want! And you should be willing to hear it, to try to make things right with me." She was quiet, so I continued. "It's like you refuse to consider the impact your choices had on me. I mean really, Mom, how could you have just left us like that?"

"Azure, you know how your father was. I had to do it that way for my safety."

"But you could have taken Jake and me with you!"

"No, I couldn't have. Plus, it seems to me that I was the one he abused!"

"For your information, children witnessing abuse is also abuse. Waking your child up to make them console you because you're abused, is also abuse. Participating in the food stuff was also abuse, Mom!"

"Come on, Azure!"

"No, you come on!" I flew up off the couch and began pacing back and forth across the house as though I were making an impassioned speech. "Here's where your argument doesn't hold water—if you're so scared of your husband that you have to leave in secret because you fear for your life, why do you think it's okay to leave your children with him? It doesn't make any sense. Here's another one for you. You were so scared of him that you went into hiding, no communication with Jake or me to let us know you were alive, whether we would even see you again. But I bet you still went to work."

She didn't answer.

"You did, didn't you?"

"Yes." Her voice was quiet. We had had this conversation so many times, I knew we had reached the pouty phase where she would give only one-word answers in a sullen tone. *I know what you're doing! Don't try to manipulate me!*

I sighed, already starting to feel sorry for her, feeling that my anger and holding her accountable was being mean to her. Our relationship always felt complicated like that, like I was the older one. When I spoke again I willed my voice to be calmer.

"Look, Mom, I don't want to get mad at you. It's just that I will never be able to understand how you could have left us there with him. It was such a betrayal. And beyond that, you have never apologized, never acknowledged how leaving me there made things really bad for me after. I mean, who do you think he started treating like shit after you left?"

She was silent for a good couple of minutes before she said, "Do you think you could just accept it and move forward?"

"Wow, you are so predictable! You're right, the problem isn't with you or your choices, the problem is with me."

As I pulled the phone away from my ear, I noted the absence of pleading correction from her. I furiously pressed the red button. I would have thrown the phone through the wall if I didn't need to check work email every few minutes.

"Bitch!" I yelled out loud, the house's emptiness reverberating back to me with the subtle echo of my own voice. Furious and repulsed with myself for being upset, I let my body fall onto the couch and my head into my hands.

Where is Sean when I need him? If he were here, he'd put his arms around me. He'd begrudgingly let me vent to him. And when he felt he had enough of sentimentality, which realistically would probably only be two and a half to three minutes, and definitely before it was appropriate to do so, he'd make jokes about my mom's quirks to try to make me laugh. He'd talk about how people who wear fanny packs are always hiding something and how you can never expect people who wear pencils in their ears to hear you. And I'd laugh and snot would come out of my nose the way it does when you laugh right after crying. And I'd feel better. Why did he always have to be gone?

When I thought my missing Sean couldn't get any stronger, I felt Trixie's wet nose on the flesh inside my elbow, and then her narrow snout, which was doing something between a sneeze and a snort as it worked its way in. I lifted my elbow and Trixie's little face peered up at me, her tan eyebrows cocked in a concerned way against the black fur of her face. She put her little paws that looked like tan strawberries on my leg and reached with her snout and licked the salt water off my chin and the sides of my face.

"Ah, Trixie," I smiled as I pet her, "you have a way of turning everything into an opportunity to get attention." I laughed, grateful for her. "She simply refuses to get it, Trix. She has no idea what it was like for me after she left. You do though, girl, you were there for some of it."

~

"Get the goddamn hell out of the way, fat ass!" Dad hissed through gritted teeth before he plowed the grocery cart into the back of my twelve year old legs. Bang!

I turned and glared at him, not just for doing it to me, but for doing it so *publicly*. I think that was part of the thrill for him—to mortify me and also show his power, as if to say "watch me do this and have no one stop me."

"Move!" he demanded. I turned and continued walking, trying to veer off to the side but clearly not enough—

Bang!

I tripped forward.

Bang!

I stumbled forward again. He was going to make me regret standing up to him even if it was just with a look; whenever I did, he always was sure to beat me down harder.

"Hey!" I heard a voice say.

We all turned.

She was a middle-aged lady with short frizzy hair wearing a trench coat over business slacks. She raised her index finger and pointed it in my dad's face "What are you doing to her?"

"Hey lady, butt the fuck out—"

"I had a father just like you!" She turned to me. "Don't worry, you will be out soon. Leave and never look back!"

He stepped between us, back to me and facing off with her. "Listen you old, haggard, ignorant sack of shit, turn your ass around or you are going to wish to goddamn hell that you had."

She moved her head to the side and gave me an apologetic expression before she turned and walked away.

We continued through the store. I tried to appear normal but was delighted on the inside. It *had* happened, someone *had* noticed and *had* even said something. Even though it didn't work, I was still with him, and she was probably in her car crying, I was eternally grateful to her for advocating for me, even if just for a moment.

We continued through the store, picking the things he wanted. I stayed quiet as usual, not expressing any wants or needs, especially nothing as vulnerable as needing feminine products. If I ever needed or wanted something, it was always used against me.

"I have a rain check," Dad stated authoritatively as he handed the checker the folded up piece of paper. Rain checks were just one of his relentless commitments to save money. We also collected condiment packets from fast food restaurants, watered down our shampoo, used Motel 6 bars of soap when we bathed, which was less often than other people, and Dad would say Jake and I were years younger than we were to get a better rate. It always puzzled me because Dad would always brag to us about what a "big shot" he was, that he was already financially retired as a self-made man, owning rental properties, having a good stock portfolio and possessing the most important type of creativity there is: creativity with taxes.

The checker eyed the single bottle of gin and the single bottle of tonic on the belt and then the cart full of bottles of both before proceeding to enter in a bunch of numbers on his register, the keys clicking crisply.

"Having a party?" the checker asked casually.

"No," Dad responded abruptly, annoyed.

The checker's eyes widened slightly and quickly returned to the keyboard. Without looking up from it he asked, "How many tonic waters?"

"Twenty-four."

Click click.

"How many bottles of gin?"

"Twelve."

When we were leaving, I gave the checker an apologetic expression, always embarrassed by my dad's behavior. But I was jealous of the checker at the same time, just like I was of any waitress or any other public person who he was rude to. To them, Dad was just some asshole that they would have to wait on for 5 minutes and would never have to see or think about again. I had to go home with him.

After we got home, it was clear he was going to make me regret that woman's intervening, that I had made his punishment of me too visible.

"You fat, stupid, ugly, spit-in-your-eye bitch!" he called me.

I had been hearing that line for a while now, but it still bothered me, mostly because I knew at least some of it was true, and feared all of it was.

Because he seemed to regard fear and sadness as weakness, I held his eyes firmly, giving him my best Clint Eastwood. "Don't call me stupid!" I enunciated each word slowly and clearly in a demanding tone.

He leaned forward and repeated, "Stupid!"

"Don't call me stupid!" I yelled as I slammed my hand onto that god-forsaken table. I glared at him, fury radiating from deep within me. But my conviction only seemed to register as weakness to his robotic, deadened eyes that looked like they belonged to a great white shark.

He leaped up and lunged towards me, trying to make me flinch.

I shifted my eyes down.

His head was near mine like a drill sergeant's and as he continued on, a spray of spit droplets showered my face. "What's that, Stupid? ... I can't hear you, Stupid... Oh, cat got your tongue, Stupid? ... Stupid? ... Stupid!!!"

Don't do it! Stop it Azure! I told myself as I felt my eyes welling up with tears. The telltale glistening in their whites spelled "mission accomplished" to him. He sat back down laughing and added a final "stupid." I flared my eyes up at him again, causing the tears to break free and ricochet down my cheeks. This really lit him up. In fact, little seemed to give him more pleasure than to kick someone, me mostly, in the proverbial balls. Seeing my tears was like blood in shark infested waters. It made his eyes crazed like the wild animal he was. I wondered what he would do.

He puckered his lower lip out like a pouting child and quivered it. "Oh, did I make you thad?" he said in an Elmer Fudd voice as he smiled sadistically.

God, I fucking hate you! I thought as he started to mimic a baby's cry, "ah-eh-ah-eh-ah-eh-ah-ehhhhhhh." I shook my head, breaking eye contact with him, ashamed that my emotions had betrayed me yet again. Maybe I *was* stupid, if I couldn't control them. I wanted so badly to be unfazed by his comments, for my lack of giving a shit to drive him crazy. Instead, my tears were free flowing now.

"You should really learn to rise above your emotions," he cackled.

I didn't answer, just looked down to the floor and to the right. I agreed with him.

"You have a real screw loose," he continued as he got up, went to the kitchen and poured himself a gin and tonic.

He's fucking nuts! I thought. *Or what if he's right, what if I am the one who's crazy?*

When he came back to the table, he slurped a little off the top of his over-full drink to keep it from spilling. I shuddered. I hated the way he sounded when he ate or drank, always loudly slurping, burping, sniffling, clanking his silverware and chewing with his mouth open like a rabid animal raiding a campsite. My eyes fell to his plate. Half of it was a flattened pancake of nonfat cottage cheese with so much black pepper that it looked equal parts black and white. The other half was burnt boiled brussels sprouts that gave off a lifeless gag-worthy stench.

After a few bites, he walked out the front door saying, "Jake, I have to get something from the car." He didn't address me at all, to him I wasn't worth addressing.

I knew what he was doing. It turns out that I wasn't the only one who snuck things. He was off sneaking cigarettes.

I wished I could have used that as my exit, but that would only royally piss him off. I was not allowed to leave the table until he was done with me. *When he comes back, don't say anything back, maybe it will be over faster that way.*

The capiz shells on the chandelier jingled when he came back inside and recommenced. I wished that cigarettes calmed him, from Mr. Hyde back to Dr. Jekyll, but Dr. Jekyll was reserved for people whose opinion he cared about: work, a couple people he considered friends, though their relationships were laughably superficial, family in Seattle, and sometimes the general public. One thing was clear: he was going to put his metaphorical cigarettes out on me.

He mumbled, repeating things he had already called me, musing, talking to himself, before finally saying, "A wise man knows himself to be a fool." This was one of his favorite lines and was so classically Dad in its twisted logic: to imply it would be a sign of intelligence for me to admit that I was stupid, but at the same time granting him license to call me stupid because, after all, I had admitted so myself.

"Are *you* a wise man?" I asked, unable to help myself. "Can *you* admit that you are a fool?"

He laughed.

"No, really I want to know. What are *your* faults? What are *you* a fool about, Dad?"

He just laughed.

I crossed my arms furious and in pain.

"Jake, tell your sister what a bitch she is."

I looked at Jake, realizing, more than ever, that I was now her, my mother.

"Don't, Jake!" I yelled, not for my sake but for his. I wouldn't be able to stand it if my dad tainted Jake's gentle nature into *anything* like him.

He leapt up and lunged at me and poked me in the fleshy part between my chest and shoulder, just like he used to do to my mom.

"Don't bring Jake into this!" he growled at me. *Fucking crazy. He is fucking crazy. Did he really already forget that he was the one that brought Jake into it?*

Sorry!" I said, not because I was, but because I was afraid he would really hurt me.

"No, you're not, but you will be," he said.

Fear rushed through my veins.

He went back to his place at the table and took another drink, gears moving, thinking of what to say next.

I tried to remain unmoving. *Azure just take it.* But he only continued. "You ain't nothin' but a negative number! You got that, stupid? That means you are even less than nothing… that having you around is even worse than having nothing at all." He said it so matter-of-factly it was as if he were teaching me math.

I cannot take another minute of this shit! I got up.

"Siddown!" he bellowed.

"This isn't right, Dad! This is abuse!"

"You don't know shit about abuse… What I went through, now that's abuse!"

"Abuse doesn't have to be physical!" I said gulping every other word through my hysterics. God knows that everything he ever said to me was a poke, a hair-pull, a punch, a sock, a kick in the gut when I was already down on the ground. Is abuse to the psyche any less legitimate than to the body?

"I could report you!" I said.

He clenched his fist, slammed it on the table and left it there for me to see. "Listen, you fat sack of shit, you're going to wish to goddamn hell you were never born."

Too late, I thought and looked down, tears still streaming down my face. *Why don't you ever learn your lesson? Why do you always have to say something to him? Because*, I answered myself, *I can't let him treat me this way.*

He always had to win, would do anything to win, and tonight, just like any other, was no exception.

"Let me ask you something fat-ass," he said with a laugh. "Have you ever tried *not* eating?"

I looked down at my brussels sprouts and cottage cheese. I wanted to throw the plate against the wall. *I will never eat again! Not tonight, not ever! They will have to put me on an IV to keep me alive because I am never, ever, ever eating again. He will see. He will be sorry. He will see me looking anorexic and be concerned for me. He will say, "I'm sorry, please just eat a little something."*

Not being allowed to leave the table, I tried to do so with my mind. I hated that fucking table—thick and heavy and immovable. It sopped up the energy of every single verbal or physical beating that had taken place there, making it heavier and heavier; so heavy it trapped us with its own gravitational field. Almost instantaneously, I found my plate appearing fuzzy. I knew what was happening, it happened all the time lately. I was leaving my body and going to the void of timeless nothingness that I called the nothing place. The nothing place had no sound, not even the muffled trumpet sound of him continuing to call me names, no sight, no smell, no taste or touch or thought, and most gloriously of all—no feelings.

Sooner or later, as the high of his amusement at my plight wore off, he got up out of his chair, and like a hypnotist's snap of the fingers I came to. I was always tired and drowsy coming back to earth, but as I settled back into my body, the senses would come back, and so did the emotions I tried so hard to escape. He made his way around the table, and passed the space between me and the stairs to go toward the living room. I thought as he passed, time seeming to slow down, *I could lunge up behind him right now and push that thing with enough force that he would fall down the stairs. But what if he survived? Azure, how could you think this way? Grandma wouldn't even recognize you!* But still, it felt like the only way out was for him to be dead.

He hadn't told me I could get up from the table yet. After the TV was on for a few minutes I figured he was done with me. I gathered myself up, emotionally raped, and quietly and swiftly threw the dinner away, washed my plate and made my way to the slightly less unsafe haven of my room. Once there I leaned against the closed door and began to sob. "Why?" I cried in a loud whisper, as my shoulders bobbed up and down involuntarily. "Why?"

I went over to my dresser and looked at myself in the mirror. My despair was so alive in me, so flush in my wet cheeks, so burning and swollen in my crimson, tearful eyes, leaking nose, and quivering lips. "Why can't he just die!" I whispered in desperation. "Why can't he just *die*?" And I meant it.

How can I possibly endure six more years of this? Then suddenly and inexplicably, my breathing slowed and a calm washed over me like an invisible shower. "It's only a few more years," I said aloud as if the voice coming out from my mouth weren't even my own. "You're going to get out of here and he's going to see, they're all going to see!"

As the emotion went back into its cage, a familiar feeling took its place: hunger. *Just ignore it, Azure.* But it got stronger and stronger and I, of course, broke my vow to never eat again. In fact, I didn't even make it the rest of the night. I just *had* to eat. Between my tippy-toeing and the deafening volume in which my dad watched TV, I made it back to my room with a mostly full half-gallon container of nonfat mint chip ice cream. At first, I ate it with anger, crunching hard on the chocolate bits, but quickly my eating was smoothed into swallows of gusto and momentary freedom in my prison cell. It was as if I had grossly misunderstood the proverb to be "the way to this man's heart is through my stomach." As I ate, a movie played inside my mind, a love story where my *other* dad played opposite me.

He has kind eyes the same color as mine. In fact, not only do we look a lot alike, but people tell us we act so much alike too. He smiles and laughs a lot and we have a lot of inside jokes. He and I have this tradition of getting ice cream and not telling my mom. He always gets jamoca almond fudge and I get cherry chocolate chip. He cherishes me. Even though I am in middle school, he still insists on hugging me when I leave the house. He cheers me on from the bleachers at my swim meets. He answers my questions on my homework when I ask, but otherwise trusts that I am capable. When he's mad at me, he just tells me very directly with a reason why, which is always that he loves me. If he ever accidentally hurts my feelings, he apologizes and is empathetic. I love my other dad so much, and he loves me.

13

POPCORN AND CHIMICHANGAS

"**R**eady to go to the gym?" Sean called to me that Sunday morning from the kitchen.

"Yeah!" I called from the bedroom though I was only wearing a shirt and undies with my dimply butt exposed. I sat on the bed, watching TV vaguely, really thinking about the disastrous conversation with my mom, which I hadn't mentioned to Sean yet since he seemed annoyed that I was talking about my family too much.

"Okay, let's go!"

"You mean now?"

Sean laughed but I could tell he was irritated. "Yeah, I mean now."

"Okay, hold on!"

Twenty minutes later, when I was able to peel myself away from the TV I insisted on watching while sluggishly getting changed and brushing my teeth, I finally got in the truck. I could feel Sean's frustration as he quickly turned the ignition and sped down the road.

"Are you mad?" I asked him.

"No."

I could tell he was but I decided to not to push it. *Wouldn't it be cool if we were one of those couples that worked out together and traded off on weight machines with matching gloves and treated themselves to shots of wheatgrass afterwards?* Instead I could tell Sean was counting down the minutes before he could get away from me. I wished Sean and I could be friends in every day circumstances the way we were at concerts, B-string hockey games, micro-breweries and road tripping in Ireland, Kauai and San Luis Obispo. *Why is home and everyday life so much harder for us?* I felt like the answer was right in front of me, and should have been obvious, but I couldn't, for the life of me, see it.

We got to the gym. I had been really looking forward to swimming, it had been a long time since I had been in the water. The lanes were full, so I surveyed them for one I could share. I settled on the lane a body builder was using to swim laps. I waited at the pool's edge until he approached. "Excuse me," I asked, "would you mind if I split the lane with you?"

He looked annoyed, perhaps unaware of the common practice of sharing lanes when swimming in a lap pool. He looked me up and down making no secret of assessing my mass while making a face as though he smelled something bad. "I'm going to splash a lot for you, I think you'd be more comfortable in that lane," he told me as he pointed to the people practicing water aerobics.

Why does this have to happen wherever I go? "Actually, I'm a good swimmer."

He threw his hands up and said, "Okay, sure, fine, you can try, be my guest," as he pushed off and began swimming back down the pool.

"Be more comfortable in that lane." Just because I look this way, I can't swim? Prick! Not just to judge me but to judge the water aerobics people too! People do that for all kinds of reasons—arthritis, pregnancy, building strength, recovering from an injury, or just plain preference. I got into the pool the way I always did, sitting on the edge, so no one could see my butt, quickly unwrapping my towel and slipping in in one smooth motion. Splashing at my size was a no-no. I began swimming and quickly caught up with him, passed him, a couple of laps later caught up with him and passed him again, and on and on.

At some point during my workout, he was at the wall at the same time I was. He asked, "What college did you swim for?"

I didn't answer that question. I instead told him, "You know, stereotyping isn't cool, and when you stereotype, the only person that looks stupid is you."

"I was going to apologize about that."

"Seriously dude, not cool."

I didn't wait for a reply because I felt myself starting to cry. I pushed off the wall and swam, my goggles filling with my own salt water, my breaths gasping when I turned my head.

Even though I was proud of myself for saying something, I didn't feel like swimming much after that, but made sure to wait until my lane partner was done before calling it quits.

In the truck on the way home, I turned to Sean and asked, "You think my eating disorder is a real thing, right?" Driving, Sean looked straight ahead and took one of his signature long, pensive pauses. Whenever he would do this, the uncomfortable silences were so long that even after so many years with him, I would be tempted to ask if he had heard me.

I didn't ask him that, not this time, I could see the gears turning in his head. Part of me wondered if he was just seeing if he could ignore me until I stopped talking.

His voice was high and strained when he finally started to answer. "I think it's real, but I also think it's about mindset."

"What do you mean?"

"I think if you really want to do something, you do it."

"So, you think I have control and am just choosing this?" *Is he for real?*

"Not exactly. But you know the code I live by: Can you change it? If yes, change it. If no, forget it."

If I have to hear that shit one more time...

"So, you think I am making this hard on myself?"

"In some ways, yeah."

123

I cannot believe this guy right now. "Not to bring up your past but you believe drug addiction is a real thing, right?"

"Yeah, of course."

"Yeah, well, it's no different. All I want is the same respect for myself as someone with those struggles."

"I hate to break it to you Babe, but people don't generally respect drug addicts."

I growled in frustration.

"They respect drug addiction as a legitimate affliction, though. I just wish people would with this food stuff too."

"I am not sure it is the same thing though."

I started to cry. "My parents don't think this is real and apparently even you don't think this is real.... I am married to someone who doesn't believe that my struggle is real.... Wow."

"Babe," Sean tried to console, but it was too late.

"No," I bit the inside of my lip and looked out the window, even though inside I was begging for him to continue on, to tell me he had just been struck by lightning and got it now, to fight for me, to fight for us.

When we were home, Sean and I avoided one another. Why was this so constant in my life, to not be taken seriously? To have my feelings labeled wrong? To be told it was as easy as Sean's stupid flow chart? *You know what they say about women and their fathers. Maybe not abusive but not super sensitive either... No Azure, Stop. Sean is nothing like Dad.*

I tried to shake the thought, but it was too late. I was sucked by vortex into my childhood room.

~

"Clean this fucking shit up!" Dad yelled before he swiped his forearm across the dresser. He turned and walked down the hallway and, still half-asleep, I got up and picked things up off the floor. Because I was sure he'd come to re-inspect, I kept the light on and sat with my back against the bed. But he didn't come. Instead, I woke up a few hours later, stiff necked from being crooked back against the bed, light still on, door still open.

On the way to school, I counted down the seconds until I'd be away from him for nine hours. That's not to say, school was paradise. My dad's new understudy to replace Bianca Garcia was Greg Bishop, who called me lots of fat names, but mostly Kirby after the videogame character who inhales stuff. And Jake was now in Miss Schinzinger's class, or Miss Shit Stinker as Dad and Jake called her. Jake had just started talking again after going nearly mute after mom left. Miss Shinzinger had recently called CPS after noticing my skinny brother stuffing chocolate chip cookies and cubes of cheese into his pants pockets at Back to School Night. When CPS called my dad, he let out a full body laugh. My brother, though thin, ate plenty, having inherited the get-away-with-eating-anything genetics from my mom's side of the family, although I'm sure that the rules for me and my eating must have affected him to some extent.

"My boy certainly gets enough to eat, he just has a hollow leg," my dad laughed with the phone to his ear. My boy. As often as I heard that, it always made me sad. To me, *my boy* carried more pride in possession than I thought my son did. But Dad never referred to me as *my girl* or even *my daughter*. It seemed like he just referred to me as little as possible. There was some element of him that denied me, refused to claim me. I knew a lot of it was because I was fat, why else would he point it out so often? I resented his resentment of me being fat, I resented being fat, and I resented my fat leading Miss Schinzinger to be concerned for the wrong kid. It was a slap in the face with my own blubber.

After school, Dad picked us up and took us to Rusty Garless's office. Rusty was a therapist assigned to us by the divorce court. Jake and I wondered how old he was, but concurred he was well into his hundreds based on his hunchback, suspenders and how his voice sounded just like Yoda—high, squeaky, and growly all at the same time. Jake and I had a really hard time not giggling when in his presence, which probably gave Rusty the impression that things were fine at home. Rusty would surely have realized otherwise except that my dad persuaded him to let himself be present during our first sessions. Extremely effective at getting what he wanted, my father introduced himself to Rusty Garless as a doctor himself. Eye roll—Dad was an engineer with a double PhD. But it prompted the whole "Where did you go to school?" conversation before Dad snickered, "Yeah, there's some BS court requirement that my kids do this." Rusty Garless laughed too.

"Can I ask you something?" Dad started in that smooth talking voice. "So many entitled kids know that all they have to do is say the word and their parents get punished. How is anyone supposed to raise children these days?"

Rusty nodded. "Back in our day, we learned about the consequences of our actions." He trailed off. They both chuckled in a commiserating, back-in-our-day-we-walked-five-miles-to-school-in-the-snow kind of way. "Yeah," Rusty said in that odd voice, "often in divorce proceedings nowadays, one parent instructs the children to claim abuse to sway the outcome."

Another one bites the dust. I noticed once again how my dad sealed the deal with his confident, insider manner and Rusty bought it hook, line, and sinker.

This wasn't a new phenomenon, though the willingness of others to believe Dad's façade never ceased to amaze me. He may have looked like Robert Redford, but he was no actor. It baffled me that people didn't even seem to notice the tension in his mouth and jaw which, to me, was so clearly his attempt at holding in the stream of insults. Similarly, they never seemed to consider the syrupy quality in his voice when he was trying so hard to be nice or the way he smiled straight to their face as he fed them a line of bullshit. It seemed like Jake and I were the only people who could see how fake he was in settings like this, the doctor's office, parent teacher conferences and the biggest con of all: Take Your Kid to Work Day. The way he treated me was directly proportional to how much he cared about what the audience thought of him—work was always number one, then family friends, teachers and other professionals, our family in Seattle, people at the YMCA and other members of the public like waitresses at Denny's.

After burning as much time of our session as even gullible Rusty Garless would allow, Dad offered a final, "Since we all know this is just a formality, I'm sure you don't mind me sitting in here." To my amazement Rusty allowed him.

Every time I lifted my eyes to answer one of Rusty's questions, Dad made sure to let me know he was looking at me. I had been the one to threaten to say something, after all. I wondered why Dad cared so much about losing us when at least I was treated the way I was. It didn't make sense. Was he was afraid to lose Jake but could care less about losing me? Or perhaps it was in a power of possession way, like 'if anyone's going to abuse my daughter, it's going to be me.' Whatever the reason was, there was one because it was clear that losing us was a fear of his right up there with being audited by the IRS.

Dad had nothing to worry about, though. Rusty Garless never asked a question that even remotely went there. He had already been persuaded and he got to know excruciatingly little about us during those weeks.

The time with no contact from my mom felt like an eternity, an expanse wide enough to completely separate our lives. No calls, no letters, nothing. When she finally showed up on Valentine's day, it at least put an end to the questions: *Was she still alive? Was she still in California, or even the US? Would she sneak back and get my brother and me in the middle of the night sometime? Was she even thinking of us?*

By the time she came back around, she was no longer herself. She was wearing a fresh new outfit and her hair was cut short. She was gloating with happiness as she strutted over to me in the YMCA locker room. But I was no longer myself either. The towel-wringing contractions of mourning had finally subsided, having birthed my new, worse life, where I played the role she used to: the target.

"What the hell do you want?" I asked.

Her smile faded. "I just wanted to see you, sweetie. Aren't you happy to see me?"

"Not really."

"Come on, sweetie!"

"I have to go to practice," I told her, leaving her standing in the locker room. I wanted her to cry, but she would never. I only heard her call one final "Sweetie!" after me.

I swam fast and angrily that day. Stroke, stroke, breath, stroke. *Who the hell does she think she is, showing up here and expecting me to run up and hug her or something?* Stroke, flip turn, stroke, breath. *And what did she think was going to happen when she shows up and her hair is cut short? Am I supposed to be happy for her and be all like, Mom you look great?* Flip turn, stroke, stroke, breath, stroke, stroke. *She completely changes herself and yet I'm supposed to miss her?* Flip turn, stroke. *After all we had been through, after all the times I wiped away her tears?* Flip turn, breath. *I don't even know who is* worse, *him, or her for knowing better and leaving us with him anyway.*

I guess my dad must have known that my mom was going to show up, because she said Ryan and I were to go with her for the weekend as part of the new custody arrangement. We made the 45-minute drive to my mom's new house, which was furnished with all the stuff she had taken with her when she left. On top of that, she was regaling the tale of how my uncle Ronnie had lain in wait on the street parallel to ours, watching for my dad to drive by with my brother and me on the way to school that morning. How they signaled the movers to come around the corner and work the whole day at taking everything she had carefully planned on taking. A list that my brother and I were not on. She was so proud telling this story, thinking herself really something clever. But it just made me madder and madder.

"I wished I could have seen the surprised look on his face when you all opened the door and saw everything was gone, and the guy handed your father the divorce papers," she said.

It was clear she had no regard for the fact that my brother and I had shared the same shocked expression.

She finished with "When I shut the door for the last time, I thought 'I'm free, I don't have to hate him anymore.'" Her nostalgic smile now was surely the same accomplished grin she had on her face when she shut that door instead of sobbing for what she was about to do to her children.

I could barely even look at her, although Jake seemed fine. I wondered if it was the difference between ten and twelve.

There were a few things I did like about Mom's cookie-cutter house—it was more peaceful, it had a pool, and there was no shortage of food—microwaveable popcorn and chimichangas, blocks of cheese, rainbow sherbet, and girl scout cookies, that I was suddenly allowed to eat. And so I did, chewing the slightly elastic flour tortillas, pulling cheese apart like taffy, licking popcorn salt and butter from my fingers, and consuming sleeves at a time of Thin Mints. In those moments, Mom's house was especially bearable, before the conversations commenced.

"Would you like to play a game of scrabble?" my mom would ask in too chipper a tone.

"No," I'd say with my teenager attitude dialed all the way up.

"Don't speak to me that way! I am your mother and mothers should be treated with respect."

"Oh really? You're my *mom* now?"

"Stop it, Azure."

"You suddenly want that title after being so quick to give it away? I know, by the way, that you didn't even fight for custody. He showed me the paper."

"Come on, Azure, you know it had to be this way."

"You couldn't tell me?! You could talk to me about killing my dad in his sleep, but you couldn't tell me you were leaving?"

"You would have told him! And then he could have killed us."

I thought of the neighbor's dog who my dad hated for its incessant barking and howling. The dog had been found hanging from a tree.

"I *never* would have told!"

Even though she was crying too now, I knew it was for herself. She had no choice: that was her story and she was sticking to it. She looked away, likely thinking the same thing as I was: *She does not get it, she never will.*

14

SMOKED SALMON CASSEROLE

Erin and Adam, Gemma and her daughter were over along with some other friends. Sean had smoked a couple of chickens and I made smoked salmon casserole, a dish of my own creation with egg noodles, cream cheese, smoked salmon of course, white sweet onion, asparagus, and Pillsbury crescent roll dough on top. The weather was warming, so we all sat out on the patio at the glass-top table.

"You have to give me this recipe!" Erin said as she took a bite and made the same type of face I did when I ate.

"It's super easy! I'll text it to you."

Sean and Adam agreed, practically in unison. I thanked them and told Sean the chicken was really good too.

Sean smiled proudly with his mouth closed and his chin up. I smiled back. Sean and I were doing well in these moments when the playful, childlike parts of us came out. In fact, it was as if our damaged, addicted inner teenagers completely and totally got each other, him imbibing and me noshing. And it felt like when we were both our adult selves, we were a dynamic duo, like business partners brainstorming career strategy in a conference room. The problem was when we were out of synch, which was often, when one of us was in adult mode and the other in teenager. In these circumstances, we found each other annoying, irresponsible and impossible to deal with.

During dinner we talked about music and concerts, showed each other funny YouTubes, and laughed more loudly than the neighbors surely liked. The sun set and gave way to the warm glow of the Christmas lights that hung on the bottom of the deck overhead. Sean took empty plates inside. "Thank you, Babe," I told him. The guys followed him and when they came back out, their pint glasses were full.

Gemma lit up a cigarette and Erin followed suit.

"How's it going?" Erin asked me pointedly, now that the guys were out of earshot.

"Oh fine!" I said in my usual chipper tone. She looked at me in a knowing way.

"Bullshit!" Gemma called me out loudly. We laughed. Gemma was always a little rough around the edges and tended to vocalize what most people just thought.

"Well," I started with my voice low. "I've actually been having a hard time with Sean. You know how I'm going to therapy for the eating disorder? Well, Sean doesn't seem to think of it as a real thing. I just don't know how to reconcile that. But I don't want to bore you guys with the details."

"Shut up! You're not boring us!" Gemma said and Erin agreed.

Truthfully, I was relieved because I really valued their opinion on Sean because they had known him for so long. Erin especially was like a sister to him. He had even introduced her to her husband, Adam, and Sean had I had co-officiated their wedding.

I continued, "I guess I expected him, of all people, considering his past, to understand and be compassionate toward me." I started tearing up and adjusted my hair so the guys wouldn't see me crying.

"Oh, Azure," Erin started as if there was something so obvious that I wasn't seeing. "Sean is just a super straight forward person. Things are very black-and-white for him. He's not all grey and weird and fucked up like us."

We all laughed.

"Don't take it personally," she continued. "Did I ever tell you the story about the time he quit smoking?"

I shook my head.

"He and Adam got back to the old apartment, climbed the stairs and Sean was out of breath. He turned to Adam and said 'I think I just quit smoking.' Adam laughed it off but Sean never smoked again. And look at us."

She took another drag and blew it out to the side away from me, the non-smoker, and said "It's annoying as hell for us too!"

I snort laughed.

Pleased that she had lightened me up a little, Erin explained "I've known him for a long time and he's just one of those people who once he makes up his mind about something, that's it. That's how it was when he quit smoking, that's how it was when he quit meth, and that's how it was when he met you."

I gave her a sincere half smile, remembering how according to Erin, Sean had come home the night he met me and told her that he had met The One. He denied this to me of course, saying that what he said was that he met the "coolest girl" that night. But I believed her. I wanted to believe her anyway, especially considering how challenging marriage had been for us.

On the other side of the patio the guys erupted in laughter at whatever they were talking about.

"I totally get what you're looking for from him. You want him to be there for you because this isn't easy for you or for most people, for that matter. Most of us are Start Mondays."

"Yes!" I agreed emphatically, feeling so understood.

"And talking it out is what girls like me are for," Erin said.

"Hey! What about me?" Gemma asked.

"Sensitivity is not exactly your forte."

"Touché," Gemma laughed in the wheezy way she always did.

Erin was not the first person to tell me that I needed to focus on my female relationships because women would most likely provide the type of support I wanted. Someone like Sean who has linear thinking wouldn't satisfy my emotional needs. And of all my friends, from the Bay Area to So Cal, Erin was the one who understood me the most, family structure, the love of food, the creative side, the searching for something more in life, all of it.

I thanked her and asked her "But how do I get *him* to understand? I don't know if I can go through this process without Sean's support. And if he doesn't understand then he can't be supportive."

"I think you should talk to him about it again," Erin said, "but not when you're pissed, not in a fight. Catch him when he's calm… You know Sean loves you for you, it's not about how you look, right?"

I nodded, even though I only partially believed it. I knew he loved me, but there is a difference between a dedicated type of love and a spicy attraction. Did Sean now love me like a sister or a friend? Was there any of that attraction still there? Were guys ever really actually attracted to larger girls?

I thought of a guy at a bar who had pointed his arms at me like he was holding an imaginary rifle and mouthed "bang" before trying to pick me up, telling me he liked big girls. Big game hunting, likening me to a rhinoceros in the Serengeti and not even hiding it.

Erin put her hand on my shoulder and rubbed it. "Call me more!" she insisted.

"What would I do without you?" I asked.

"About that…" Erin answered with an uncomfortable look on her face.

"What?" Gemma and I asked in unison.

Erin explained that she and Adam were thinking of moving to Nevada, that California was too expensive and that if they moved they'd be able to afford a house and be able to go do things too.

I told her I understood and was happy for them, and I was, though, selfishly I was sad at the idea of having her and Tiff both an airplane ride away. By that time it was way late, too cold to be out on the patio.

We all made our way to rooms, spare bedrooms, the couch, and air mattresses.

~

When I woke up, it was with the dead feeling of someone hungover, but I wasn't, only sleep deprived. I never have been much of a drinker, probably because I was an eater. I stumbled into the kitchen, Sean and Erin already awake and drinking coffee and talking in low voices to one another. *Is she telling him what I said? Is he confiding in her about his desire to leave me?* Others were stirring, others still dead to the world. I began to make my breakfast feast of two dozen eggs, bacon, sausage, well-buttered sourdough and bloody Marys. Hungry kids dished up first, then adults then teenagers who had slept the latest. Even though the energy was much quieter than the night before, I loved it—the faint sound of the cartoons and children's laughter, the clinking of silverware on ceramic plates, the swish of the back door opening and closing, the laughter, the mumbled talking, the slurping of coffee, the sounds of family. A family of our own creation.

Regaining sober lucidness, our family started to disperse, leaving just Sean and me, and a messy, profoundly empty, silent house which would get even lonelier in a matter of hours when Sean was gone again.

~

The following Saturday in my next session with Sylvie, I complained about Sean's lack of understanding and help even though I had not yet even tried Erin's suggestion of talking to him. *Sometimes we need a glass of whine*, I justified to myself.

To my great annoyance, Sylvie kept directing the conversation away from Sean and back to my mom.

"I know you don't think this is related, Azure. And I know you have some resistance to going there, but I need you to stick with me," she told me.

She looked sure of herself, staring at me head on with eyebrows raised a little. I raised the laptop up to the arm of the couch, an electronic equivalent of sitting up straighter.

"Azure, I get the sense that you don't want to be mad at your mom, or maybe be mad period, but I want to remind you how important it is that you not bypass your anger. Our anger protects us from harm. Your anger is saying 'what my mom did is not okay!' I want you to own your anger."

"Right now?"

"Right now."

Sylvie seemed to realize she would need to coach me through this and asked me "Did it piss you off that your mom didn't take you?"

"Hell yeah it pissed me off!" I responded automatically.

"And you're still pissed off?"

Shame. The apple doesn't fall far from the tree. My eyes dropped. *Yes.*

"I can tell anger makes you uncomfortable, but the anger that you just expressed is actually among the healthiest statements I have heard from you in our work together. Remember, our anger is an instinct that protects us from harm."

"Yeah." *Why does Sylvie have to be right all the time?*

"Remember what we learned about emotions—they want to surface, be fully experienced, and only then dissipate. Otherwise they calcify inside just like that steak we talked about at the beginning."

"Yeah."

"After your mom left, you must have experienced some anger."

"You have no idea," I answered in a mischievous way, feeling the horns sprouting on top of my head.

Sylvie smiled. "Tell me more about that."

I told her about a day when I was thirteen when, as soon as I got to school, I changed into my black velvet Elvira dress and Doc Martens from Hot Topic, applied white makeup, being careful to avoid the safety pin in my nose, and added a trickle of "blood" from my eyes with a red lip pencil. I never even made it to class. Vice-Principal Vernon, stopped me in the hall. "I'm going to need you to change," he told me.

"Um, this is my cultural expression," I retorted with every bit of thirteen-year-old sass.

"Is that a safety pin in your nose?"

"Maybe."

"I can't have that here either."

"This is part of my religion. You are not allowed to not let me do something that's part of my religious views."

"Come with me to the office," he sighed.

After a visible eye roll, I followed.

He had me sit in the same blue plastic chair with metal legs that we used in class, while Mr. Vernon went back behind the waist-high counter to his office. The administrative staff were wide eyed when they noticed me, which is what I was going for, of course. Mr. Vernon came to the counter and asked me back to his office where I sat in the much more comfortable guest chair while he sat behind his big brown desk. "Your dad is coming to pick you up."

Fuck! I thought, *he is going to kill me.*

"Azure, I've known you since you were young," Mr. Vernon continued. "You're a sweet girl. Why are you doing this? This isn't you."

I had no idea how to even begin to answer that question, so I just stayed quiet. *What am I supposed to say, that if I were loved, that would make my entire life bearable? Not even bearable, but validate my very existence on the planet. That I am fucking angry at... the world, at God for doing this to me? For birthing me to my parents? For making me look the way I look? For no one ever helping me, ever? For living in a world where my real life is a secret, for being told that the part of me that is visible is too visible? That I am so sick of hearing people say what I am or am not? And yet simultaneously wanting everyone, to tell me what they want me to be so I can just be that already. What do you want me to be? Just tell me! And since the only person you people are only ever worried about is my brother, what the FUCK is the point?*

"What do you think about what I asked?" he pressed.

"I don't know." I folded my arms.

Dad was pretty quiet when he picked me up and the ride home was silent too, but that was typical before he had his first drink. When we got home, he remedied that. He then told me to "get that thing out of my nose," which was more painful than putting it in, if that was possible.

I sat at the table and waited to receive my punishment. After a few minutes he sat back down wearing the faded navy blue polo shirt that was at least as old as I was and khaki hiking shorts. My eyes fell to his large feet and his three middle toes which were webbed, just like my brother.

He then sat across from me at the table for a while in his contemplative pose, which he did from time to time. It was something like Rodin's The Thinker but involved him staring off into space with a haunted look and rubbing his mustache which crunched the way rubbing straw between one's fingers might sound. I always wondered where he went when he slipped into this other world. It always seemed like wherever it was, it was more past than present.

When he came out of it, he picked up the phone and dialed my grandma and told her what had happened. Even though she wasn't on speaker, I could feel her shock, disappointment, and confusion. She would have agreed with Mr. Vernon that this wasn't me. Except now, it was.

A week or so after getting suspended, we road tripped to Grandma's house. These trips always started the same way: Me having to pack Dad's bottles of gin and tonic in my luggage, Dad making us stay up until one in the morning when he was done packing, him yelling at us to go to bed as if we were the ones keeping *him* up, and going to school sleep deprived before an eight-hour drive to Ashland.

At our fast food stops, Jake and I were reminded that we were to order one item off the dollar menu, and then I was made to feel guilty for ordering whatever I ordered. "You won't lose any weight eating that," he'd gibe, even though I'd be given no other option. *At least we aren't at Denny's* I'd tell myself, thinking of the way he would speak to the wait staff and how he'd not only not leave a tip but steal tips off of empty tables. Then for entertainment, as in his own entertainment, Dad would tell his favorite racist and sexist jokes in addition to his vacation variety of criticisms of me such as "having you along is like bringing a suitcase of diarrhea," which made my brother laugh at the word "diarrhea." In these moments, I hated Jake and that Cindy Crawford beauty mark of his because it was the same as Dad's. But I still shared the pack of peanut M&Ms I got from the vending machine at the Motel 6 after Dad had drunken himself to sleep. Not that I had much choice in the matter. Jake had caught me sneaking back into the room and threatened to tell unless I shared. I watched as precious sugar marble after precious sugar marble clicked into the palm of his hand.

The next night, when we finally arrived to Grandma's, after an all day hike and eight more hours of driving, Grandma gave me her usual pillowy hug made of puffed up cold cream, baby powder and unconditional love. I loved her so much. I wanted to stay forever, to live with her and not go back with my dad. But that was impossible.

After getting settled, we had the traditional weighing ceremony, where Grandma would slide the scale out from underneath the stand next to the door to her room. Grandma always weighed herself too, so I wasn't the only one. "He just wants to make sure you don't struggle like he did," she'd explain. But there was nothing preventative about this—I already *did* struggle with my weight and with food. My whole life felt like a struggle, with only a few points of ease: love for Grandma, my admiration for my cousin Connie and a talent for writing and crochet. I just nodded. I loved Grandma.

"I really want to see you get there," she continued. "What if we even made it fun? What if I paid you a dollar a pound that you lose?"

This stung. She didn't need to pay me. Just letting me know that this was something she wanted for me was enough. I wanted so badly to please her and was so sad that she was confirming that even to her, I wasn't good enough as I was.

The next morning after my dad, brother, and I walked a few miles to the top of a nearby hill and back, we had breakfast—eggs, bacon, sausage, sourdough toast, and the best strawberry homemade freezer jam ever. I always helped cook while my dad sat in the recliner. I was then critiqued for all of my cooking. "Do these eggs look over easy to you? Just have one egg and half a piece of toast, no jam." This would be spoken over his plate of three eggs, bacon, sausage, two pieces of sourdough and jam.

We then went on the dreaded all-day "dumpster diving" shopping spree at every second hand store in a fifty mile radius. Afterwards, we drove to meet my grandma, two uncles, aunt, and one of my cousins at the Asian Seafood Buffet. On the way Dad counseled me, "You know what shows a lot of strength? Exercising willpower." He explained it to me in an uncharacteristically neutral tone. "Being able to sit with other people eating and to be able to just sit there…. Plus, have you ever noticed how retarded people are always fat? Why don't you show everyone that you are smarter than you look?"

Did he just imply I'm kinda smart? I was delighted. It was the closest thing I had ever heard to a compliment from him and I cherished that crumb he tossed me. *All I have to do is prove it to him by not eating?* More than anything in the world I wanted my father's respect—I knew earning his love was too farfetched, but respect seemed doable, as long as I did the right things. Like not eat.

So, I didn't. At the restaurant, the waitress asked, "Are you sure you're not hungry, darlin'?"

"Yeah," I said, lying.

My aunt looked over at me. "When you don't eat with us, it feels like you don't like us," she said.

"It's not that—" I started.

"If she doesn't want to eat, don't make her eat!" my dad jumped in.

"She looks hungry," my aunt continued.

He gave me a conspiring look.

"Why don't you just have a little something?" my aunt asked again.

"I don't want to be fat, okay?" I snapped. "Haven't you ever noticed how retarded people are fat?" I parroted what Dad had said earlier.

I immediately regretted it and hated myself for saying it. How could I have repeated anything he said? He was the most prejudiced, bitter, bigoted, angry, hurtful person I knew and almost had ever heard of, except for genocide-committing dictators and child-raping murderers. Apparently, I had the capacity for speaking like him too. I didn't share his sentiment at all, though, and was so ashamed that I sold myself out for the prize he held in front of me. I looked up at him and he gave me a little smile, one of only a few I had ever seen, let alone directed at me. I wasn't sure if it was a twisted sort of pride in me or gloating at his power over me.

~

Sylvie interrupted.

"Great vulnerability today, Azure. We are at the fifty-five mark. It goes without saying that anger was a particularly unsafe emotion to express in your family. Your anger was punished by your dad, and labeled as wrong by others like your Grandma because they were of the philosophy that 'nice girls don't get angry.' Plus there is the fact that any emotion you *did* see from your father was anger."

"Yeah, you're totally right. I never thought of it that way before. And I really don't want to be anything like him. That is seriously my worst nightmare."

"But being angry does not make you like him. Being angry helps you set boundaries, not become an abuser. In fact, *not* dealing with anger makes it more likely you will eventually explode and say something hurtful to others."

"Yeah that makes perfect sense."

"And, I also want to remind you that narcissism is a family disease, not just the narcissistic individual. Family members cater to the demands of the narcissist and treat them as though they are healthy individuals, which inflates their egos even more."

"This really makes me feel better. Growing up, I was always wondering 'Am I the only person who is seeing this?'"

"And you may have been the most clear. In these types of families the children tend to fall into two categories- the Chosen Child and the Rivaled Against Child. You were the Rivaled Against child and the gift in it is that you see the dysfunction the most clearly and have the highest likelihood of escape."

I thought of Jake and felt a twinge of guilt.

Sylvie closed her file and looked up at me.

"I just want to say: what you are doing is so hard and very few people do the hard work that you are doing. You should be proud."

I nodded genuinely.

15

ICE CUBES AND SARAN WRAP

"**B**abe, can you scratch?" Sean asked desperately as he sat on the bed with his bare back to me. He must have seen that I had woken up as I sometimes did when he was getting ready during what everyone but Sean considered the middle of the night.

I propped myself up on my elbow, leaned forward and ran my nails along his back vigorously. He didn't have to tell me higher or lower or curl his back like a cat. I knew the spot he wanted by the black brindle pattern and peach globs of flesh that looked like large candle wax drippings. I wondered how many more years of me scratching at them it might take before a teeny piece of gravel that I was sure was in there would finally work its way to the surface and pop out into my hand.

This road rash, as well as the grid-like pattern on his forearm from a skin graft and the foot long, inch thick surgery scar on his hip came from the car accident that both saved his life and nearly took it.

I remembered Sean telling me the story shortly after we met: how he had finally fallen asleep in the passenger seat with his seatbelt only partially on after being up for several days on drugs, and how he had been ejected from the car when they had a blowout on the highway on their way home.

"I'll never forget the way my mom looked at me," Sean had told me, "when I woke up from the coma in the hospital and didn't know where I was." I would never forget the look in his face either, when he first told me this story—the regret, shame and disgust in himself for having done that to his mom. It was so vulnerable, so human, and it made me want to dive into him and learn everything there was to know about him. I had so many questions. What was being in a coma like? Did he remember conversations taking place around him or have a glimpse of heaven like in paranormal TV shows? "Nope, just blackness," Sean had answered as a matter-of-factly. What had being in a wheelchair for months been like? "Shitty." What was learning how to walk again like? "Hard." How did he think he was different after the accident? "Other than wanting to get clean, my short term memory took a dive," he had answered.

I stopped scratching and touched my palm to his back. How close he had been to death. How close we had been to never meeting at all. Had he lived so that we could meet and he could help me overcome my own addiction? I hoped so. But it felt like he wasn't interested in that. It felt like he just wanted to live his better, normal life and didn't want to revisit the old, drug stuff, even if it would help me.

I got a little sad. What had happened to that vulnerability between the first time he told me this story and now? When had he closed off his heart to me? Had drugs killed it in some delayed death after an incubation period? Had it ever been there at all or had I made an assumption that just because he understood my family, that he was understanding?

"Thanks, babe," Sean said as he stood up, wafting the pungent smell of man body wash and began putting on his shirt and expensive watch. Sean really did have that successful man thing down. He always looked the part, which I assumed was because he was so confident and self-possessed. In fact, Sean looked like he belonged so much that he was mistaken for a local when we traveled to Kauai, Fairbanks and even Ireland. I on the other hand felt like I had to practically talk my way into the building at work. *No really sir, I work here.* And that was just the tip of the ice berg when it came to Sean and my differences. Sean was always fifteen minutes early. I was always fifteen minutes late. Sean ate the same thing for breakfast lunch and dinner. I could barely commit to the next meal. Sean always made the bed in the morning. I was lucky if I got clean and unstained clothes on. Sean loved being the center of attention. I was incredibly shy in group settings. Sean was content. I was hungry, always hungry for more. Sean didn't take life too seriously and enjoyed antagonizing people who did. I was one of those people.

I wanted to be like Sean so much. I know that was a big reason why I married him. I figured if you are who you hang out with you *really* are who you are married to. But it hadn't worked. I hadn't magically taken on Sean's qualities through osmosis. But I longed for Sean to show me the way, to take me under his wing.

"See you Saturday," Sean said just above a whisper before leaning over and giving me his Monday goodbye kiss.

Stay! Don't go! I shouted in my mind, before answering, "Drive safely."

After I heard the front door click faintly, I felt like I could chew through the walls. I got up and headed for the kitchen. Standing in front of the open fridge, I thought *Same ol' Azure. You never change. You say you want to change. Swear you are going to change every single Monday, birthday, wedding, girl's trip, bikini season, Christmas Party and New Year's Eve. But you never choose differently. Look at you right now, looking for food. No wonder you get stuck in Eat and never make it to Pray or Love!*

I wanted to be like Sean, a success story, deliberately transformed. I had known occasional moments of that myself and I wanted that moment, that *feeling* again.

⌒

I was determined to transform myself in the summer between junior high and high school, making it my full time summer job. Thinness, to me, was like the American Dream—if I worked hard enough, it was attainable and I was going to work my ass off this summer, literally.

In the it's-already-this-hot heat of the San Jose summer mornings, I began the day by awkwardly passing the roll of plastic wrap from left to right as I wound it around and around my abdomen at the waist, hips, saddle bags, butt, and each upper thigh. After clumsily tearing the stretchy plastic, I attempted to move but was stiffened by the transparent layers which didn't glide over one another as I for some reason expected. Rather, they clung. *Duh! It is called cling wrap!* I pulled up my stretchy pants and lowered my shirt, the plastic swishing and catching in a squeaky way. I inserted my "Jagged Little Pill" cassette into my boom box, clicked play, grabbed my hand weights and began running in place, sounding like a squeaky, screaming grocery bag with every movement. I tried to drown out the sound by angrily singing along with Alanis.

When I could no longer stand to run in place another moment, I laid on the floor, and proceeded to do one thousand leg lifts, left leg, right leg, then a thousand uncomfortable crunches. The sweat that trickled down my spine was both hot and chilly at the same time. The plastic wrap looked as sad as a used condom when I was done—saturated, disgusting and half falling off. I removed it and noticed a colony of red bumps all over my now itchy skin, which I assumed was from my body reabsorbing sweat that was unable to evaporate under the plastic. My skin was cool and clammy as I changed into my swimsuit for the pool portion of my workout: running through the resistance of the water, treading with my hands above the water, and pulling, kicking and swimming laps. At breaks I sucked on ice cubes. *Make your body work to heat it up*, my dad had told me. When I could no longer stave off my profound hunger, I made my way wet-footed back into the house to dip some raw broccoli, cauliflower, and baby carrots into a dab of dressing. After lunch, I hung up the swimsuit and began wrapping the plastic wrap around me again, initiating round two of the entire sequence. I would go on to rounds three or four.

Between working out, I helped my mom, who is something of a hoarder, declutter. I trashed old xeroxed teaching materials with ease, and put excess books in the Goodwill pile gladly. I chucked useless knick-knacks and piles of catalogues without a second thought. I was making real progress when I came across a mysterious shoe box among her files. I lifted off the black lid and saw my mom in four by six staring back at me. She was folding down her bottom lip exposing a gouge where her bottom tooth had been shoved into it. Not too long after that picture was taken, the root died in that same tooth and she had to have a root canal. I reached my hand in and chose a different photo, this one a close up of a bruise on her arm. Next, a post-it with "1-12-93 kicked me in the stomach" scrawled on it. I chose a different photo, this one of a bruise on her thigh. I chose another, a cascade of bruises down her shins from when he would kick her under the table. Another of bruising on the fleshy part between the chest and shoulder he liked to poke so much. Another of her thumbnail black and blue and wavy from him squeezing it with all his might. It remains wavy to this day. Another of black and blue toe-nails from him stomping on her feet. Another of a patch of hair missing where he had pulled it out. I shut the lid and held it there frozen for a few moments. Beyond the obvious reason, I knew why she had this box.

Next to the volatility and the violent tendencies, the thing that was most frightening about my dad was his supreme intelligence. When he was in high school, he was a juvenile delinquent who failed almost all of his classes but in a standardized test, he tested highest in the state of Washington, according to family lore. He went on to be valedictorian at University of Washington and after that to earn a double PhD in physics and electrical engineering. He was cunningly clever and he approached everything as if it were a game of chess. Oftentimes, he would do something puzzling that didn't make sense in the moment and then later it would. My mom always told my brother and me about when they traveled to Australia, there was a huge spider the size of a person's hand in their room. Rather than asking the people at the front desk to get rid of the spider my dad fell into perfect character. "My wife and I are entomologists. Would you mind capturing the spider that's in our room and putting it in a jar on the table for us to study?" Afterwards, my mom asked my dad if he was crazy. He said, "I wanted to make sure they did it, otherwise the spider could still be loose in the room." He was always calculating, two steps ahead, which applied to the abuse too. My mom never went to work with a black eye, a busted lip, or anything people would obviously associate with beatings. He was too smart for that. Instead, her bruises were often in places that would be covered by clothes.

Holding this box of proof, all so carefully documented, I was nauseated and terrified at both the horror and the power that it possessed. And I could exercise that power if I wanted to: unfit for primary custody of children. I remembered the same familiar nauseating feeling I felt when CPS pulled me out of school to ask about my dad, the same deep sickness when the police officer came to the house and asked me if my dad hurt us. I felt the same sour sensation of knowing that the wrong word could break up my family, the same twisted knots of terror of being grateful that *someone* had called the police, yet knowing that the neighbors, who were my dad's renters, must have heard the yelling and screaming for years and had decided not to.

I then surprised even myself—I gingerly and reverently placed the box in the trash pile.

I understood even at fourteen what most people do not about domestic abuse—that the emotions are so much more complex than you can imagine. Some of the few friends I'd confided in over the years would say things like "If my dad did that to me, I would hate him." I imagine if a random person comes up to you in the street and assaults you, it's easy to hate them. When it's your parent who does it, it's not binary like that- love or hate, but *both* simultaneously. I did hate him, and yet I didn't. I don't think that what I felt for him was *love*, exactly. It was more of a longing for him to love me, mixed with admiration and obligation to do right by him. Plus, there was the brainwashing about foster care and other things. Besides, since my mom left, he was a stand-up single dad, as far as anyone knew. Part of his genius was to expertly install self-doubt.

After decluttering, I took the trash bags out to the twenty yard dumpster Mom rented for this task and one at a time, coiled the bags behind my back and flung them an irretrievable distance into the pile of trash. I then recommenced my workout regimen which took me well into the evening. Doing sit ups and leg lifts in the dark while watching infomercials, a woman said "I never feel hungry!" while pulling out the waistband of her way-too-big pants by her thumb. "What the hell does hunger have to do with it?" I asked aloud.

~

I didn't recognize Greg Bishop's voice when he called me at the end of that summer. Even though we had gone to school together from elementary on, and he'd tormented me for years, we never talked on the phone.

"Is it true?" he asked me.

"Is what true?"

"That you're hot now?"

I giggled. *Oh my God! Was someone saying that about me? Does that mean it worked? All that hard work over the summer?*

"So, it is true," he stated more than asked.

"I dunno!" I laughed, "I mean, I do look different."

"I hear you look like Britney Spears now."

I laughed. "I don't know about that!"

"How do you look different? What are you wearing?"

"Well, I have blonder hair now, and am thinner, and wearing white shorts, flip-flops, and a seafoam green tank top."

"I'd love to see that."

Wait—was Greg Bishop trying to *flirt* with me?! He *hated* me, had even bullied me by the stricter 1990s definition. "Yeah," I said, "maybe a bunch of us can get together sometime, since we're going to different high schools."

"How about now?"

I laughed. "What do you mean?"

"I'll drive over there."

"You have your license already?"

"Yeah."

I was one of the youngest people in my class so he must have been a solid year older. Had Greg repeated a grade? It would have explained the chip on his shoulder. My dad was gone for the night at a singles dance since he had started to date again.

"Sure!" I said, and shrugged.

I heard Greg's car before I saw it. The subwoofers were so loud that my mirror, which I was obsessively primping in, vibrated as well. *Why am I trying so hard? I don't even like Greg!* But just because I didn't like him didn't mean I didn't want *him* to like *me*. Greg rang the doorbell and I answered. He was wearing a white cotton shirt with a plaid shirt unbuttoned over it, jean shorts, and tennis shoes. Unlike me, he had not transformed over the summer. He was still beefy himself, pimple-faced, and hopelessly arrogant.

"Hey, come on in," I said.

"It is true!" he said, making no secret of looking me up and down.

I looked away and laughed nervously. I had zero interest in Greg but was really enjoying feeling desirable, especially by someone who had tormented me so much. After awkward conversation and showing him around the house and me nervously wondering if it had been a mistake because I didn't want him to take it as an invitation to put the moves on me, he asked, "Wanna go on a drive?"

"Sure," I was anxious to get out of the house in case my dad came home. If I were gone when he got home, he'd be mad; if there was a boy in the house with me when he got home, it would be my ass. We climbed the dark stairs and into his (well, his dad's), white Mustang convertible. When he turned the key and the music came on, the rap blared and the car shook. We drove down the hill I lived on, and made our way onto the freeway. He drove fast with the top down which was both exhilarating and terrifying, since I was trusting Greg Bishop with my life. As my hair whipped around in the heat of the perfect temperature of the late summer night, I felt like my transformation was complete. I smiled and laughed and danced to "Wannabe," Greg Bishop's music. When I insisted that I had to be home by ten, he shocked me by being compliant about it. No questions asked, he turned around and dropped me off. I never saw or spoke to him again. It was as if we both became aware of the end of an era.

16

LUNCHMEAT WITH BEST FOODS MAYONNAISE

If I wasn't making progress with food, I was at least doing so at work. I had plugged the biggest holes and was now working on doing so with the medium and small sized ones. Sean and my conversations had improved. We now had a good number of conversations about career strategy. He welcomed my ideas on negotiating his promotion and raise, and was genuinely proud of me when I got my own to Director. I was pretty proud of me too. I needed that promotion so badly, because I needed evidence that I was competent at something since I couldn't be as a daughter or someone who wanted to lose weight.

And even though there was still an elephant in the room of our marriage that we were not addressing, things seemed to be going pretty well, until a Friday, when an unintentional bomb email exploded my inbox with the subject line "Tiffany and Brett's wedding pics!"

I shouldn't click, I thought before clicking.

My eyes went straight to me, the largest blob of color on the screen of girls in matching robes. *Oh God!* I thought in horror as I couldn't help but notice that Spanx were sticking out from the bottom of mine. There were photos of Tiff getting ready and us helping her into her dress. *God, I can even tell which arm is mine, fat.* Us walking down the aisle. Tiff and Brett saying their vows, then kissing. Us walking back down the aisle in our celebratory looks. *Double chin! Tiffany! This should have been deleted before being sent out. Please don't post. Please don't post! Do I seem immature if I ask her not to post?* All of us posing outside the venue. *Fattest freaking person there.* More pictures. *Gasp, you can see the seam on the dress where the emergency material was added.* More poses. *I'm so sorry, Tiff. I know you must be so disappointed I ruined your pictures.* Finally, Tiff and Brett gazing at each other. *So perfect. So freaking attractive! Unlike me, where people assume I am Sean's friend or roommate or charity case until they realize we are together and wonder how the hell that happened and what the hell is wrong with him. I knew I shouldn't have clicked. I knew it.*

When Sean came home, I burst into tears.

He hugged me. "Babe, what's wrong? Don't tell me one of the dogs died!" He looked around anxiously, counting the wagging tails.

"Nope," I snuffled. "I look so gargantuan in Tiff's wedding photos. I'm so freaking fat. It's awful!"

"Babe, you look fine!" he told me as he patted my back.

"You haven't seen them!" But I could tell he was anxious to put down his stuff and take a shower, so I added, "It's okay, I'm fine, it's nothing."

When he emerged, he announced he was hungry and since I only had kale, hummus, garlic cloves, and veggie burgers in the house, he requested we go to Slicks so he could get a burger. The memory of gasping on my jalapeño corn vomit popped in my mind. The phantom of all the bad food I had ever eaten overtop of me with its hands around my neck choking me into submission. Frightened, and realizing my heart was beating fast, I willed the thought out of my mind.

Entering the double doors, we laughed when we saw the deejay who was always there on Friday nights and placed bets how long it would be until he played "Cupid Shuffle."

Menu open in front of me, I became tense. *Everything is at least a thousand calories each. Maybe I should just have a cheat meal. No! I pigged out on Indian food a few days ago!*

"What's wrong?" Sean asked, reading my pained expression.

"There's nothing I can really eat!"

Sean shut his menu and said, "Let's go then," and started to get up.

"No!" I insisted quietly. "I'll find something."

Sean was visibly frustrated as he sat down again, which immediately became embarrassing when the waitress came over and asked, "How are you folks doing tonight? Can I get you started with anything to drink?"

"We're doing fine, thanks!" I answered overly enthusiastically trying to take the focus away from Sean and his annoyance. "I'll take a club soda."

Sean ordered a beer from Kern River Brewing Company on tap.

"Are you ready to order food, too?"

"I am," Sean said, "are you?"

I wasn't but decided I would make do.

Sean ordered a burger with sweet potato fries. I ordered a salad and fried zucchini.

After she took our menus, I apologized to Sean, "I'm sorry, Babe. I'm feeling sorry for myself for looking so big in Tiff's wedding pictures."

"It's okay, Babe."

"I have no one to blame but myself! I had plenty of time to lose weight for that wedding and I just couldn't get it together. Now it is inked in the history of her wedding photos."

"You could do something about it," Sean said just as the fried zucchini was delivered to the table. *Fried* zucchini.

"What did you say?" I asked, suddenly moving from sad to irritated. *Okay, not to be that cliché "does this make my butt look fat?" wife, but did he seriously just agree that I look fat?*

"I said that you could maybe do something."

I crossed my arms.

"Don't get mad, Babe," he insisted as he helped himself to the zucchini fries I had ordered, dipped it in ranch and brought them dripping to his mouth.

"Don't get mad?"

"Yes, Babe. Don't get mad. You know how I am, the code I live by—"

"Yeah, yeah, yeah, I don't need to hear it again."

"Yeah."

"Well, it ain't that easy for me."

"It could be. Just don't over think it. You've done Weight Watchers several times, you know their program in and out." He crunched another few sticks of zucchini. "Just count the points. Calories in, calories out. It's simple if you're consistent in sticking to it."

"Burger and sweet potato fries?" the waitress said as she placed the plate in front of me.

Of course, she assumes that since I am the fat one, that I ordered the burger and him, the salad.

"I'm the salad," I told her with as much composure as I could as I passed the mouthwatering burger and the aromatic sweet potato fries over to Sean.

She sat the salad down at my place at the table. Once she was out of ear shot he asked "Are you okay?"

"Yeah," I answered in a pouty way, embarrassed for doing it publicly and unable to stop myself.

"Come on, Babe."

"Yeah, I get it okay. Calories in, calories out. It's simple. You're right. Let's just drop it." *It's simple, so very simple. If I have to hear one more freaking time from anyone on earth how freaking simple this is and what a moron I must be for not being able to figure it out, I am going to snap.*

"If you're upset, we can just get this to go."

"No, it's fine!" I insisted. I grabbed a stick of zucchini and proceeded to peel the fried bread crumbs off it, thinking of the unforgiving yellow bridesmaid's dress. *Why couldn't I have just done the work to look nice in it? I should have just gone back to injecting myself again. Azure, have you made no progress in therapy? I wish I could go all the way back and learn how to eat like a healthy, normal person. And if that's too much to ask, I wish I could go back to one of the countless times I've lost weight and just realize I was there, at the finish line, instead of always thinking I was still ten to fifteen pounds away.*

～

In high school, I think it started with the fact that my best friends, Carmen, Natasha, and Shelby were petite. It wasn't their fault by any means, but their natural bodies made me feel mine wasn't. I was reminded that there was still more weight for me to lose, that I wasn't quite there yet in carving out my American Dream Body. I was always told by my family that I was the type who "could just look at a piece of cake and gain ten pounds." Maybe I shouldn't have looked at my friends as they ate their pizza and Flamin' Hot Cheetos for lunch and McDonalds after school. Meanwhile, I brought a slice of bread, a handful of baby carrots and had water polo practice for three hours a day and supplemented with hours of cardio at the gym. Even with the indiscretions that would follow days and weeks of restriction, I had to be netting a calorie deficit, right?

"Think of food as fuel," my dad would tell me, "nothing else." I wanted that too. To approach food as calories in, calories out. Protein, fat, and carbohydrates. I wanted to exercise the perfect control over my food, to think of food as completely devoid of pleasure and emotion and connection, rather than joy, consolation, a good laugh, a good cry, a pat on the back, a hug, an 'I love you.' I wanted to see the world in non-food terms. To be able to drive and navigate by street names and not restaurants—turn right at See's Candies, make a left at Taco Bell, if you get to Max's you've gone too far.

Still, my friends offered me something else invaluable to me— a window into what other dads were like. Shelby's was nice, innocuous, quietly supportive. Carmen's was more vocal and traditional and protective. Natasha's dad was the most like what I fantasized about. He asked me questions, took interest in me, teased me even. One time, he even told me I looked like Meryl Streep. The next time *Death Becomes Her* was on

TV, I mentioned to my dad that I'd been told I looked like her. As Meryl Streep's character pranced around having drunk the potion of youth my dad replied "Everyone knows Goldie Hawn is the hot one."

One afternoon, as I tried to close the fifteen pound weight gap between me and my friends at the YMCA, Bob, my former swim coach, came into the cardio room and leaned against the black arm bar on the machine next to me. "Hey, Azure," he started. His voice was apprehensive like someone who is about to break up with you.

Winded exhale, inhale, "Hey-Bob," I answered in one blurred word followed by a gasping inhale.

Bob was a pudgy guy, bald on top with an auburn band of hair wrapped around his head.

"Hey, listen," he started, "you've been here for a while."

In the silent space that followed, save for the hum of the stair climber steps retracting and stretching, I wasn't sure what kind of break up this was, but it sure as hell was one.

Winded exhale, inhale, "Yeah," inhale.

He darted his eyes around the room a little nervously. "We're going to have to ask you to leave."

Winded exhale, inhale. "Leave?"

"Yes, you have been here for over three hours and we think you are over-exercising."

Yeah, duh! I have weight to lose!

He stood there in solidarity, firmly but kindly, in that parental way where they think it is for your own good.

"Okay?" I said as I pressed the big red stop button on the machine, annoyed and hurt.

This wasn't a breakup between me and him as my coach, or me and the YMCA, he was breaking up with me on behalf of exercise. Without another word and without wiping the machine, I walked out of the room and the YMCA, pissed off and desperate. *Over-exercising! Is that even a thing? What a stupid policy! Was it even a policy? It has to be arbitrary. Show me the fucking sign that says the maximum time someone can be here! How do they expect me to lose weight? As if wanting to lose weight is something bad! The freaking gym, the very place that supports societal pressures of needing to lose weight, is also the very same place that is kicking me out? Just another no-win mind-fuck. May as well go home to Dad.*

Feeling alienated from the YMCA, I decided to try out for the wrestling team at school, having been dared to by a guy I knew. I came to find out that there weren't exactly *try-outs* for the wrestling team at my school, especially for girls, or should I say girl. They basically took all who showed up. I was the first and only girl to be on the wrestling team in the school's history, I think. So, thirty boys and I crowded onto the musty, dusty mats in the small room that I don't think had been opened once since the year before.

The coach, Ben, thick-necked and cauliflower-eared with an upstate New York accent, gave a lecture about how wrestling would turn boys into men. I wasn't sure what it would turn me into, but was pretty okay with whatever transformation awaited me, even if I would be manlier. I had lately wondered if the issue my dad had with me was that I was female. My dad had recently told my brother and I that he had been married in a shot-gun wedding when he was barely out of high school and had a son who died shortly after being born. Perhaps Dad was resentful that I had been born a girl and not a boy who would live out the life his first son had not been able to. And perhaps if I could become more of a man, able to be tougher in my dad's presence, to do masculine things, then I would earn his respect. Ben told us about the weight class system, equally important as the wrestling techniques we would learn. We all would soon get to a lower weight class, with the grueling practices we would be enduring, and there was no reason why we shouldn't be able to drop significant weight. Music to my ears—become tougher, earn my dad's respect, and lose weight.

He finished with a "So, if any of you pansies are scared, there's the door, go home to your mommy." No one budged. "All right ladies, time for your first weigh in." I gasped audibly. I am not sure why this was so surprising to me since Ben had spent so much time emphasizing weight, but I assumed it would be on the honor system, that we would weigh in at home and monitor ourselves. The thought of weighing in in front of everyone froze me in embarrassed horror. Although I'd made progress lately, I was still far heavier than what I guessed the other girls at school weighed, weighing 132 instead of 115. And I didn't want any of the guys to know how much I weighed. I wanted them to think I didn't weigh anything, just as I hoped they believed girls didn't poop but somehow magically relieved ourselves through our skin like sharks do or something. A girl's weight should remain one of the classic and enduring mysteries.

One thing I was learning fast: wrestling was not a sport of modesty. I let as many of the guys go in front of me as I could, but reasoned that it was better to go in the middle of the crowd. If I went last, all their attention would be focused on me. When I stepped on, Ben told me, "All that weight-loss stuff I was talking about, you don't need to listen to that, just show up and learn to wrestle."

Why, because I am a girl? If the guys are going to, then I am too! I am not here to get special treatment! Of course, I didn't say any of this to Ben, I just nodded shyly and did my usual holding of breath and playing with the way I leaned forward or back, just as I did in weigh-ins at home, which my dad was still doing. I was curious whether any of the guys on the team were peaking, trying to see how much I weighed, but I could tell Ben was the type of guy who would not tolerate that. It then occurred to me how silly that thought was because Ben, himself, was a guy and witnessing my weight, but he looked kind and objective as he wrote it down on his clipboard.

I threw myself into wrestling, now fixated on the weight loss it would surely provide. I wanted to learn the ins and outs of wrestling—well, rather every nuance of the weight loss strategies of wrestling. Practicing with thirty sweaty, stinky guys in a room for hours with the door closed so it became a natural sauna was effective. As was eating only a bowl of rice a day, not eating or drinking the day of the weigh-in but rather swooshing water around in my mouth to relieve the cottony feeling before spitting it back out. Every wrestling match began with feeling faint, exhausted, nauseated, and dehydrated. I loved it in a hurt-so-good kind of way. My enthusiasm for the boot camp aspect of practice eclipsed my interest in or enthusiasm for the fireman's carry and half nelson.

Because everyone was trying to lose weight, we layered clothing during practice. I usually wore two pairs of spandex pants on top of one another, a pair of shorts to keep them from sliding down, a thermal shirt under a large band shirt and sometimes a sweatshirt over that. When we were really desperate to cut weight, we would also cut a hole in the top of a garbage bag and wear it as a sweaty poncho. We ran around the room in circles, we ran up a hill adjacent to campus. We did drills which consisted of football runs (which, as a girl, was basically twerking before that was a thing) and then whatever wrestling move Ben called out, before leaping back up and recommencing football runs. We paired off and wrestled each other, practicing certain moves over and over so they would become second nature. We were paired more for who was standing near us than by weight so we could stretch our abilities. Since the door was closed for the sauna effect, it was an especially sweaty mess and for me a hairy, sweaty mess. Having long hair doesn't work so well for a wrestler, I put it in a tight bun, but it would almost immediately get pulled out when practicing with an opponent. I would re-do it and re-do it. Wearing a swim cap only ripped my hair out in the process, so that didn't work. And my mop wasn't the only hair making workouts a mess. Sparring with sweaty hairy guys became the norm for me.

At weigh-ins, guys would often get down to their underwear because every ounce counted. Once a guy was naked "cupping his junk." I left the room if I was warned, but wasn't all the time. It was like being a fly on the wall in the guy's locker room. It was everything I had imagined—nudity, teasing each other harshly, socking each other in the arms, slaps on the butt, attempted slaps in the crotch with flicked towels, dirty jokes, and talking about how hot so and so's mom was, and teasing him every time she picked him up.

One day before practice, I sat on the cement ledge outside the door, already changed into my practice clothes, doing some homework.

A friendly voice interrupted me. "You like 311?"

I looked up. It was Vince, the best wrestler on the team, who played football as well.

"Oh, this is just a shirt I wear to practice," I answered shyly, not sure whether he thought it was cool that I liked the band 311.

Despite my nervous response, he continued being nice to me and when he asked me out on a date toward the end of the season, I was so surprised. We saw *Shakespeare in Love*, well, I should say we were inside a theater playing *Shakespeare in Love* while we were making out. We fell in love hard and fast. So fast in fact, that I don't remember the first time it was said. It felt like it was always that way. Vince was really funny, sweet and affectionate, and we were inseparable in that high school romance way.

When the season was over, Friday nights soon became filled with parties and late- night Jack in the Box runs and eating and loving with abandon. He would do things like make candlelit dinners for me on a table he set up in his room. He wrote me notes during class and always hugged me strong. We walked to his house after school with his brother. His house was always so comfortable. There was at most a little bickering but otherwise felt so remarkably peaceful to me, in comparison to my house. Vince was a redhead, like his mom and his step dad, and the one who stood out was Vince's brown-haired younger brother, Hugh. I really enjoyed them all. Susan was an independent woman making a creative living as a home designer, Red was in construction, and even though introverted, Hugh was sharp-witted with a very dry sense of humor and I loved talking with him. And they had cable TV and good, regular food. Spaghetti with meat sauce, sandwiches on Dutch crunch from Woodside deli, *real* mayonnaise, which I had never had before. When the boys got home, they just made themselves something. It astounded me how *free* they were with food, making things like pigs in a blanket, which I had also never had before. I ate dinner there as often as

I could. Too often probably. I always felt guilty for imposing on Vince's mom, but didn't know how to tell her it was that or burnt boiled brussels sprouts.

On Fridays, my mom would pick me up late from Vince's after a date with her boyfriend. Sometimes after Vince fell asleep, but before my mom got there, I would sneak to the kitchen to eat slices of ham, slathered with mayonnaise and rolled into little meat taquitos. Full bellied, I felt so full of love—for Vince, his house, his normal family, his cat, his dog, and for Best Foods Mayonnaise.

When it came time for prom, I thought of it as a dress rehearsal for the wedding we'd have when I turned eighteen. Vince looked amazing in his tux. I wore a baby pink gown I picked out at the mall by myself, instead of with my mom like my friends did. My dad didn't see me off to prom or ask to see me in my dress, to my disappointment, if not to my surprise. I reasoned that he probably would have just said something nasty anyway but wished he could just indulge me in one thing classically feminine. It was like he wanted me to be a tomboy but then reserved the right to criticize me for not being feminine. It seemed like he had a grudge against women in general, myself included, or rather myself especially. When he'd point out hot girls to my brother, I longed for him to notice me, in a non-Oedipus complex kind of way, of course. All the more reason to move on with Vince, I reasoned. My fantasy wasn't so much Prince Charming rescues me and we live happily ever after as much as it was tenacious girl and her kind, supportive boyfriend start their life together young and work hard to be successful and happy. But that day was so far off. Aside from magical nights like prom and fun nights at Vince's and out with friends, things were still as bad as they ever had been with my dad.

Have you ever had an intense craving and tried to stave it off with something else, anything else, and ended up eating everything in sight since the actual craving went unsatisfied? Well, it was as if my dad's primary emotional craving was committing physical abuse and he had been trying to get by with verbally mistreating me after Mom left. The reason for this was transparent enough. He talked fairly openly about how he hated his own father for physically abusing him and resented his mother for letting it happen. He hated what he considered child abuse, as in sexual abuse and physical abuse that met his threshold. Poking, kicking, grabbing, pushing, swatting, hair pulling and physical intimidation did not meet his definition, of course. As for the concept of verbal abuse; that was complete hocus pocus made up by sensitive pansy assess who couldn't hack it in real life, like me.

I knew that for him and lots of people, being abused was like becoming a vampire—a transformation from victim to monster with an appetite for blood beyond his control. As his primal desire to be physical with me went unsatisfied, the nightly sessions at the kitchen table became longer, going on for hours and hours. There was still the matter of food restriction and compulsive exercise, which he had masterfully delegated to me, making me a vampire of sorts myself, only I was the kind thirsty for my own blood. However directly or indirectly it was, it was clear that he was trying to bend me, my will and my body, like a paper clip back and forth, back and forth, back and forth until I broke. And when that didn't work, the manual labor began.

High school weekends became a montage of unpaid hard work on my dad's rental properties and land. Dad always justified not paying for this work because we would be inheriting the property eventually and was always sure to remind me I was a selfish bitch for questioning it. The easiest tasks involved helping my dad do electrical or plumbing work, though the electrical always made me nervous because Dad always did things his own way, disregarding some standard safety practices as being "made up by dumb shits who didn't know a goddamn thing about electricity." After all, he was a PhD level electrical engineer who had worked as a lineman before attending college. More difficult tasks included ripping up carpeting, tiling bathrooms and painting rooms with 15 foot high ceilings in houses with three stories and lots of rooms. The most difficult tasks included staining decks and hauling cut oak limbs weighing well over a hundred pounds each to a brush pile on the hillside to prevent erosion. It was days like these, wiping away dirty sweat, nursing cuts and scrapes and bruises, flicking away spiders and ticks and trying to get relief from the hot, stagnant air that I wondered if my dad saw having me the same way homesteaders did in the 1800s—as free labor. It would have explained a lot—his disdain for me, his begrudgingly providing me shelter and his withholding of food.

At least my brother worked too. I respected him for it, not that he had much say in the matter, and despite the fact that he always seemed to get the inside jobs while I was baking in the sun working on the decks. I'd pass the back end of a saw forward and backward in the spaces between the two by fours of every deck and step, creating little parallel rows of dirt, leaves, fungus and dead bugs in its wake. Then, once that was completed, I would take a wire brush and scrape the wood surfaces on my hands and knees. I especially hated this because the scraping had a nails on chalkboard quality that gave me goosebumps no matter how many hours went by. There was one good thing about jobs like these, though, and that was the degree of solitude they offered, stretches of time free of insults where I could luxuriate in fantasies of the future life I'd create for myself with Vince by my side.

After Vince and I get married when I turn eighteen, we can get a little place in Santa Cruz. He can be a carpenter and work towards getting his general contractors license while I'm in college. After college we can start having kids before I turn thir—

"Hey shit for brains!"

I looked up and saw my dad put his coffee mug down on the deck railing.

"What do you think you're doing?"

"I'm doing what you told me to do," I answered dumbfounded.

He came at me swiftly and shoved my head forward trying to smoosh my face into the wood itself. "What the hell does that look like?"

I didn't answer. I had no idea what he was talking about and thought answering would sound like I was trying to be a smart ass, which I never did while his hands were on me.

He let go. I winced and looked at my palms when I got up. Not only were they blistered and calloused from carrying five-gallon buckets of stain over from our house but now had deep splinters as well.

"You didn't go with the grain right here!"

"Sorry!" I said exacerbated.

"Fix it," he said turning and walking away. He turned his head sideways and added over his shoulder "and chop chop, we don't have all day."

I could feel my veins dilate letting in red hot, angry blood.

"I don't see *you* doing anything," I said unable to help myself.

He turned.

I continued, "Jake and I have been working since 9:00, 9:30, and I have yet to see you lift a finger. And what time is it now, 2:30?"

That was the curious thing about my dad. The times I expected him to hurt me, and braced myself for it, he often just chuckled. Perhaps like lions that live alongside wildebeests in the Serengeti, he only felt the urge to attack when the element of surprise was there.

He just laughed and offered a simple explanation, "I'm supervising."

When he turned to walk away, my eyes narrowed and I flipped him off.

At least I'll probably lose weight, sweating this much, I told myself.

I worked my way from end to end of deck after deck and the stairs that joined them, steadfastly wishing that my other dad would suddenly reveal himself, all cute and old and wise and tell me the real Karate Kid reason for this grueling work, but needless to say, he never showed up. At what I guessed was around six; however, the real one did.

"Commere!" he called to me, voice gravely before clearing is throat.

I got up, stiff and exhausted and wiped my forearm across my forehead, smearing brown across my arm like water color.

We didn't get breaks so I was nervous for what fun task was in store for me. I followed him to the makeshift stairs on the side of the rental house that were made by railroad ties. As I followed him down the hill, I noticed a rectangular door open on the side of the wall.

He stopped just past it.

"Get your ass in there and get that rat's nest," he said as he pointed to the opening of the crawl space.

My stomach clenched and twisted itself into a pretzel. It wasn't the first time I'd felt fear working on the property, but this fear felt different than when he whacked me with the long metal rod end of the sprayer for taking a break. It was even different than the frightened shock of freshly cut oak limbs narrowly missing me as they fell to the ground. I wanted to decline, but refusing wasn't an option with him. He retrieved a pair of gloves from his pocket and handed them to me.

I swung one foot over the crotch high opening as if I were getting on a horse. While doing so, I had the distinct feeling that if my life were a horror film, this was the point when the audience would scream "No, don't do it!"

Once inside, the gravely dirt made a crisp sound as I began to lose my balance.

"Where is it?" I asked, catching myself and looking around.

"How the hell are you in Advanced Placement classes?"

He shown the flashlight way off into the dark corner, illuminating a messy pile of pale pink insulation.

I wanted to ask him how he expected me to see it when seeing it required a flashlight, but thought better of it.

I turned to him and asked "Shouldn't we call an exterminator or something?"

"Like hell we will! Put it in these." He handed me a wad of cheap plastic grocery bags, the kind from the produce section.

I stepped forward into the darkness.

"Watch the beams overhead for brown recluses and black widows," Dad said.

I instinctively ducked down and he laughed. He was enjoying this way too much. I turned around and when I saw his smile, I instantly realized why I had a visceral reaction to this place.

We had a crawl space at our house too, only the door was inside our house instead of outside like at the rentals. It was in the bottom, third level of the house, almost to the bottom of the stairs. Even though it wasn't a basement, it was always dark down there, the hallway dimly lit by a creepy light fixture that looked like candles with flame shaped lightbulbs. The door was small as if it were more appropriately sized for a hobbit, rather than a person. The iridescent pattern of the koa door gave it depth like Tiger's Eye gemstone, making it look like it concealed a world within it. And there was perhaps no time in which it was more fitting. I remembered hearing Mom's muffled cries on the other side of the door. I remembered imagining her laying on the dirt floor since it wasn't tall enough to even sit up straight in. I remembered imagining the pitch blackness and the horrifying tickle of spiders crawling across her skin. I remembered telling her it would be okay, not being sure if she could hear me, and not being able to repeat it louder in case Dad heard. I remembered wishing the door had a handle rather than a lock that locked exclusively by a key so I could let her out. I remembered feeling so sad for her because I knew how claustrophobic she was and being trapped in the coffin like space was literally her worst nightmare. And I remembered knowing how making nightmares manifest was one of Dad's specialties.

I realized my breathing was fast, mind re-focusing on my surroundings. How could I get out of here? "I'll probably do it wrong," I started. "Why don't you or Jake do this and I'll hold the flashlight?"

"Quit your bitching and get your ass over there and do it."

I wondered if this was a moment he had waited for—an opportunity to lock me inside, to teach me a lesson for ever talking back or protesting my treatment, his chance to make me plead and beg. I decided it was best to hurry, before he acted on it, because surely it had already occurred to him.

I walked forward until I knew I had to be close because I could smell rat pee but couldn't see the nest, only my own shadow and a skewed silhouette of light like a figure in a religious painting. "I can't see it," I called to Dad.

"The light would reach if your ass weren't so fat."

"Prick," I muttered under my breath.

I turned sideways and saw the illuminated nest, speckled with so much rat poo, it looked like it was part of the fiberglass pattern.

"Make sure they aren't in there and don't breathe in the fiber glass or the rat turds, they carry disease you know," he snickered.

A mask might have made sense, I thought.

I took a breath and held it and gave the nest a little kick.

"Roar!" He let out.

I flinched and my breath left me.

My dad busted up laughing and the light started bobbing all over the place.

Great, now I'm going to catch bubonic plague.

I turned my head as far away from the nest as I could and took a gulp so deep my cheeks bulged out like a puffer fish. I grabbed pieces of the nest trying to make sure none touched my arms beyond the gloves and shoved the gobs of filth into the plastic bags as quickly as I could. I practically ran back to the entrance, sticking my head out the door to take a huge breath of air. I tried handing the bags out to him but he said "I don't want it," and gave me a disgusted look. I left them on the floor and climbed out.

I didn't thank him for not locking me in, but was grateful, not because I thought I deserved it but because we both knew he could have if he wanted to. I wondered why he hadn't, and reasoned that it was probably because we were at the renter's house and the chances of me being heard was much higher than at our house. He was so cunning that way, a regular abuse actuary, constantly calculating risks of getting caught. And then it hit me: was our crawl space inside our house instead of outside and with a key lock and no door handle because when he was building the house he knew he'd want to be able to put my mom in there whenever she made him mad enough?

I stepped away from the entrance, wanting to get as far away from him and any confined space as possible.

"Since I've already put in a full day's work and got this nest, I am going to clean up and head out," I said.

"You ain't going no where."

"Dad! I've already worked eight hours!"

"We work until the job is done."

"But Dad, people are expecting me."

"Tell them you'll be late! All the more reason to get your ass moving and finish up."

I let out an exacerbated exhale and turned and headed toward our house.

"Where the hell do you think you're going?"

"I'm calling my friends to tell them I'll be late."

"Get your ass back here."

"But you said!"

"You'll call later."

I recognized the look in his eye of an almost orgasmic satisfaction from his power and control over me, as if I were a wild mustang just made to take the saddle.

He had always denied my treatment as abuse, let alone physical abuse. But, was this not abuse of my body? Even if I wasn't walking around with busted lips or broken arms? Was he not gaining pleasure from every scrape, bruise, blister, cramp, drop of sweat and aching stomach that I got against my will, even if the pain had been inflicted by work he made me do and not his closed fist?

Defeated, I went back to work, rolling out stain on the decks with a long pole while telepathically trying to communicate to Vince who my plans were really with to please forgive me for seeming like an inconsiderate flake.

Dusk came, then the darkness, then the cold.

Finally, I was done and headed back to the house carrying the much lighter empty five gallon buckets, painter's tray, and roller brush. I put it all in the garage, said a wordless hello to the freezer, and headed to the house.

My dad and Jake were already eating and I could tell Dad had had at least one gin and tonic already.

"Where have you been?" He asked with a slight smile. "We thought about waiting for you."

I glared at him.

"Thanks a lot for ruining my plans," I said sarcastically.

"You'll see your friends Monday you spoiled brat."

He called me a lot of things and a lot of them bothered me, but to be called spoiled, when I was treated the way I was, was a slap in the face.

"I am not spoiled."

"You go on trips, you have a car, you screw off with your friends and boyfriend all the time."

"I never asked for you to take me on those trips and they aren't great anyway, because the way you are here is the same way you are in Hawaii; the only difference is the palm trees! Ever notice how you make me cry every single day whether we're on vacation or not? What is it—some kind of daily ritual for you like brushing your teeth or something? As for the car, getting Mom's old station wagon to take Jake to and from school so you don't have to doesn't really count. You act like I have a new car, daddy's credit card, and spend every spare moment at the mall or something!"

"You completely failed Jake! Got that imbecile? Every time you could have helped him you have decided to go fuck off instead, you air headed bird brain."

My eyes fell to the floor. Even though he was meaning something different, he wasn't entirely wrong. Given the choice of keeping Jake company in that house or spending time in a place where I wasn't called stupid or fat constantly, I chose any place but home. And I felt incredibly guilty for doing so, but I saw few options when I, not Jake, was the target of my dad's hatred. And that was the mind-fuck of the whole thing- Jake and I were very different from one another: me outgoing and assertive, him shy and introverted. It was clear that I was basically being told to turn Jake into me even though I was simultaneously being told how terrible I was. I didn't see how it was possible to change Jake anyway. Jake was the way he was and I was the way I was. But I did feel responsible for him now, just as I had all those countless nights when I took him to my room and told him it would be okay when Dad was abusing Mom. The truth was that I wanted to save us both and just like people who get stranded in the wilderness, sometimes the stronger more able person has to leave the other behind temporarily to get help.

"You're a total failure as a mother!" he yelled.

He's actually fucking nuts! I thought. *Does he actually think I'm my mom? Or was that a delusion or a Freudian slip or something?*

"Maybe that's because I'm *not* his fucking mother!" I retorted with every ounce of teenager's attitude I could muster.

"Everybody knows that an older sister is supposed to think of her younger brother as her child! That she helps raise him! Everyone except you!"

"But I'm a kid too! I'm only a year and a half older than Jake! I just want to do things regular people get to do, like hang out with my friends! And I'm being punished for it! You're just mad because Jake isn't where you want him to be and you're blaming it on me! *You're* his parent."

He flew up out of his chair and reflexively, I flew out of mine. As he came toward me, I backed up until my back was against the wall. He then stuck his finger in my face, so close I thought he might poke my eye out.

"If you ever," he poked me in the cheek, "talk to me that way again, you're going to wish you were dead!" I thought of the crawl space. He twisted his finger to really dig hard. I did my best not to wince at the bruising pain. He looked at me with murderous rage and I did not doubt that he could and maybe even had before. I had always wondered about how the neighbor's dog came to be hung from a tree.

"Got that, fuck head!?" His spit flew in my face on the "F." He poked me one final time before turning and going back to his chair.

"Hey Jake, your sister should really learn when to shut up." He erupted into laughter. Jake laughed nervously, trying to diffuse the tension.

I yelled, "I can't take this anymore! I'm leaving!" I started toward the stairs to get my keys and clothes.

"Not in that car, you're not!" he answered, gloating as if he had been waiting for this moment for months. And I did not doubt that he had, given how analytical he was. I imagined a 'good one' occurring to him at work and him pulling out the little notebook he kept in his breast pocket and jotting it down to use later.

"But it's my car!" I pleaded.

"You leave, I report it stolen, you go to jail. Got that, dumbbell?"

I continued downstairs anyway. To my amazement he didn't follow me. For years and years, I had wondered what would happen if I just left the table, and when it came right down to it, nothing happened? That couldn't be. He was probably just finishing his drink and contemplating what he would do to me. I would have to be quick.

How could I get out of there? It was not like my mom would pick me up. I picked up the phone and called Vince's.

"Hello?" Vince answered asleep.

I hadn't realized how late it was. Well past midnight?

"Vince?" I asked, voice quivering slightly above a whisper.

Vince woke up suddenly; his voice went from groggy to alarmed. "What's wrong?" he asked. I could hear the fear in his voice.

"Things are really bad," I sobbed. "Can you come get me?"

He knew what I meant, knew from the bit that he had witnessed that I wasn't exaggerating to get attention as I had been accused of previously when trying to confide in a friend. And even though I was so grateful for that, I knew even then that the opinion that mattered most was my own because being abused is a bit like a paranormal experience—someone who has truly gone through it says, "I don't care whether you believe me or not, I know what I experienced."

I packed a few things in a backpack and snuck out the side bathroom door. After what seemed like an eternity, the whites of the headlights came around the bend, followed by a light blue Volkswagen Bug. I am not sure why but it shocked me that Vince's mom, Susan, was driving. Vince got out on the passenger side, pulled forward the seat, and I jumped in. He was still surprised to see me, I thought. I was visibly a mess, snotty, eyes swollen, and my body shivering. The car ride to his house was sleepy and quiet. When we got there, I whispered "Thank you so much" to Susan and we all went to bed.

I loved Vince's house. It felt cushy and comfortable there just like Vince's borrowed sweatpants I wore as we lounged, watched movies and didn't talk about It the next day. I must have looked to all of them as a normal teenager who just had an argument with her dad. Late that afternoon, Susan alone drove me back up the hill. I felt sicker and sicker as we got closer, as if I were getting closer to a dangerous toxin.

"It'll be okay," Susan offered, sensing my hesitation as I got out of the car.

I said "thanks," even though she had no idea what I was dealing with and I had no idea how to even begin to tell her. Crushed, I trudged down the stairs toward the entry and took a final breath of freedom before opening the front door and heading in. Dad and Jake were at the table, as usual.

"Well, look who decided to show the fuck up. Where the hell you been?" Dad asked before immediately answering himself. "I'll tell you where you been—at your boyfriend's house!" sarcastically squealing the last part like a teenaged girl.

I looked down, which only confirmed his suspicion.

"Lowlife, two-bit slut," he said with disgust before continuing on. "Why don't I just call up Grandma right now and let her know what a whore she's got for a granddaughter?"

Don't! Please! I pleaded in my mind, upset at the thought of the one person who really, really loved me, thinking differently of me.

"You know, you could learn a thing or two from your cousin," he continued, mouth full and bits of pasta stuck to his chin. "She's coy and knows how to manipulate men to get what she wants. And she doesn't pick losers. You on the other hand got yourself a real winner. You two deserve each other, Tweedle Dee and Tweedle Dumb. Vince must be real hard up. What's the matter? You're the best he can do?"

Tears running down my face, I yelled, "You don't know anything about what it's like to actually be happy with someone! Or to be happy period! All you know is misery and how to make other people miserable!"

His eyes lit up. *Eureka!* I could hear his mind say, *I found the perfect spot to twist the knife.*

He laughed in a mocking way. "Happy, poor but happy. That's what you'll be. Do you believe in the Tooth Fairy too? I can see it now, you in a flea-bit apartment, working some dead-end job, having never amounted to anything, never being able to go anywhere or buy anything, being the total failure that you are, but you'll be happy all right!"

"At least I won't be here anymore!" I bellowed.

"Let me ask you a question: do you think your children will be *legally* retarded?"

I scowled at him as he twisted his face, crossed his eyes, and said, "Duhhhhhhh."

"I fucking hate you," I said flatly as the fact that it was.

"You think," he said as his snorts gave way to smoker's wheezes, "I give a shit what *you* think?" He laughed and wheezed harder.

I looked down and shook my head in flabbergasted shock, and then realized he probably thought I was answering his question and stopped. There was a satisfaction to him then, he had gotten to me, he had won. Even though he did every time, it never got old for him.

I hate my life! Please, God make me somebody else! Anybody else! Please God! I can't do this anymore!

I was just like my mom now. I remembered all the times she whisper shouted "I hate my life" and pulled her own hair or hit herself on the head.

"Get the goddamn hell out of my sight!" He said with disgust.

No need to tell me twice. I thundered downstairs and called Vince. It was late again.

"Vince?" I sniffled. "It's really bad ag—"

"Azure?"

Sniffle. "Hi, Susan."

"Azure, no, I'm sorry, we cannot come get you. You will have to figure this out with your dad. Goodnight."

173

I could hear a muffled "Mom!" in the background before the click which almost echoed in its magnitude.

My sobs returned. "Why won't anyone help me?"

And then inexplicably a robotic wave of calm came over me, my mind shutting down so as to preserve something else. As my breathing slowed, and despair subsided, I felt the wave of familiar hunger take its place. *Ah yes, food. Food will help me, always. Always food.*

17

JACK IN THE BOX

"**I**'m so glad we finally did this!" Blair exclaimed rubbing my forearm.

I smiled enthusiastically and told her "me too," overjoyed to have some girl time after feeling so isolated.

"I just wish it were under different circumstances."

"Me too!" I added, though I was still in denial about Erin and Adam picking up and heading to Nevada.

But that's a short flight! I told myself. *About the same amount of time it took to drive here to Santa Clarita. I'll see Erin all the time. I hope. No tears though, this is going to be a happy evening.*

And I was happy to be with Erin, Blair and Gemma and some other friends at a fun, upbeat restaurant. Even though they were now in the maintenance phase of Weight Watchers, Blair and Erin still consulted each other about what they were going to order. They compared point values of appetizers, drinks, salads, sushi, and entrees. Blair decided she was going to get whisky on the rocks because it was the biggest bang for the buck in terms of percent alcohol to points. Erin ordered a light beer, because she just could not do straight alcohol. They would split a salad with dressing on the side and an order of sashimi.

You have to split a salad and sashimi? Dear God! Still, I felt guilty when I looked back to my menu. *I don't want a salad! I don't want sashimi! I want a burger with jalapeño poppers! No, just get something responsible.* I compromised and settled on a salad with a side of jalapeño poppers. *If they ask or look at my plate disapprovingly, I will tell them I'm just eating part of it and bringing the rest home.* I ordered and tried to pump myself up like a coach in a locker room. *Salad on three, salad on three, one two three Salad!* Didn't work. *I don't want salad*, I whined internally as I cracked a joke about a pastrami sandwich that Sean and I had shared recently which gave us food poisoning. "I lost ten pounds in twenty-four hours and I have a natural aversion to pastrami now, so needless to say all I need to do is figure out a way to give myself food poisoning with mac and cheese, sour cream, all casseroles, and Reese's. Do they still sell ipecac?" The table erupted in laughter. I smiled too. Even if I had to play the funny fat friend, I loved being funny.

When the food arrived, the salad didn't look any more appetizing than it did before my rah-rah internal monologue. I looked around the table and surveyed the burgers and sandwiches and fries and ranch. I looked back to the salad. *They are allowed to have it because they are skinny*, I told myself in the same tone my very formal Grandmother used to tell me. This was a universal law to me, just as what goes up must come down. When thin girls eat delicious food it's deserved, either because they earned it by hard work in the gym or they got lucky in their body constitution. "How darling!" Society says, "The skinny girl can eat whatever she wants and not gain weight. Look how cute she is with her huge burger, mound of fries, and bowl of ice cream. Can her cute little hands even fit around that burger? Where does she put all that food? It's just so cute!" Or they think, "This must be a cheat meal. She's worked so hard for this. Enjoy it, honey." When fat girls eat delicious food it's not deserved, not allowed, because it's assumed that that very meal is why she is overweight. In this case it's "No wonder she looks like that. I can hardly stand to look at her. So sad. She should put the burger down and go to the nearest gym. And even when she loses weight, she should know she has to watch it because her body puts on weight easily. Poor thing."

I hated this universal law, not just because I was on the losing end of it but because it was based on pure speculation that didn't include some of the other possibilities. Perhaps some of these thin girls were bulimic and purged after indulging, and perhaps the overweight girls did in fact eat healthily and work out, contrary to popular belief, and this *was* a splurge for them.

Even though I was unsuccessful at willing my salad to taste like a burger, or put my suspicions of everyone's judgments out of my mind, I felt successful for exercising willpower. I remembered my dad telling me to use my willpower to not eat while at the restaurant in Seattle with our family. *Put that out of your mind too, and just eat your salad and enjoy spending time with Blair and Erin.* Our glasses clinked, we laughed, Blair danced around the table when we approved of a song they were playing even though it wasn't that type of restaurant. I admired her fearlessness. I wished I could be more like that. I twirled my wedding ring as I often did when I was nervous and noticed the athlete's-foot feeling underneath it. It was so tight now but I just didn't have it in me to have it cut off to be sized.

When it was time for our checks I asked for a box. "This salad was just so filling! I couldn't even eat one jalapeño popper, I was just so full!" *Azure, as Dad would say, no one is dumb enough to buy your bullshit.* We walked out into the warm Santa Clarita air and noticed the palm trees rustle in the breeze. I hugged Blair and turned to hug Erin. "I can't believe you're leaving!" I said as I hugged her extra-long and took in the sweet smell of her conditioner.

"I miss you now! How are we going to live so far apart?" she told me in our embrace.

"I have no idea. I am going to miss you so much, I am actually a little scared!"

It was the truth, I knew there was a big difference between seeing her a weekend or two a month vs. a few weekends a year.

"You'll be fine. You and Sean."

"Thank you!" I replied so grateful for her optimism. "I hope Nevada is everything you dream it to be."

She thanked me and we let go of one another and looked into each other's faces. Overcome with emotion and not wanting to go there, I said "we'll still see each other all the time, plus the phone. It won't be too different, I promise."

With leftover box in hand, I crossed the street to where I parked. Cars waited for me at the crosswalk. As always, I power-walked, feeling the drivers' frustration at my presumed slow speed because fat people are always expected to be slow.

When the car door slammed closed after I plopped onto the seat, my world seemed extra devoid of sound, the sound of laughter and clinking of the dinner, the sound of friendships, the sound of connection. *Why was I too busy thinking about food to just enjoy my time with them, especially Erin?* I scolded myself. I started my car and made my way to the freeway. So lonely. I called Tiffany. Voicemail. I turned on the radio, kept it on the chattiest station I could find. *An hour and a half drive, just me and my thoughts.*

I side-eyed the brown takeout box, with its flaps folded like an origami. Keeping my left hand on the steering wheel, I attempted to unfold the flaps with my right. After several attempts and a box tipped sideways, I got it. There they were, the jalapeño poppers now with salad dressing on them, spilling out of the box and onto the seat of the car, and salad behind them. At seventy miles an hour, with half an eye on my lane, I righted the box and one of the three poppers fell back in, while the others fell onto the seat. People had sat there but that didn't stop me from picking them up and after a brief glance for obvious signs of butt, taking a bite, then another, then the second jalapeño popper, then the third. After my "ah" moment (not to be confused with an "ah-hah") moment, I leaned over and opened the glove box, grabbed a napkin, and wiped the seat. It was still a little shiny in the places where the poppers had landed. Next the salad. I reached over and began pinching the salad between my thumb and index finger and brought it to my mouth over and over, most of it making it inside, some of it ending up on my shirt, pants, or in that gap between the seat and the center console. I could feel myself weaving in my lane on the freeway.

You are such a pig, I can't even believe you are eating your leftovers before you get home and without even silverware. You are going to get pulled over again. Just like that time you were pulled over for suspected DUI and it was just eating while driving. When the food was gone and all that was left was the empty container, my messy clothes, and the dark Mohave desert road in front of me, I felt satisfied that it was finally gone and no longer taunting me, and also wanting more, wondering if I should stop at a drive-through. *I should have ended with the jalapeños, not begun with them.* I always liked ending disordered meals with whatever I saw as the naughtiest item, the most dessert like. Ending with the salad contradicted this. Once in Palmdale, I pulled over at Jack in the Box, comforted by its familiar red sign that reminded me of Friday nights in high school.

In the drive-through, I held the phone up to my ear. *I can't believe you're doing this, I can't believe you're doing this.*

"Welcome to Jack in the Box, would you like to try our new buttery jack burger?"

"Uh, yeah, yes, please."

"Meal or just the sandwich?"

"Meal."

"Curly fries or regular?"

"Curly."

"What to drink?"

"Can I please get a soda water?"

"What?"

"Soda water."

"Soda water?"

"Yes, water with bubbles."

"Okay, will that be all?"

"No, hold on… Hey, what did you want from Jack in the Box?" *I can't believe you! You aren't even a good actress, you know? The drive-through lady knows exactly what you are doing. So freaking transparent. This is a new low. Even for you.* "Okay, I'll see you at home, bye. Okay, we'll also have a sourdough chicken club meal with curly fries and a seven-piece stuffed jalapeño."

"What to drink?"

Make it different than soda water! "Dr. Pepper, please."

"Does your order look correct on the screen?"

"Yes." *Oh my God, it worked it actually worked! She probably knows! I mean, what is she going to do, kick you out of the drive-through in complete disgust?*

"I'll have your total at the window."

"Okay, thanks."

I avoided eye contact with the drive-through lady at all costs although I noticed she was not a small woman herself. *She sees through you. She knows what a disgusting pig you are!*

"Any sauce?"

"Buttermilk, please." *Oh my God, can this torture ever end?*

She handed me one large drink then the other, and then we sat there awkwardly beside one another while the food was still being prepared.

"Just a minute," she offered.

"It's okay, no problem!" I said with a nervous smile. *Did she know what I was about to do? Is that why she had told me it would just be another minute? Just another minute before you gorge yourself like the gluttonous pig that you are.*

She tossed a handful of little rectangular containers with teal tops in one of the two large bags she handed me.

"Thank you," I said

She didn't answer, just closed her window. *She knows, she has to know!*

I pulled forward and back onto the road. I reached in and retrieved a little container of buttermilk and held the steering wheel with half my left hand while peeling off the lid with my right. I sat it in the change holder in the center console near the gear shift and sifted through the bags until I found the container of jalapeños. I dunked and bit, over and over again. Then I ate the curliest of curly fries, only selecting the ones that looked like perfect potato slinky toys. Then the chicken sandwich, ripping off the edges of the bread and biting into the mayonnaisey chicken inside. I slurped some Dr. Pepper. *So full! You got it, you eat it!* I moaned before I bit into the buttery jack sandwich, which true to name, leaked oil all over my shirt. *Fuck! Oh well, too late now.* I took another bite.

I was full to the point where I actually thought I might burst when I pulled up to the house, lights off, Sean already in bed. I sighed at the intersection of pain and numbed pleasure. There were still uneaten fries but I wasn't bothered the way I normally would have been. I shoved the salad leftovers box into the brown bags and crumpled. I got myself out of the car and waddled to the garbage can and threw it away thinking, *Hey, at least I cleaned up after myself.*

I quieted the dogs who growled and came to the door when I let myself in, kicked off my flip-flops, and took off my pants, letting them land on the floor wherever they did as I walked. I kept my shirt and underwear on and curled in bed with extra pillows behind me, having learned that sitting up prevented the acid reflux that tended to accompany binging. I immediately fell into a deep, comatose sleep.

The next morning, I still felt like I could barely move, a brick slowly digesting in my stomach. I felt so physically full that I actually couldn't imagine eating breakfast. I burped and tasted onion and ketchup. *Maybe warm coffee will help me digest.* When I went to the bathroom, I saw the stains on my shirt and congealed sauce on my face. *You are so freaking disgusting. What the hell is wrong with you?* I stumbled to the kitchen and called "Babe?" No response. I peeked out the window and noticed his car was gone. Presumably at the gym. *Like you should be right now.* I went into the kitchen and looked at the clock on the microwave, 9:45. *You have a session in fifteen minutes!* I drank some more black coffee and burped and farted uninhibitedly on the couch, waiting for my session.

181

When Sylvie came on, I felt the relief of stepping into church. *Sylvie, save me from my sins!* Sylvie asked me how I was doing. I told her I had been so bad. She took a moment to lecture on the importance of not assigning subjective and moralistic labels to my behavior like good or bad and instead say I ate a large meal. Even though I could have argued that was also a subjective label, I told her fine, I ate a large meal, well, meals: three. She asked me to explain what had happened. I told her about Erin's going away dinner, how nice it was seeing them, how much fun I had had. And then how silent the car ride felt, how lonely. And then eating and then needing to eat some more.

"What did you get out of this binge, Azure?"

Normally, I would have been indignant when faced with a question like this, but instead answered "I felt so content at the end. I don't know how else to describe it. It was like the ultimate relaxation."

"Food is very grounding, so I can see that entirely."

Can you? I wondered. I had a sneaking feeling she could not, stereotyping her ballet background and thin body.

"And how are you feeling today?"

"Other than gassy?"

We laughed.

"I feel guilty and mad at myself. I say I am trying to lose weight and then I go and do shit like that. And Sean probably knows and it just proves his point that I am not doing enough about this."

"Hold on, explain please."

I told her about Sean's annoying code that he lived by and that I am not doing enough about my problems.

"Do you think Sean will eventually be tired of seeing you do this to yourself?"

"Duh, *anyone* would at some point, but especially him with his over-simplification of the healing process."

"Let's go there. What would it feel like if the worst-case scenario took place?"

My stomach twisted and dropped out of me.

Presumably seeing the look on my face, Sylvie asked, "Can you describe what's going on in your body right now?"

"It's the same feeling I had when Vince and I broke up, the same feeling that happened when my mom left, and mixed with panic because I feel like it is looming before me."

"What was that like?"

"When Vince and I broke up?"

"Yes."

"Horrible. Even though I don't have feelings for him anymore and it's been fifty-million years, I'll never forget it. We had been arguing and I spent way too much time over at his house since things were so bad at home. I was totally suffocating him. So, I should have seen it coming, but I didn't. It completely hit me from left field." I adjusted myself on the brown fabric couch and continued. "It was one of those relationships that probably should have ended when high school did, but I was just so in love. I was so sure that we were going to get married, that we were going to be that high school sweetheart couple that actually made it." My eyes dazzled with the idea of it, even now, ever the idealist, more in love with a story than the actual characters. "But instead I got my heart broken big time. Even though I know it was for the best in retrospect, at the time it was the literal end of the world: 'We can't get together tonight, I've met someone else.'"

"Ouch! And Vince was your first love?"

I nodded.

"Eesh," she said and winced.

"Yeah!" I laughed. "It took me a good couple of years to get over Vince. You know, that whole it takes half the time of the relationship to move on from the relationship? And then I really went through an unlucky-in-love phase. I've had some doozies!"

"So, what I want to know is—" Sylvie had that contemplative look on her face as if twisting a pencil eraser on her chin— "what you took those break ups as saying about you?"

"Oh man, Sylvie!" I complained like a teenager.

She smiled but again in a way that let me know she wasn't going to let me tap-dance around this. I took a breath.

"I always knew it was related to my weight. With Vince, I look back at pictures and it's amazing what a change I went through in four and a half years. I look at one picture of me in a short black dress at the peak of my fitness, I look at another and I'm thicker, and then another and I'm slovenly, way bigger than Vince and busting out of the pants that were digging into my side, with unkempt hair, and wearing clogs for God's sake!" I laughed at the memory of the clogs but I shook my head in shame at my weight. "And with Nathaniel, a guy I was in love with in college, I always suspected a lot of it was that I was a thicker girl. The thing was that I was always one of those girls who was super close with a lot of guys and they would always say things like 'you're such a cool girl,' and I knew even if they didn't say it aloud, there was always a 'but' and the 'but' was always the same—my weight."

"So, you think people have to be thin to deserve love?"

"No! I don't think that of other people at all!" I paused, "… just me, I guess." My voice trailed off and my eyes stared into space.

"You've been thin before, right?"

I looked back at the screen. "I don't know about *thin*, but yeah I've been 'normal sized.'" I fingered air quotes.

"You think you were more deserving of love then, versus now?"

I sighed in a long exhale. "I don't know."

"I know this is difficult, take your time, *really* feel into yourself."

"Well, part of me agrees, part of me doesn't. I agree because I have evidence for it. When I was skinny, guys treated me differently, and that happens to be when I met my husband, so in a way, yeah, I agree. But then there is this other part of me that's like fuck you, Society, because I am the same person whether I am heavier or lighter. How can I be the same person and not be deserving of love in one body configuration or another? Is someone more or less deserving of love if their hair is brown instead of blonde? No. If their skin is a certain color and not another? No. But somehow weight is different even though I think it's no different." I shook my head. "I just have a really hard time with that." My chin started quivering. *Don't cry, Azure! Stop fucking crying!* I told myself harshly.

"What does that bring up for you?" Sylvie asked gently and reassuringly.

Voice shaking, I said, "I just can't stand how people are with weight. I think most people acknowledge that it isn't right to discriminate against someone for their gender or race or if they are physically disabled, or ill, but with weight, it's different. I mean, I know we're talking love here, and who's attracted to what, and you can't dictate that. But it's all just so surface level and unfair and not about who the person *actually* is! It's not just dating, it spans all types of love and relationships and just plain existing in society. People hate fat people. Hell, when I'm fat, I hate myself, and I then hate that I hate myself. But I learned that hate from people, through their treatment, not just my dad, but people in general. And that hatred and ugliness happens every day. At work, at the store, with friends, with family, *anything* to do with food or body, people think, 'Well, she *chose* to be fat. She's fat because she's lazy and only eats junk food and doesn't exercise, so she *deserves* the ridicule, passive aggressive comments, stares, whatever we dish out to make her feel uncomfortable.' And the worst part is that I think many of these people actually think they are helping me because maybe their comment will be the 'motivation I need' to start losing weight. And I will be the first to admit I am not perfect with my diet, but that is not every day. Between binges I'm eating kale and gluten-free vegan, and working out a couple hours every day. I know a part of my body being this way is the compulsive over-eating, which I am working on, but part of it is that it's just my body. I was always a thicker girl who struggled with my weight. To be skinny for me is just so exhausting because it requires an extraordinary amount of effort compared to other people.

"Like, when Vince and I broke up, I was overweight. I had gained a lot toward the end our relationship from the stress of not getting along with him and things being so bad at home and eating fast food way too often. He never said anything, but I'm sure it had an effect, because it always does. I went to Seattle shortly after breaking up with Vince and on top of the usual inappropriately open discussion in my entire family about my weight and diet, I was also treated to an *intervention* by Wendy, an old family friend who I'd only met a few times. She told me and my dad *all about* Weight Watchers and my dad ate it right up because it came from Wendy. It just makes me mad looking back on it. That every time I was up there, my entire life, my weight was the main topic of discussion the same way the weather normally is. It was *such* a convenient deflection from the abuse and dysfunction, nobody ever mentioned that.

"And the worst part is, I totally bought into it too. Weight Watchers sounded so much better than Herbalife and the other things I had done in high school, so I threw myself into Weight Watchers just like it was a rebound relationship. Even though my allotted points per day was 25, I decided to eat 18, the lowest permitted amount, and to make it extra effective, I didn't add more points as we were instructed to do after exercising, which I was doing at least two hours per day. So, I was starving constantly and would drink a couple cups of coffee just to have something in my stomach before heading off to class. By this time I was going to community college. Needless to say, I spent more time studying for Weight Watchers than any of my real classes.

To be successful I brought my usual to school—a single slice of bread with margarine and a bag of baby carrots, but on weigh in days, I didn't let myself have that either, at least not until after my two-hour workout and evening weigh in, when I would show up on the verge of passing out. When out to dinner, I would eat a bag of baby carrots in the car, then drink a carafe of water myself, so I'd be really full by the time the food arrived. I didn't think my body registered fullness like other people, so I was still after the food-sitting-at-the-top-of-my-esophagus type of full feeling and carrots did the trick. Yeah, I know, that's neurotic, but at the time I called it dedication. I finally made it to my goal weight of 135 pounds, but it didn't feel like enough. I wanted to know what it was like to weigh 125, so I strived and strived and strived. I was pretty well stuck at 135, but then the pendulum swung, hard.

"I can't tell you a particular event that caused that shift in the pendulum, but I do remember the effects. Now that I think about it, it must have been actually making it to 135. Not really knowing to how to maintain weight, only how to be an expert gainer and sometimes expert loser, I started to gain weight again. First it was back up to 150, then 175. The higher it went, the more it seemed that my life was careening out of control. To me, a thin life was an ordered life, so when the barometer went up, so did the chaos. Unlike people probably assume, I wasn't "letting myself go." I didn't declare 'screw dieting!' It was like holding onto the jungle gym bars with sweaty hands that start to slip. The more I tried to grasp tightly, the more I went downhill.

"Of course, like attracts like, so I had plenty of friendships with weight-obsessed girls like me. Hot gossip included things like which birth control results in gaining the fewest pounds, how to trick your body into not gaining weight right before your period, and wouldn't it be awesome to try this eating disorder as a diet where you chew food and spit it out, like a girl I saw on Montel Williams. And, of course I endured all the oh-my-God-I'm-so-fat's from girls way skinnier than me."

"How does that make you feel now?" Sylvie asked. "You seem a little distant."

I covered my face with my hands in shame. "It was all just so crazy. Let's try this eating disorder as a diet? How crazy is that?" My voice choked with emotion.

"Azure, Azure," Sylvie interrupted in a reassuring way, "this is great! This is actually what we have been waiting for!"

My confusion stopped my tears. "What have we been waiting for?" I asked through my sniffles.

"Azure, when I first met you, you were so deep in disordered eating, that I am not sure you would have seen just how unhealthy it was, the extreme lengths you went to lose weight. This is excellent progress! We are really getting somewhere!"

I was quiet, contemplating what she was saying.

"What are you feeling right now?" Sylvie asked.

"Not sure. I hear what you are saying. I guess I just assumed break-throughs would feel, well, more like what I imagined a breakthrough to be. *Ah yes I see now, the sky really is blue and not a morose gray.* What I feel is so much more subtle than that."

"But isn't that subtlety what this is all about, Azure? When you have disordered eating, it's a disease of extremes, being ravenousness or busting at the seams, being completely numb to feelings or drowning in them? But see, the gradations in between have in fact been there all along, you were just not used to registering them because being numb to emotion was part of the life-saving response you had to your trauma. Being able to identify them now, and more importantly *feeling* them now, is evidence of your progress! It's wonderful, actually!"

A little smile crept up my cheek. For the first time since starting this process, I felt a sensation that was almost like a tickle from deep within me—not happiness, that was too surface level, but similar, purer, and coming from my core.

18

OREO COOKIE BALLS

I cracked up when Sean showed off the pair of three parallel lines in his hair that his mom, a former hair dresser, shaved into the side of his head. He put on his open metallic shirt and genie pants, MC Hammer costume complete. He struck a pose to me, lit by the bulb lights above the vanity of my in-laws' guest bathroom. I laughed. Sean lived for Halloween, mostly because it was an excuse to get into character and put his inner twelve-year-old on full display.

"How much longer are you going to be?" he asked.

"Ten or fifteen minutes."

When he left, and I turned back to the mirror, my smile faded. I remembered telling myself *I will never weigh more than Sean*, just as I blew right through that stop sign to the wreck my body was these days. I dressed up as a fan girl with a puff-painted white shirt with fray cut at the bottom. *Do I really have to go?* I thought as I adjusted my side ponytail and applied another layer of hot pink lipstick. I had fallen a long way since the year I made my debut as Sean's girlfriend at the Halloween party in my pinup outfit. How could I even bear to show my face there, the way I was now? I shuddered at the mortifying thought, took a deep breath and told myself in the mirror "You're going, even if it's uncomfortable. Maybe feeling embarrassed is the motivation you need." *Sylvie would not approve of that last statement*, my inner voice whispered.

Sean was the center of attention as usual from the moment he got out of the car. I wished I could break off a small piece of his self-assurance for myself. I followed him, self-conscious and bracing myself for the "what happened to you" stares, trying desperately to look like regular hellos. We hugged friend after friend, couples dressed up as Popeye and Olive Oyl, Frankenstein and Lady Frankenstein, Bonnie and Clyde. I couldn't help but notice the girls wearing skirts hemmed right beneath the crotch or ass exposing leotards as naughty nurses and Playboy Bunnies. The last time some of these people had seen me, I was skinny, by my standards anyway. Now I was the matronly wife who had gained a ton of weight overnight looking at those girls with longing eyes.

Each arrival felt like another thin girl being pushed in my face to taunt me. *It's no one else's fault you have this issue.* I took a sip from my solo cup and heard Sean's laugh across the yard. I was annoyed that he was being carefree when I could not seem to be that way myself. Couldn't he see this was hard for me? I turned, opened the sliding glass door and went inside. Holly, the hostess, wife of Sean's childhood best friend, otherwise known as sexy Lady Frankenstein, hugged me and thanked me again for coming. She was one of those beautiful petite moms with a cool job that you can't help but love because she was so sweet. I stood there, not being of help except as moral support, while she refilled the hors d'oeuvres in the kitchen. I insisted on helping to set the plates and display towers back onto the table. She washed her little hands, dried them, reached into a bowl filled with some kind of brown paste and began rolling a glop of it between her palms in a circle. I asked if she was sure she didn't need any help and she said yes, but to keep her company. *I wonder what it's like to be small like that. I bet Gavin carried her over the threshold when they bought this house, like in the movies. I wouldn't have let Sean if he tried.*

"These," she explained, "are Oreo cookie balls. They're so easy. You just take Oreos, a block of cream cheese, and mix it all up until it's this kind of pasty, like this." She showed me and I pretended that I hadn't already noticed. Between forming dark brown blobs, she reached over and stirred a pot on the stove filled with something green.

"It's white bark chocolate with food coloring," she explained as she took the spoon and ladled the green chocolate over the balls on the dish. She put the plate in the fridge and exclaimed, "in a few minutes, they will be done!"

All I could think of is how I would never be like her: small and sweet. How I was big, and though also sweet, I felt bigger parts insecure, sad, and sometimes even jealous. I helped her place the green balls onto the serving dish. She excused herself to say hello to some folks she hadn't spoken to yet. So, I served myself snacks, including the cookie balls in a cup instead of the paper plate so they could be more concealed. Afterward, I returned to the backyard and searched for Sean amid the sea of scantily clad and cellulite free bodies like I had once had for a fleeting moment, and lost. Was there anything more humiliating than having to show up as I was? To be held accountable to what I had done to my body even if there were reasons, exquisitely good reasons, that no one else knew and I couldn't very well share. Sean glanced up and our eyes met. He came over. "What's up, Babe?"

I shrugged. "I dunno. It's just really hard to be here."

"What do you mean?"

My eyes welled up. "Can we go talk?"

He sighed and his eyes circled as if looking to the sky for an excuse. "Fine, let's go," he said, clearly annoyed.

"No, it's fine," I retracted.

"No, let's go." His voice was firm.

We went through the house and to the front door acting as naturally as possible, as though we were just grabbing jackets from the car.

As the car doors shut Sean asked, "What?"

"I just don't know if I can be here, it's so hard for me." I saw Sean make a face. "And I know you never get to see your friends, so go back in and have fun. I'll stay here. Just tell them that I feel sick."

"No." He rolled his eyes. "Why do you have to do this? Why can't you ever just have a good time?"

"I don't think I you understand! Do you have any idea what it's like to be me here?"

He was quiet, so I continued. "Remember that year I came as a pinup and you came as the bumble bee from the Simpsons?"

"Yeah."

"You remember what I looked like?"

"Yeah. I got high fives from my friends because you were so hot."

"Okay, that's weird and kind of gross, but proves my point exactly. Can you imagine what it's like to have been that and then to have to show my face here as this?" I waved at my body.

"Then change it! If it bothers you, then change it!"

"I'm trying! Don't you see that I'm trying? I do therapy every week, I eat kale, I go to body combat!" *So much for the calm conversation Erin had suggested.*

"When you're not going to fast food or hiding candy wrappers under the bed."

I gasped. Even the truth, perhaps especially the truth, slaps you in the face.

Sean continued, "You're such a hater, you know that? Can you ever just be happy for people without thinking 'poor you' for not having that?"

I was quiet. He had a point, though I didn't know any other way to be.

"I'm sorry!" I cried, bursting into tears. "I wish you understood!" I wailed through heaves. I looked up and through my saltwater-logged eyes I saw a pained look on his face. It was clear he hurt because I was hurt and he was unable to fix it for me. "Do you know what love tastes like?" I asked him. "For me it tastes like Grandma's shell macaroni or mac and cheese or Reese's peanut butter cups. Do you know what frustration tastes like? It tastes like barbecue kettle chips, the really crunchy kind. Do you know what despair tastes like? Boiled brussels sprouts and nonfat cottage cheese. Do you know what deprivation tastes like? Kale and hummus. Do you know what desperation tastes like? Two Melba toast crackers and a syringe of HCG. I have a food pairing for every scenario, every emotion. Food isn't just food for me!"

I looked up at him. He looked like he was watching a horror movie.

"You're so lucky," I sniffled, "that food is just food for you. And you don't even know it."

"Babe." His voice was consoling and apologetic. *Finally, a little compassion!* He reached over and placed his hand on my shoulder. "Let's go," he said.

"No, you're right, I can't have good time right now. I don't know what's wrong with me. But I don't want it to affect your night. Please go have fun with your friends."

"No, I'm not leaving you here. Let me go tell people we're taking off." He opened the car door.

"Okay," I conceded, "tell them I'm not feeling well."

"Okay." The door clicked shut.

I watched him as he walked toward the house and navigated around the garbage cans. Garbage cans. Why was Dad lurking in everything?

$\sim$

"Take this to your mother's," I remembered Dad demanding, dropping two bags of garbage at my feet before plopping down in his chair. In his relentless pursuit to save a buck, he had canceled his garbage service, and instead took bags with him to the YMCA dumpster, or had us kids take it to my mom's house, even though I was now nineteen, making it seven years since they got the divorce.

"She doesn't want your garbage," I remembered telling him. The audacity of making such a request of the woman he abused and screwed over went completely over his head.

"You think I give a shit what that cluck thinks? You better keep an eye on your drinking, bird brain, or you'll end up a crazy wine-o just like her."

"Oh, you're right, never mind the gin and tonics you drink every day, it's her wine that's the problem!" I retorted. "Back to the issue at hand, it's her garbage can and she is not going to be paying for your garbage."

"Put it in your goddamn car!"

"No."

He leapt out of his chair and over to where I was standing in the family room near the front door. He recoiled his hand to poke me in the chest as he had done so many times, but this time I grabbed him on the outside of the elbows and squeezed them. Then with each step I moved forward, he moved backward, in some kind of abusive ballroom dance. I demanded, "You. Will. Not. Touch. Me. Like. This. Ever. Again!" I pushed him.

I looked down at his surprised face attached to his older body that once seemed so powerful to me and now had just been tossed onto the white couch visitors never sat on. I glanced at my hands. I had been the one to put him there. Me! I felt so powerful in that moment. I was half expecting him to bound up and throw me down the stairs, but I think what stopped him was the very same knowledge I had just come to learn myself—that if I ever needed to defend myself, I could finally take him.

I moved out a week later, bound for university. Most people I knew were escorted to college by their parents, who helped them select a place, take care of the deposit, and carry boxes inside. Although my university was five hundred miles away, the moving assistance I got was a don't-let-the-door-hit you-on-the-way-out type of goodbye at the top of the driveway.

"See you, Jake," I told him as he looked down at the ground.

"Bye," he mumbled back to me, not making eye contact.

I hugged my brother and thought of all the times in my room where I told him it would be okay, all the times he helped me sneak food, all the times I had now forgiven when he had gotten me into trouble. *I'm so sorry, Jake,* I tried to telepathically tell him. *I don't want to leave you, but I just can't be here anymore. If you ever reconsider, please move down with me and get out of this hell hole.*

"Bye," I told my dad coldly.

"Bye," he replied as he stepped forward. *Oh my God, is he actually going to* hug *me?* I was completely shocked. He rounded his arms way out into an awkward I-guess-we-are-supposed-to-do-this hug, making as little contact with me for as short a time as possible as he gave me a brief and awkward pat-pat on my back before practically pushing me away.

I had always imagined what it would be like to hug him and now it had actually happened. But instead of feeling elated as I got into my car and started the eight-hour drive to San Diego, I instead felt completely weirded and grossed out. *He hugged me! Did he feel obligated to because that's what parents do when their kids head off to college?* One thing I was not confused about was whether it meant he'd give me money for food or gas.

Trixie and I moved into the only vacant place I could find around campus that allowed dogs, a filthy room in a wing of an eccentric Greek widow's home in La Jolla. The house must have been fancy in its heyday, but it had been many decades since then. I was to park on the street and walk the long driveway which had all kinds of palms and exotic plants lining it. I about leaped out of my skin when I noticed the first pair of eyes peering out from behind one of the trees and sighed with relief when I realized it was just the first of many large stuffed animals: tigers, gorillas, cockatoos, and others.

The house was a series of four long hallways that made a square surrounding a courtyard. My room was at the bottom right corner and had an outdoor kitchen and no bathroom so I crossed the courtyard into my landlady, Mariam's part of the house to use the facilities.

Mariam was in her eighties, and dyed her hair black but not very often because there were long white roots showing. She covered her plump body with colorful muumuus with nothing underneath, as I learned by seeing her bare ass when she reached underneath it one day to scratch her back, not realizing I was behind her. When she did see me she said, "Why, hello, dear! Come here and visit with me." Even though she was so different from my grandma, I have an affinity for old women and was happy to keep her company.

"What are you studying again, dear?" she asked.

"Animal Physiology and Neuroscience" I answered, sitting awkwardly on a stool, trying not to disturb her cluttered stacks of newspapers.

"Oh!" she replied, impressed. "What made you want to do that?"

Well, I want to impress my dad who was an electrical engineer, but there's no way I'd make it as an engineer. But, I took this amazing psych class taught by a neuroscientist and I thought a neurosurgeon would be the next best thing. How could my dad not respect me if I am a neurosurgeon?

"I am just fascinated by the brain and I really want to help people." *That was truthful enough*, I thought, trying to convince myself.

"That's great, dear. Are you going to be a doctor?"

"That's the goal!" I laughed as I darted my eyes around the room, nervous for some reason.

"That's great, dear. My Spiro, my late husband, he was a doctor of horticulture. That's why I have so many splendid exotic plants in the yard coming up to the house."

"That's cool!" I said with more enthusiasm than I felt, remembering the creepy, lurking stuffed animals.

"And this house is a historic home, you know. We have the plaque on the house, I'm not sure if you noticed."

"I did see that," I lied, having been too focused on wondering how on earth I'd be able to keep vermin out of the outdoor kitchen.

"I had better let you get back to studying."

"Yeah, I probably should get to studying," I told her, even though I didn't have much intention of it.

When I stood to leave and helped her up from her recliner, she placed her hand on my forearm and said, "Honey, you are a sweet girl and have a good heart, I can tell."

"Thanks," I said, and smiled genuinely.

"When you become a doctor, don't lose weight. Having you a little fat makes you relatable."

My smile faded into the dumbfounded meets offended face I am sure I always made when I got these types of comments.

"Uh, thanks," I managed.

"You're welcome, dear."

At least I am not in his house anymore.

Although my dad was now five hundred miles away, he still wielded control over my life, most notably, his portion of my school tuition. He devised a budget whereby he, my mom, and I would each pay a third of my education. He explained that I would be given the balance of my college fund when I was in my mid-thirties, a promise I immediately knew was bullshit. The budget was perhaps better suited for when he was in college without inflation factored in, since it included three dollars a day for food. Although I was expected to cover a third of my education, I was also inexplicably expected to not work and to focus on my studies. His being a multi-millionaire disqualified me from receiving any financial aid, not that our lifestyle was ever what most would call privileged, so off to work I went, personal assisting and working in a lab.

UC San Diego turned out not to be the school I had expected or hoped for. I had envisioned it as difficult, sure, it's college after all, but was expecting it to also have a mix of fun and social opportunities. It immediately became clear just how rude my awakening would be. UCSD was an extremely competitive environment, especially in the sciences—especially in my major—since it was such a highly rated school. Where was the fun that I saw in the college movies? Nowhere to be found at UCSD. Teachers gleefully declared that they were going to weed out the wannabes.

Transferring from community college to UCSD for my junior year had been a major mistake, not that I had much of a choice since that was Dad's mandate, to save money of course. All of the students seemingly already had their friends from their years in the dorms, for which I was too old and ineligible anyway.

Although I had always felt alone, since my real life was a secret, living in San Diego was a state of being *truly* alone. No friends, no family, no roommates, no one. I woke up in my dirty old room alone, except for Trixie. I made instant coffee in my kitchen alone, I drove to school alone. I sat in crowded class halls that held several hundred students beside people I did not know and would never see again. I performed personal assistant tasks alone, I counted cells in my lab job alone. I went to the gym alone, I drove home alone, I cooked and ate my food from the Dollar Store alone in my outdoor kitchen, and I studied alone, with Trixie by my side and the TV on.

This will be good for me, I reasoned, *to learn how to be on my own.* The truth was that I was terrified to be by myself. Nighttime always made me super anxious for reasons I wasn't clearly tuned into. TV was a mildly effective antidote. It was an El Nino year, and as winter rains flooded my outdoor kitchen and winds whipped about, I would just lie in my bed and pray: *Please don't let the electricity go out. Please don't let the electricity go out.* Then I'd scold myself for being scared of the dark, though it wasn't really the dark I was afraid of, it was being alone with my own thoughts.

In bacterial plating, little white dots form on a gelatin inside a circular dish. These little white dots are colonies of thousands of bacteria cells. As the bacteria grows, the colonies multiply, and more white dots form. There then comes a point called confluence where individual colonies are no longer distinguishable from one another and there is instead an entire moss of bacteria that has taken over the plate. This is what loneliness is like. It starts as a small thing, a spore, but grows and grows until it has completely taken over your life confluently. I knew from the looks people gave me at school that I was now that lonely strange girl, which only made me hunch my shoulders more, look down at the ground, ashamed and not wanting people to be able to see the darkness that was the real me, which only made me even stranger. Of course, evolution takes place quickly on the micro-level and loneliness very quickly mutates into its cancerous offspring: anxiety.

At first these attacks would only happen at night. But then, the relative calm of day crumbled beneath my feet. I would find myself sprinting out of the auditorium and barely making it to the bathroom in time to throw up. This would happen before every single test, then at random. I found myself hyperventilating in my car when I would see a gleam in the sky that I was sure would turn into a terrifying streak as the asteroid entered the atmosphere. I felt my heart racing as I tried desperately to not fall asleep since I was convinced I would die in my sleep. The very sound of an airplane flying overhead, especially the military jets that do daily fly-bys in San Diego, would cause heart palpitations.

Anxiety is a shapeshifter, born of your own imagination but looking so identical to your own worst fears made manifest that it's able to convince you in an instant. As my anxiety grew, so did that familiar empty feeling that took residence inside my gut and just like any monster, it demanded to be fed.

I had developed a bit of a Chipotle problem since anxiety had confluently taken over my life and could time my responses perfectly, not needing to hear the hair-netted college kid's prompts:

"Burrito, please… white rice… no beans, but could I please have fajitas?… steak… mild salsa and also the corn… extra sour cream, cheese and guac… yeah the extra charge for the guac is fine… side of chips and guac and a drink please."

I was always so embarrassed when they had to make multiple attempts to close the over-full burrito. I would eat the chips and guac on the way home and the burrito once I got there. In the moments when I was with the world's most perfect burrito, even if it wasn't the most authentic, I wasn't lonely, I wasn't majoring in something I shouldn't have, an asteroid wasn't going to hit the earth, and I wasn't going to die in a plane crash. I was just experiencing contented bliss.

I would wake up in the morning with the brown paper bag on the bed, the aluminum foil wadded up and the tissue papery lining ripped up and half eaten by Trixie. My body felt like it was about to give birth to some species of whale. I gained fifty pounds seemingly overnight, because I think it *was* overnight—nights like these were happening in alarming regularity.

Still there were unending class assignments. I went to the computer lab to work, as I didn't have internet at the tropical hideaway house. Avoiding the latest research paper due tomorrow and barely begun, I went to check on my grades. I saw the icon that looked like a little piece of paper illuminated in red; I clicked.

"The purpose of this letter is to inform you that you have been placed on academic probation due to poor academic performance. As you know, University of California at San Diego is highly competitive, and maintaining the integrity and reputation of our institution is of the utmost importance. If your grades do not reach a minimum of 2.0 next quarter, you will be academically disqualified. We strongly suggest you seek out the services of a guidance counselor at Thurgood Marshall College. It is our sincere hope that you will be able to become academically successful."

What's happening to me? Academic probation? I don't even know who you are right now! He's right about you—you're fucking stupid! You will never amount to anything! You are a failure! You got that! A total failure! A negative number!

I looked up at the ceiling, shook my head and sighed before glancing back down at the screen. I gasped audibly when my eyes fell upon the address line—my father's address. *Fuck! No! Please no!* I pleaded to God, the Universe, anybody who would be able to listen and answer a prayer as I logged out, bounded up the stairs as fast as I could, and sprinted halfway across campus to my college's office: Thurgood Marshall, one of six at UCSD.

"Can I help you?" asked the guidance counselor lady behind the counter. She was a kindly, motherly sort of woman.

I had stopped out front to try to catch my breath and not look like the gasping overweight girl that I was, but I was still breathing hard.

"Yes! If there is a letter when I logged into my account, do those get physically mailed?"

"Yes, those were sent out yesterday by certified mail."

Oh fuck!

"It was the first letter, right?" she asked in code since there were other students around.

200

I nodded, trying to fight back my tears.

"Don't worry, honey, lots of people get the first letter. Your parents will come to understand. I would like to meet with you and make a plan to get you back on track."

I nodded, completely distracted and socked in the gut. We made an appointment which took entirely too long considering I needed to hit the road immediately.

I drove home as fast as I could, threw Trixie and a couple things in my Camry, and sped on out of there. *He's going to kill me! He's actually going to kill me! Azure, get a grip! They just mailed it yesterday, that means that the soonest it would arrive is tomorrow.*

Jake and Dad were still awake when I got home at one in the morning. I let myself in and Trixie bound over to my brother in that still-puppy way and started scratching at his leg for him to pick her up. I smiled at their sweet love for a brief moment before I heard my dad speak.

"What the hell are you doing here?"

"Uh, I have a few days off between classes, so I thought I would come up," I lied. I would be calling in sick to my personal assistant job tomorrow and my lab job. As for class, they didn't know that I was even alive, let alone in class.

"What's up, Jaba the Slut?" Jake asked me.

I returned a classic "Shut up."

The next day, I waited and waited and waited at the house until 3 p.m. When the doorbell finally rang, I raced to the door.

"Hello, can you sign for this?'

"Yep!" I answered trying to hurry him along before my dad got back from a walk.

Envelope in hand I sighed the hugest sigh of relief, feeling like a regular Double-O-Seven. I stuffed the envelope into the bottom of my bag. Now that that was done, I didn't want to be there anymore. Not at the house anyway. But in the Bay Area, yes. I called up my friends and made arrangements to get together.

When I tried to leave, Dad said "See, Jake, what did I tell you? She's not up here to see you, she just wants to run off to see her friends and use this place as a free hotel." *Not entirely untrue, but acceptable in my situation. Most people's parents aren't like you*, I thought.

"If you leave that little turd factory here," he said and looked pointedly at Trixie, "you're going to come home and find it's neck snapped." He wasn't kidding. I took a seat at my place at the table and braced myself for whatever he was about to dish out.

Dad started, "I have a friend."

Coworker, I corrected in my mind.

"And he has five kids are all doctors, pharmacists and dentists. All I have, on the other hand, is a fat, and getting fatter, flunky, party girl."

Flunky? Does he know? Or was it just a coincidental word choice?

"You'll never understand the feeling of getting an advanced degree and knowing that you are second to no one."

The hoods of wrinkled skin that made his eyes look even angrier than they normally were seemed to disappear and for that moment there was a brightness in his face I don't think I had ever seen before. I knew he had overcome his own obstacles. He had recently revealed to Jake and me that when his first baby didn't survive, he took it as a second chance, causing him to go back to school and go on to earn his PhD. I wanted that feeling he was talking about—to accomplish something so spectacular that I would never feel second to him again. That way, we could finally be equals and have a respectful relationship.

When I got back to San Diego, I met with the nice guidance counselor lady.

"I see you're a transfer student," she stated as she peered through her glasses at a paper printout of my transcripts.

"Yeah," I responded nervously, bracing myself for what she would say.

"You were quite a strong student."

"Thanks," I replied, not really knowing what to say because I knew that a *but* would follow.

She studied the paper a bit longer before removing her glasses and letting them fall dangling by the colorful eyeglass holder necklace with Kenyan design she wore.

"Have you considered changing your major?"

"No!" I replied, taken aback. "I haven't."

"Animal physiology and neuroscience is a very difficult major and perhaps transferring to such a competitive program is taking its toll on you. Lots of people change their majors."

"Yeah, but, …" my voice trailed off, though my mind continued. *My dad is an engineer, he wanted me to be an engineer but there was no way I could hack it, so the next best thing was biosciences. In fact, he once admitted that he could never have done biosciences, that he doesn't have the memory for it. I really need this. If I don't do this major then I will never do some spectacular thing that he couldn't have done himself and I will never earn his respect and I will never be his equal. And then, we will never have a good relationship. I will be a failure, and he will have been right about me all along.*

"It's your choice. I just want to help you be successful here. Can I ask you how things have been as a transfer student? Do you find yourself homesick?"

Homesick? If that is wanting to go home, back to that table, hell no. If that is wanting to be back with my friends and where I knew people and was known by people, yes.

"I don't know anyone here. And it is an adjustment." My voice was quivering. *Don't cry!*

I looked around her office at the eclectic book collection on the shelf, the binders labeled as different form numbers, and her outdated computer.

"Transferring is a very difficult process. Some students find that going through student health services and receiving some counseling really helps."

Rusty Garless flashed into my mind followed by my dad's voice saying, "Shrinks are people with a screw loose that couldn't handle a *real* profession. Anyone who goes to a shrink is an imbecile. Do you believe in God too? How about Santa Claus?"

"...and although I can't make any promises, the Dean and the board that makes decisions about a student's ability to remain at UCSD despite poor academic performance are usually compassionate toward students who are seeking help for any psychological health struggles they may be having."

Sold. "Is there a list of counselors?"

"As a matter of fact, there is." She got up and fingered the binders in her book shelf before pulling a thin one that read "Campus Service Referrals." I noticed that she was a big girl herself but seemed like one of those confident and self-accepting types. *Her parents must have been different.*

She pulled a slip of paper and with a highlighter made a big orange circle around the underlined section reading "Psychological Services."

The night before my first appointment, I drank a bottle of wine and the morning of, I took some swigs off a bottle of cough syrup because food was no longer able to stave off the monsters that lived inside my gut and mind. *I can't believe you right now,* but I screwed the cap back on and decided to slip it into my bag, just in case.

Nate was a pretty boy and shockingly young, thirty tops. The brassiness in his reddish blonde hair, his slight but muscular build, and the tight way he wore his button up shirts made me think he was a surfer. Although his features were classically attractive, I did not find him so. Guys that were too nice or clean cut grossed me out. After the heartbreak of Vince's rejection, guys that I was into had to have an edge to them whether it was a dysfunctional upbringing, illicit drug use, violent punk mosh tendencies, or general emotional unavailability. Nate's office was immaculate with so few effects that I suspected it was shared. When I told him the truth about drowning at school and how there was no way to tell my dad because he is abusive, Nate seemed inexperienced and uncomfortable and said things that made it clear he just didn't get it, like, "Do you really know what your dad's reaction would be?" I explained to him snippets of my life growing up, but it was like he never grasped that there was absolutely no way for me to be transparent with my dad and get any form of understanding from him. His naiveté might have been cute if it weren't so maddening.

During later visits, Nate would say things like, "So he doesn't come to understand, is that really the end of the world?" I would explain that yes, that he would cut me off and I would not be able to afford school, that his income level prevented me from getting financial aid, that the system is messed up because it assumes that if your parent has money that they will give you any. I confided to Nate how I longed for my other dad, who would slip twenties under my car shade for me to find, by surprise when they fluttered down. And that my real Dad's voice was the voice inside my head, that even though I had physically gotten away, I hadn't really escaped at all. After a few weeks of seeing Nate, he told me that he finished his intern hours and would be leaving and no longer able to help me—not that he ever was much help.

I decided I was done with therapy and inexplicably, over time, my anxiety started to dissipate. I ended up moving to a place in Ocean Beach, OB. I loved the relaxed, hippie vibe. My place was a block from the beach that allowed dogs and near the main drag with bars and restaurants and pier. It was a cute townhouse with a fenced-in front lawn with a couple lounge chairs and a hammock. The place was almost as cute as my new roommate, Kelly, a southern belle from Mississippi. She was my age, while her husband Chase was a few years older and an officer in the military. Kelly had the most charming accent that matched her natural comfortable-in-the-spotlight charisma. She was a beautiful singer and guitar player and dreamed of being the next *American Idol* discovery. She had an angular face like Reese Witherspoon, a wide toothy smile and the body I coveted—petite with muscle tone and still feminine. Chase was part Pacific Islander and very fit with that perfect tan skin. Being military, he was very clean and regimented. I of course was not so clean and not so regimented. He started each day with fifty push-ups and a hundred crunches and he despised butter, cheese, even cream cheese, sour cream, and mayonnaise. I wanted to ask him if he knew how different my life would be if I didn't like those foods. I hoped Chase would rub off on me, or that I could at least find a hypnotist to help me get nauseated every time I even thought of dairy.

Life in OB was good. Coming home from school to the chill vibe and the smell of the ocean dissolved much of the day's stress. I was doing better with my classes, finally, and the relief felt like the sunlight that burned off the fog. And I loved the way of life there. I took Trixie to the dog beach a couple times a week and to the farmers markets every Wednesday, where white pop up tents lined Newport, live reggae music blasted, and the air was perfumed with fresh chicken kabobs, fish tacos, and kettle corn. I always made a beeline to my favorite booth, bypassing the beautiful flowers and fun jewelry and cupcakes. This booth had fresh-catch filets of different hues splayed in long trays and towers of dips mounding over the top of an open ice chest. I always got two tubs of dip—smoked salmon and smoked tuna. I kept the tuna dip for the week, but the smoked salmon dip never once made it home. Taking a couple sample pieces of pita from a nearby booth I walked to the end of the street and sat on the rock wall that framed the beach and brought a couple of tablespoons to my mouth at a time. It was heaven made from a piece of flakey, freshly caught, smoked salmon whipped into fluffy cream cheese. I let it slowly dissolve in my mouth like salty ice cream. It was rich and briny and creamy and light all at once. But then all of a sudden, he was there: *I never met somebody who could just stick their finger into a stick of butter and eat it. It's enough to make a person vomit.*

Weeknights were relatively quiet at our house. We made dinner and watched TV together, me with textbook open on my folded knee. On weekends, though, after watching beach goers and listening to Kelly jam on guitar, we'd walk to Newport, grab a slice of the Hoff pizza which had a spinach, mozzarella, feta, and a huge dollop of ricotta and then bar hop. Six weeks or so after moving in, Chase and Kelly and I went to Sunshine, a bar on Newport, for Halloween. I never saw Kelly in an outfit that didn't look amazing on her and her Halloween costume was no exception. She was a Greek princess and Chase a shirtless Trojan, which wasn't altogether different from his usual "civvies," or civilian clothes. It seemed like I only saw him shirtless. I had dressed up as Little Bo Peep and had a little sheep costume for Trixie, who I left at home.

Sunshine was always a great time, crowded but comfortable, and no one was pretentious. It was a big, crowded, casual bar, where darts and pool tables were in the back, an open roof patio was upstairs and the rest of the bar sang along to classics from eighties and early nineties. It was a mixed crowd— college kids, former college kids who thought they still were college kids, and beach bum hippies. It was especially rowdy, being Halloween, as a mostly costumed crowd laughed and clanked their glasses freely since they were disguised as their alter egos.

In the main room, the DJ hosted a costume contest and bar goers formed a large circle inside which contestants would strut their stuff with the DJ providing commentary on their outfits as though it were a fashion runway—sexy tongue rolls for the girls dressed in cat costumes, not so subtle sexual innuendos about the guy dressed as a cowboy looking for something, or someone, to ride, police car sounds and begs for a pat down for the girl in the sexy cop outfit. I was looking on when I felt a large roommate shove in my back that sent me lunging forward into the circle. Although painfully shy in these types of situations, I tried to make the most of it by striking a cute pose and then I heard it: "Oh no! Miss Bo Peep ate her sheep!" There were gasps and open mouths, slow, stunned laughter of girls that said "I can't believe he just said that... but that's still funny as hell," and then some cheers and laughs from the douchey military types. Mouth agape and body frozen in mortification, I looked up at the DJ who was at least 300 pounds himself and dressed in black with his face painted red with horns sticking out of his temples. "Come on, let's go!" I heard Kelly say as she pulled my arm and made a point of storming out through the circle so everyone would see her visible protest. She was feisty when she was pissed and her southern accent became more pronounced. Kelly led me to another part of the bar and Chase was just behind us.

Chase and Kelly didn't say anything and I didn't either, other than "Malibu pineapple" when Chase asked what I wanted to drink. I tried to act as normal as possible, as though I had shrugged it off, although I was fighting back tears and plastering a fake smile on my face. It was something we all just wanted to forget happened. But my mind was racing. *How could he do that to me in front of hundreds of people when he's overweight himself? I mean I know I'm fat, but why do I need to be publicly humiliated? Nothing like this is ever happening to me again, ever,* I stewed. *I am going to lose weight. Everyone's going to see I'm so much more than they think I am.*

19
FROSTING FLOWERS

My mid-morning Sunday session was an emotional replay of the previous night's Halloween party, the disagreement that Sean and I had, how alienated I had felt from him, from everyone, from the Universe for making me defective. It was a session of streaming tears that collected and dripped under my chin, snotty nose, and red, swollen eyes. A session where I couldn't get comfortable on the fabric couch. I was cold and lay our teal blanket over my legs, then hot and threw it off, then cold again. I kept adjusting in my seat, sitting on my right foot, then with my feet on the floor. Sylvie stopped our session earlier than usual. She took a moment to be quiet and ensure the tone was serious. "I want to talk to you a bit about where we are," Sylvie started.

Her serious come-to-Jesus tone was rather startling.

"You have significant clinical depression and I think at the very least you need medication."

"Medication, really?"

"Yes, I think you really need it, Azure."

"Oh my God. I mean, I know I have issues but I didn't think it was to the point of medication."

"It is."

"But I want to really do this, not just take medication."

"We will still do the work."

"Yeah, but I want to be better because I *am* better, not because I took medication."

"I know, but a good medication isn't a short-cut and it won't change who you are. It just takes the edge off."

"I'll think about it."

"I can't prescribe it to you, I need you to make an appointment with your primary doctor and tell them that I said you were depressed and that I recommend Prozac."

"Okay."

~

I begrudgingly went, and told the doctor that Sylvie wanted me to talk to them about getting Prozac. I said it half rolling my eyes. The doctor asked if I had been crying more lately, was lethargic, experienced loss of interests. *Check, check, and check!* "Yes," I answered.

"Which?"

"I guess all of them to varying degrees."

Without a word the doctor scribbled on the prescription pad, ripped it off, and handed it to me.

After filling the prescription, I held the pill in my hand, and bobbed it up and down as if measuring its weight. It weighed nothing, and yet to me, it felt like it carried the weight of failure. *Fine, let's just do this.* I flung it into the back of my mouth and took a swig of water, every bit the sore loser. *This isn't even working* I thought as I watched TV just before the curtain of sleepy numbness descended. I felt as if I'd drunk an entire bottle of wine or more, but somehow less relaxed. The very thing that was supposed to make me feel less anxiety was in some visceral way making me feel more so for not having control over myself.

~

Sylvie asked how it went as soon as our next session started.

I told her I filled the prescription and had tried one, but didn't like the way it made me feel.

"It takes some time to get used to," she told me.

"I don't know."

"Do you think you will continue to take it? Realistically?"

I shook my head. "Probably not."

I sensed her frustration with me, so I justified my decision: "I just want to do this naturally."

She seemed tense, but trying not to be. *For someone who tells me to own and express my feelings, she seems a little hypocritical right now.*

"You understand my opinion and my professional recommendation. Since you are not comfortable with that at this time, I am requesting that you seek out an Overeaters Anonymous meeting and commit to that process. I'm sure you already know this but at the risk of being repetitive, the twelve steps is the most successful program when it comes to bringing addicts into recovery. I really want you to supplement our work with OA."

Addict.

The next weekend I ventured down into not the best part of Bakersfield to a church. I followed the signs in the corridor to the meeting in a '90s-era rec room. I sat awkwardly and anxiously in an uncomfortable blue plastic chair with metal legs which called me fat through the mortifyingly loud creak it made as I plunked down. Our chairs were vaguely in a circle. I watched the women slowly file in and waited for the meeting to start. It was the middle of a heat wave, which in Bakersfield means well over a hundred degrees. My legs were sweating against the plastic chair to the point where sweat droplets cried down the sides of my legs. Whenever I felt their tickle, I would attempt to rub the sweat tears away quickly, embarrassed that others might see.

Another came in who looked like she was perhaps playing Cruella de Vil in a Broadway production of *101 Dalmatians*. She was slim in a cartoonish way with lanky limbs, a short jet-black bob, long skirt, dramatic mannerisms and voice. "Why helloooooooo!" she drew out as she walked through the doors and across the stage, I mean room, slinking in a way that almost looked like a waltz or tango. I smiled at her uncomfortably for the briefest of moments and looked down. There were a few middle-aged women with short hair and unisex dresses, and there was another girl in her twenties like me. I couldn't help but wonder how similar our struggles were. I couldn't imagine anyone was dealing with something as bad as I was.

Then the leader came in, hurried as she was running late but assertive and clearly in charge. She announced she was Jill and this was Overeaters Anonymous. We new girls looked around the room shyly.

"I see a few new faces here," she said warmly which seemed out of place in the dark room. "Welcome. Anne, would you like to start in order to show the newcomers how it's done?"

One of the middle aged ladies answered, "Hi, I'm Anne and I am a food addict."

"Hi, Anne," the room said in unison. I don't know why but I was surprised. I've seen it in the movies of course, but the thought of everyone saying "Hi, Azure" made me slink down in my chair a little.

"I've been struggling a little bit," she continued, "I just really have been craving foods that I shouldn't be eating and then I find myself overeating later. I feel a little out of control…"

As she continued, I found my mind drifting back to college, after the Bo Beep Ate Her Sheep incident and after I threw myself full throttle back into Nutrisystem and then Weight Watchers while training for a marathon. I sprung out of bed, and went straight to the bathroom to pee and weigh myself, hopeful that there had been progress from the night before. I was disappointed when the scale registered the same as the night before. My stomach growled. I was already so hungry and it was going to be a long day! I threw on some gym clothes and packed a few extra shirts in my backpack and went downstairs. Chase and Kelly had already left. I made a cup of instant coffee and was grateful that the hot liquid temporarily soothed away the dull, preoccupying ache of hunger.

I opened the bread bag, held it up to my nose and inhaled deeply. It smelled so good. I could have eaten half the loaf at least, but restrained myself. I buttered a single slice with margarine, folded it in half inside a plastic bag, and headed out the door.

I got to campus and headed straight to the gym. I pulled out my notes from my backpack, got on the stair climber and stayed there for an hour studying and sweating. Afterward I changed my shirt, and briskly got myself over to my class. Then back to the gym for another hour and a half, studying and sweating some more. As I stepped off the machine, I could feel I was getting a little shaky but I had to burn that fat and couldn't let myself eat yet.

A girl stopped me and asked, "Excuse me, how do you do that?"

I was puzzled. "How do I do what?"

"Sweat so much?"

Because I'm fat, duh! "Oh," I laughed nervously, unsure of whether I should be offended or flattered, "lots of water and really pushing the intensity." I was a girl who longed to be visible but once noticed wanted to blend into the wall.

After another shirt change, I headed to class. On the way I picked off and ate little pieces of my bread, savoring every morsel. I got to the auditorium, took a seat, survived another panic attack and proceeded to bomb my midterm.

Walking from there to my next class, I thought: *That guidance counselor was right, I should change my major! Nutrition would be nice. That way I can figure out how to get and stay skinny. Maybe I could also become a personal trainer and then I will be forced to stay fit.*

Somehow, I got through my next two classes and work. One more stint at the gym and this time I would have to be stingy with my water to not add weight. *Thank you wrestling for this weigh-in wisdom!* Final shirt change, then I hopped in my car and drove to my weigh in at Weight Watchers, shaking off the dizzy spells.

"Wow, Azure! You're down another five pounds!" the meeting leader exclaimed. "You're almost there! What is your secret to having such great success?"

"Thanks," I smiled. "Just following the program and working out when I can." *As in literally every free moment*—cardio before, between and after all of my classes and work, followed by leg lifts, butt isolations and crunches while watching TV at night. I also neglected to tell her that I was only eating one slice of bread during the day and chicken bouillon with a few peas in it for dinner most nights.

By the end of February, I had lost almost 70 pounds and was only a few pounds away from my goal. How could I be done already? I really was proud of myself but I by no means felt *complete* with this. *How am I almost there and still feel the same, unchanged, empty?* Where was the version of me with long thick hair, who didn't mind being the center of attention, who tans easily, who's doing well in all her classes and who all the guys like? I couldn't be at goal yet, because I was still... me.

Tears started rolling down my cheeks, while driving home.

"I should be so happy!" I cried. The tears turned to sobs. "After *all* this work, *all* this sacrifice to be someone else and I am still my shitty fucking self!" And then I heard it—the grumble. This time it would not be ignored. My usual Dollar Store meal would not cut it.

I stopped at Chipotle, the convenience store and the grocery store that night to get the largest meal consumed without being a spectacle at the fair. I managed to shove all of it inside my backpack to sneak past my roommates who invited me to eat dinner with them.

"No thanks, I already ate," I lied, holding my Chipotle cup. "I actually have to study, I'm heading up. Midterms." I shrugged apologetically.

"Okay, good night!"

"Night!" I called as I climbed up the stairs.

At 2:30am when I awoke to the familiar blue glow of the TV, my stomach, which I'd so painfully shrunk over the last six months, was distended and pregnant looking. *That was a mistake. How could I do that to myself and ruin all my progress?* I headed to the bathroom. I recoiled when the light came on, not just because it was bright but at the sight of myself. *You are so disgusting! You should be ashamed of yourself.* I opened the medicine cabinet and retrieved the bottle of laxatives. I poured out three instead of the prescribed one. I needed all of this stuff out of me as soon as possible. I needed to be absolved of this. *Tomorrow will be different. I will be so controlled with food that I will be free from it. I am never doing this to myself again!*

~

"How about you, Pamela? Would you like to go next?"

Was it obvious that I was totally spacing out?

"Sure!" Pamela, Cruella de Vil, answered with excitement. "My name is Pamela and I am a compulsive overeater."

"Hi, Pamela!"

She proceeded to tell us her rock bottom story. "I was at a friend's wedding and they had this wedding cake with these exquisite frosting roses. I ate mine. It was so good I just had to have another. I noticed the people at my table had eaten their cake but had scraped off the frosting rose. I asked the person beside me if she would mind if I ate hers. She said sure, so I ate it. I worked my way around the table and ate all of the discarded frosting flowers. But I *still* wanted more. So, I started walking around from table to table, asking people for their frosting flowers. I finally reached a woman who looked at me and exclaimed, 'That's dis-gust-ing!' and glared at me as if I were an animal. I was so humiliated and that was my wake- up call. I joined OA after that and I am proud to say that I have abstained from refined sugar for 1,259 days."

Everyone clapped.

Did she just say "abstained?" I thought, horrified. *As in zero, none?*

Jill, the leader went on to describe the Overeaters core belief of absti-nence, just like in Alcoholics Anonymous. "But what we abstain from are our trigger foods," she explained.

What if your trigger foods change? What if sometimes it's sugar, sometimes it's cheese, sometimes it's chips? What if it's different within a month, a week, and even a day? Am I supposed to just not have any of a long list of things? Why couldn't it just be a little of those things and focus on healthy things? Why does it have to be so all-or-nothing? Does it have to be so all-or-nothing?

I looked over at Pamela. Was she what I aspired to be? Did I aspire to a life where I haven't had a single piece of chocolate for 1,259 days and counting? Where a single bite of mac and cheese sends me back to day zero? I became so sad looking at her. *She's a woman in prison. We both are, really. She went from a prison like mine, one that was given to her from whatever trauma her eating issue is from, into another prison, constructed brick by brick by herself to keep herself at bay with food. Is that what I want? Haven't I been in enough prisons in my life?*

I flipped through the little book with "Overeaters Anonymous" in gold on the glossy white cover that the leader had handed to me, trying to force myself to be compliant. The first page read in bold: "I am powerless over food." *I am powerless over food*, I repeated. *I am powerless over food. Am I powerless over food?*

Is the opposite of addiction absolute abstinence? Is declaring myself unfit for society and putting myself in a cage the only way to deal with this? Is that really healing addiction or just succumbing to its powers? Is food really an addiction at all? It's food! Food is central to life—it's sustenance and celebration and love. Eating is natural, food is a friend, food even saved my life, according to Sylvie. I refuse to believe that I have to vigilantly abstain from all my favorite foods, to desperately bat food away like a pack of converging zombies. Food isn't a monster and neither is my appetite for it. Is a life with no mac and cheese or chips or burritos, or mousse au chocolat, or anything I love so passionately really a life worth living? I want to live fully—yes, full-ly!—but just not have food run my life. To be normal with food. Isn't that possible? To be able to have a little of something, like everyone else, and not the whole bag or container? But the fact is I can't do that, at least not yet. If that makes me a food addict, then so be it, but I know somewhere inside me there is the power to be as I was naturally intended, a person for whom food can just be food in a way where food is still glorious food. I am not powerless, I know I can be powerful. Power-full. (Pun intended and without shame).

I couldn't stop thinking about it while other lifers droned on with their rock bottom stories, which seemed to bore even them, they'd repeated them so often. I felt simultaneously grateful to OA for labeling overeating an addiction, an illness like alcoholism or drug abuse, and frustrated with the organization for having no other option than abstinence, as if they served junkies, bingeies and drunks (Oh my!). Binging, I knew too well, is seen as an error in morals or character, a total lack of willpower, completely shameful—and so are other addictions too, now that I thought about it. Only there was a certain glamorousness to the pop star struggling with substance abuse, and more than that a level of acknowledgement about substance abuse being a legitimate problem that food collectively did not have. Still, it is not fair to ask for abstinence from what you have to do three times a day to live. Does anyone *want* a life of Melba toast and raw kale? Doesn't it all boil down to the Finnish proverb "happiness is a place between too much and too little?"

The uncomfortable plastic chair creaked when I shifted and got out of it to slip out the door. Even though I hadn't eaten one less thing that day, or lost one of the many pounds I still felt I needed to lose, I felt strangely… lighter, more self-assured, capable even. *Who am I right now?* I smiled to myself as I walked out the way anyone who is truly done with anything does—not looking back.

20

TWO SLICES OF PIZZA

I met Sean after my six month Rocky-style-montage of
wake, scale, sweat, starve,
wake, scale, sweat, starve,
wake, scale, sweat, need to fucking eat, binge, laxative, misery,
wake, scale, sweat, starve,
wake, scale, sweat, starve.

A peculiar thing had happened as I passed my initial goal weight: guys at the gym would hold the door open for me—the same guys who would let it slam in my face before when I was fat. *Did they recognize me?* I wondered. *Was this a way of saying good job on my weight loss? Or had they never even noticed me before?* Being overweight can be a bit of a contradiction that way—you are more visible because you are physically larger, however you are more invisible because people tend to ignore your presence. *Suddenly I deserve respect when I'm no different except the way I look?* I'd think.

Guys being courteous at the gym wasn't the only unexpected thing that happened. "Don't you think you're getting too skinny? You don't look like yourself," one friend told me. "Your face looks better with more on it," another said. Needless to say, when I looked in the mirror, I didn't see this "getting too skinny, not looking like herself" girl people were talking about. To me I was the same: same saddle-bags, same dimple-butt, and still way bigger than my friends.

Unlike guys at the gym, Sean was a fresh start. He would only ever know me as After, or so I thought. Over the weeks that followed Sean and my meeting at the club and the kiss on the pier, Sean and I counted down the hours until the next weekend when we would get to see each other again. *We are just having fun*, I told myself. *Don't get too attached. He'll see who you really are at some point and it'll be all over then.* Weeks later, at Newport Pizza Sean announced that his roommate Adam had referred to me as Sean's girlfriend. "And I didn't correct him," Sean told me in his cajoling, confident manner.

I paused, raised an eyebrow and laughed, "Is this seriously how this conversation is going to go?"

"Yep!" he said giving me his best shit-eating-grin.

I laughed and punched him on the arm playfully. "Sean! A girl thinks about how this conversation will go and this is *not* how they imagine it going!"

We both laughed.

"Since you are my girlfriend now, do you want to go to a concert with me in a couple weeks? I'm going to win tickets off of the radio."

"Wait, wait, wait, what?"

Sean explained that he was lucky and that he won things off the radio all the time, once twice in a single month, and that he was probably going to win the lotto someday.

Who is this guy? I feel like I should roll my eyes at him, but he's just too charming.

Sean did win those tickets off the radio and I sat beside him in the eighth row of the sold out arena. Thereafter, our weekends were spent alternating between Ocean Beach and Santa Clarita as we took turns making the two and a half hour drive. But those weekends were the best, spent bar or micro-brewery hopping, going to the Gaslamp Quarter downtown, singing along at our favorite dueling piano bar, having bon-fires at the beach near my house or eating Enchilada Vallarta from the best Mexican food restaurant in the world. And contrary to my preoccu-pation with my lower ab pooch bulge, the first time we made love came with no self-consciousness. It felt like I actually had met someone I was supposed to be with, clothed or naked.

It was one of those nights when Sean, orange glowed beside the bonfire and strumming a guitar in a hooded sweatshirt, seemed different to me. The final synapse sparked: love. I was completely in love with him. He looked up and smiled at me, seeming to recognize the difference in the way I looked at him. I smiled back with cartoon heart shaped irises, though I told myself, *you better play it cool or you'll scare him off.*

After we stumbled into my room inebriated, we flipped haphazardly onto my air mattress, bouncing Sean right off. We collapsed into laugh-ter, but that didn't stop the internal monologue. *You're so fat you bounced him off the bed! Shut up! You're 135 now, he bounced off because it's a freaking college kid's air mattress.* When Sean's laughter faded to match mine, he got into bed, successfully this time. I nestled my head into the nook of his armpit.

"I love you," he stated, self-assured as ever as he stroked my hair.

I turned my head to look up at his face. Though it was dark I could see enough of him via the yellow street lamp from down the street. *I love you too!* I shouted inside my mind so loud I thought surely he could hear. *Wait, he's been drinking. Maybe this is what guys say when they are drinking.*

"We've had way too many Jack and Cokes to be talking about serious stuff. I'll know you love me if you say it in the morning," I said. *You're such a bitch! No, I just can't handle it to have this ripped out from under me now, not after everything I've been through.*

He kissed me on top on the head and we drifted off to sleep. Counter to physics, a few minutes later the rude, baking sunlight woke us as it turned my room into an oven. We were in the same position we fell asleep in. He was already awake and waiting for me to wake up. He pulled my chin up, kissed me tenderly, and whispered, "I still love you in the morning."

As my graduation closed in, it was apparent that I was going to make it despite the academic hiccups I had the previous year. Sean and I decided together that I would move up to Santa Clarita since he was older and already had a real job. It just didn't feel right to ask him to move to the Bay Area with me where he would be starting over and where our primary support system would be my parents.

Because college education was presented as absolutely mandatory in my family, I had assumed that graduation would be something of a big deal, a rite of passage. Instead, my parents each separately expressed their disinterest in attending my graduation because of the long drive and the hot weather. It was like the philosophical tree falling in the forest question: If no one was in the audience to be proud, would my walking across the stage really count as a graduation? I decided there was no point in participating. My college days ended anticlimactically, technically being done when I finished my last final and officially had a degree in Animal Physiology and Neuroscience.

Even if my parents weren't, Chase, Kelly, Tiff and Sean were happy to celebrate with me at the 80s house party we threw as a combination graduation and going away party. Sean presented me with the most beautiful leather briefcase, which I thought was so sweet, especially since nothing arrived from my parents other than my dad's email informing me that I had received his last check even though I did not have a job lined up yet. When I confided in Sean about my disappointment, he held me with his hands on my shoulders, looked me square in the eye and told me for the first time "You and me against the world."

I felt like I couldn't be making a better decision than starting a life with him in Santa Clarita, though we did make a pact that one day we'd move back to San Diego. The following week, I packed my Toyota Camry to the ceiling, held Trixie on my lap and watched OB disappear in the rear view.

21

FRY BREAD AND BARBEQUE

"**H**ello?" I answered.

"Yeah."

That fucking "yeah" again.

"Hi," I answered not amused and still a little on guard from my last run-in with my dad.

"I was thinking, I'd like to come down, see your house, learn more about your job, and work on our relationship."

Is this seriously my dad on the other end of the phone? "Work on our relationship?" Oh my God, is it actually happening? After all this time, after all my effort? Is this finally the turning point in our relationship that I have been waiting for my entire life? Yes! He is going to see everything I worked so hard for. He is going to see that I am actually somebody at my company, someone whose opinion matters, someone whose thoughts are taken into consideration when making decisions. He will be impressed with our house, surrounded by oaks and the family of deer just like his house. He'll see it all—all that Sean and I have accomplished on our own without his help. He'll realize he was wrong about me, that I was—am— smart, successful, and worthy of respect. He won't even need to ask for forgiveness. Just simple acknowledgement will be good enough. We will finally have a good relationship. He'll give me career advice and help Sean and me do our own renovations on the house and he'll be a good grandfather who takes our kids fishing. My dad and I will finally have our version of a happily ever after!

"Okay," I answered, much more subdued than how I felt. It always seemed best to play it cool with him.

A couple weeks later, I straightened the house to perfection—well, the closest thing to it with closets concealing heaps of crap as usual. My heart beat fast when I saw his car pull up. I opened the door in a welcoming way, but still a little guarded. Even though this was our chance to make things right, it still felt too weird to me to be openly friendly with him. We would have to build trust for that.

My dad and brother came in and set down their bags in an awkward spot in the foyer and I noticed the purple bruising all over his arms. My Grandma, who had died of leukemia had had similar bruising. I offered them a beer and some snacks in the kitchen. As they wolfed down the snacks like animals, I interpreted my dad's thoughts in his eyes—these were expensive snacks that I had spent too much money on, because I was stupid with my money, because I was stupid.

Between bites my dad said, "Man! You guys need to redo this kitchen!" My shoulders sank a bit, as the first comment he made on the house was critical, of course. He walked around the kitchen fancying himself a home inspector and pointing out what was wrong with the ceiling height, the cabinet choice, the design, the lighting, but complimented our choice of sponge. In fact, he complimented it so much that it was clear he wanted us to offer it to him. Sean and I looked at each other and smiled, but did not offer it to him. My dad was similarly disparaging of all six of the bedrooms, even the one we converted into a brewery. He was unimpressed with our large lot and it's haunting oaks. He made sure to point out some dry rot on a post of the deck and said that he of course knew how to fix it since he had built his own house, unlike us lowly consumer-types.

I looked over at Sean. He looked so calm, so cool, letting it all roll off his back, unlike me, who took each unconstructive criticism as a word bullet to a vital organ. I was dumbfounded that Dad found nothing kind to say after all of Sean and my effort.

Finally, even Sean was riled when my dad sat at the head of the dinner table. Sean made it a point to sit at the other end, facing off with him.

Sean stayed quiet, as I asked him to with my eyes.

After dinner my dad settled into the middle of the couch with no regard for where we normally sat or ensuring everyone had a place. He asked us how much we paid for cable, then told us what a rip off it was as he turned the volume up high.

Sean and I went to bed and did our best to fall asleep despite the deafening volume in the living room.

"Babe?" Sean whispered.

"Yeah?"

"Your freaking dad!"

"I know!"

We both laughed, but our giggles faded to my sadness and Sean's frustration.

"I can't believe your dad would go into another man's house and have the nerve to sit at the head of the table."

"Babe, I'm sorry. That's just how he is."

"I just want you to know that was really hard for me to put up with as a man."

"I hear you. It's only a few days."

You should tell Dad to be respectful or leave. Prioritize Sean's happiness. Stop asking him to walk on egg-shells. But this is what I have always been working for with Dad my whole life! I need Sean to stick with it just a little longer.

Sean pecked me goodnight and rolled over.

I lay there with my eyes open looking at the ceiling. *Okay, he wasn't impressed with the house, but maybe work will go better.* Dread balled in the pit of my stomach. Perhaps a premonition? Unable to sit with it any longer, I reached over and clicked on the TV.

The following day, I arranged for my dad and brother to come to an event I had organized at work as a benefit for a nonprofit, which I had done on top of performing my regular job. My dad and brother arrived late, dressed like vagrants, and headed straight for the free food. When a couple of executives strolled over, I introduced my dad to them. Mouth full, wiping his hand on his pants, my dad bragged that he was a retired big shot in the electronic world. The Head of Operations offered to give my dad and brother a private tour of the manufacturing facility.

When my dad returned, he was snickering.

"What?" I asked him as he strutted over.

"The circuits in your electronic products are archaic. It's the same types of circuits I worked on in grad school!" He laughed.

Please God, please God, please let him not have said this to the Head of Operations. Nothing surprised me when it came to my dad.

"Well, not much to see here. We're going to take off," he said, having exhausted what small entertainment value this event offered, something I had poured so much into.

Standing alone, I plastered an I'm-not-sad smile on my face for the rest of my coworkers. *He thinks our products are a total joke, so he thinks my company is a total joke. He thinks they are stupid, so of course they appointed a fellow stupid person to management and are even stupider to pay me the salary I make, which, as a stupid person, I do not deserve and will not hold onto.* The pillars I had built up crumbled and brought me back to square one—a total dumb shit negative number who would never be able to accomplish enough to impress Dad or make him proud. *Oh well*, I told myself unconvincingly, ever trying to be the optimist. *Strike two.* But he did say he wanted to work on our relationship.

The next day, sitting again at the head of table, somewhere in the middle of his umpteenth cup of coffee, my dad declared his boredom. "This is what you do for fun? Just sit around? No wonder your ass looks the way it does. Hey Jake, ever notice how some women have fat butts that have been flattened from sitting too much?"

"We are all waiting on *you!*" my brother pointed out to him.

I felt so grateful that Sean was so understanding and patient with my family's dysfunction. I wanted to tell Jake again that life didn't have to be that way, as I had so many times on the phone when I begged him to come live with us. I wanted to thank him for not acknowledging or feeding into the fat butt comment. I loved how I could still see the good in Jake, that Dad hadn't been able to blacken Jake's heart, at least not yet.

"Jake is so pig headed," Dad told Sean and me, and laughed, not considering that we might agree with Jake.

Sean drove us all to town. I reflexively sat in the back seat—my dad never sat in the back, but I immediately regretted doing it, supporting his chauvinistic ideals. When we happened upon the Wells Fargo, Dad insisted we go inside. "I have some business here."

He approached the teller while Sean, Jake, and I hung back. Then my dad waved me over. "We want to transfer this amount from her account to mine." He slid her a piece of paper with the figure which was two thirds of my annual income.

Sometimes moments stretch into long sprawling expanses, like the moment after my dad's last word. The teller looked up at me in a concerned way.

Of course, it all makes sense now. He isn't here to see our house or learn about my job or improve our relationship. He thinks of this as a business trip. He's just here to get me to transfer the money I inherited from Grandma. I thought of the emails he had sent me over the months since my Grandma's estate, demanding the money, that it was his money and should have been left to him since he was Grandma's son. I remembered my replies, agreeing to on the condition that he would go to counseling with me. And I remembered his responses. *"You would find a one on one meeting with me and a shrink a very unpleasant experience as they are sure to call you on your BS."* Of course, how could I have been so naïve? *All along, all this had ever been was one giant manipulative mind fuck.*

"Miss?"

I looked at the teller.

"This seems a little coerced. You seem really uncomfortable. You don't have to do this if you're not comfortable."

I nodded and felt my chin start to quiver. Embarrassed and had for a fool, again, I simply said, "I can't do this," and stormed out of the bank, Sean behind me.

It was a long silent drive back to the house. I think the only reason my dad wasn't giving me all kinds of shit was because Sean was in the car with us and even though we were married, my dad still considered him an outsider. When we got in the house, Sean went to the room to take a shower. Dad made himself a cup of coffee and began stirring it with a spoon, like he did at home even though he drank it black and we didn't make instant coffee. The jingling of the spoon irked me.

"By the end of the day Monday, I had better get my money," my dad said as he sat down at the head of our table.

"Dad, I have no problem transferring it, even though Sean and I could really use it since we are just getting started out, but fine, if it means you and I can repair our relationship, then fine! I will transfer it... *if* you agree to go to a counselor with me, like I have requested multiple times."

He just laughed and said, "You crazy cluck. You better transfer me the money or you're going to live to regret it."

It was like I had been standing before a banquet of promises that looked so amazing, so appetizing, so mouthwatering, only to put on glasses and see it for the disgusting slop it really was. Suddenly it was clear that this sprawling smorgasbord displayed every mean, awful and abusive thing he had ever done to me. The centerpiece was his deliberate exploitation of my undying hope that things would one day turn around for us. It was over. There was no more *am I crazy? Or is he?* This money grab had been premeditated. I was done.

I stepped my feet together and leaned forward and slowly, clearly and deliberately annunciated, "Get the fuck out of my house."

I thought this would shock him into momentary silence, but he responded right away.

"Fine! Who wants to be in this shit hole anyway?"

He must have known this was coming. He must have thought of this on the way home. Who thinks like that, how to hurt their daughter that way?

"I'm serious! Leave. Now!"

When he got his stuff, I followed to make sure he left. I was barefooted and barely noticed the painful pebble or two as I walked the path from the front door to the driveway.

"Jake, put that in there," Dad demanded.

Jake did as he was told and lifted the suitcases into the trunk of their silver Camry and closed the door.

"Jake," I said, "you can stay if you want. You don't have to go with him."

Jake shrugged looking at the ground and got into the car.

My dad stepped into my line of sight, blocking my view of Jake.

"You are the biggest disappointment of my life!" Dad bellowed at me. "You are nothing but a fat, stupid, ugly, spit-in-your-eye bitch!"

"I've heard that line so many times, Dad." I exclaimed with a wave of the arm. "You really should come up with some new material. Do you know that I found a journal from when I was eleven and I wrote then how you called me that? You probably did even earlier, but it's the first time I wrote it down."

"So what?"

"You think it's okay to call your eleven-year-old daughter that? Are you hearing yourself?"

"I called you a fat, stupid, ugly spit-in-your-eye bitch because you *were* a fat stupid ugly spit-in-your-eye bitch and you still are!"

Somehow it stunned me. I'd always wondered whether he had just lost control in those moments when he said awful things or if he truly meant them. Here was my answer.

"You are a despicable father," I told him.

"Like you'll do any better."

"I think Sean and I will be really good parents, actually."

"How are you planning to do that, put your kids up for adoption?"

At which point I lost it. "Get the fuck off my property right this instant," I screamed.

He got in the car with my brother and they drove off. I stood there alone for the longest time, noticing the strange silence. On my way back into the house, obliterated, I couldn't help but notice that the black dead looking oaks were bearing a plethora of tiny vibrant green buds.

I made my way back inside and collapsed onto the couch. "Why was I so foolish to believe that maybe one day he would love me?" I howled in despair. Sean, freshly showered, was suddenly there, putting his hand on my back, seemingly having figured it out. What could he say? This was the final garnish on the platter of all my hurts, all my disappointment. How did this weekend go from the pinnacle of everything I have always worked for with my dad, to earn his respect and his love, to this? I failed. And I had stood up to him, stood my ground, called him out, and instead of feeling strong, I felt hollowed out, like a big empty, shaking, brittle failure.

Though Sean didn't know what to say, he certainly knew what to do. "Babe, I'll be right back," he said as he hurried out the door. I sobbed into the pillow for what seemed like only a couple minutes when he returned with rustling plastic bags. When he walked by me and into the kitchen, I smelled Red's Barbeque, the best comfort food in Tehachapi. I heard Sean clanking plates and silverware before returning to me, setting down a plate on the coffee table and pulling me up to sit next to him. "It'll be okay, Babe." He hugged me.

I nodded, not believing him but not wanting to break his heart either. One broken heart was enough.

I poked the food with my fork and raised it to my mouth. It was as though I got actual hugs from the salty, savory brisket, sweet and tangy pulled pork, mac and cheese so thick, creamy, and pungent it may be the very best in the entire world, and the salty, chewy goodness of Native American fry bread. In all of their company, and Sean's, I felt I would be all right.

In my session with Sylvie the following week, I wailed, "I hate that my dad is doing this to me! As if the whole mind fuck of him coming down wasn't bad enough but now telling me that I had better steer clear of 'his' family?"

"What is the power that he has, though?" she asked. "Don't you think your family is capable of forming their own opinion?"

Sylvie looked like she was biting the inside of her lip.

"He's really persuasive. I just wish I knew what he was thinking. Does he miss me and is pretending not to? Or does he not? I mean, I know the answer is no, he doesn't miss me at all. He doesn't give a shit. But he keeps me chained in somehow. It feels like a game that I just can't figure out and whose rules constantly change. And then I am mad at myself for being so caught up with it all still. I'm just so conflicted. If it were anyone other than my dad, it would be like 'forget you.' but when that person is your dad. Man, that's hard."

"I want to see your state of being as more independent from your father."

I sniffled. "I want to be cleansed of him, of this whole situation. It's like he's made me dirty! I just want to be scrubbed clean of all of it. That's why I am doing this vegan detox and I feel really different already."

Sylvie sighed, and shook her head. "I understand," she said. "But what are you hoping to gain? You came to an excellent understanding of him last week. You called him out. Can you just let go of this person that one can barely even call a person, who has done nothing but hurt you your entire life?"

"I just want him to be wrong about me. And it's not even just him. There is this girl at work who has been emailing people calling me Ugly Helga, some big, unattractive, mole-faced, German caricature. And the worst part is that same girl confided in me that she is bulimic herself. I'm so tired of being treated this way. What is about me that tells people that it is okay to treat me that way?"

"What do you think it is?"

"Because I *am* fat, which is why I want to change that." I answered, concluding that Sylvie was just not getting it, and why would she, she was skinny, a ballet dancer. She would never understand what it was like to be anything like me.

Sylvie sighed again in a disapproving way that let me know she was frustrated with me, at my backslide, even though I knew she would deny it if I called her on it.

"I want to speak to you plainly, Azure; can I do that?"

"Of course." I braced myself, scared of what she would say.

"You came to me because you were bingeing quite often and wanted help. I believe you have reported that things have gotten worse. You've been bingeing more, correct?

"Yes, at the beginning."

"You are still bingeing with some regularity though, correct?"

"Yes."

"Since we started therapy, you have experienced more sadness that has interfered with other areas of your life."

"Yes."

"I recommended that you try using anti-depressants, you did not."

"I didn't like the way it made me feel."

"I suggested you supplement our work with going to Overeaters Anonymous, but you decided it wasn't for you."

"Correct. I don't believe that abstaining from particular foods and counting days is the solution. It's really no different than weird diets. What I am looking for is to be actually free of addiction."

"Yes, and the Twelve Step model is the most effective option for recovery from a statistical standpoint."

"For drugs and alcohol, I'll assume that's correct. I am not sure that's the case for food. I'm trying to do this the real way without medication. I want to get to the root of it. I know addicts are just sensitive people who have gone through a thing or two and who are ill-equipped to process their own emotions, so that is what I am trying to learn here—how to deal with my emotions."

"I really think you need more help than you are currently utilizing.

You are clinically depressed, but refusing medication, addicted to food but refusing the treatment I am recommending. I want to be very clear with you. I think you need to go to a ninety day in-treatment program."

I made a sound somewhere between a cough and a snort. *An in-treatment program? Food rehab? Like I am some kind of junkie? A food junkie? Or more appropriately a junk foodie? Is this some kind of place in Malibu where we learn about the joys of juicing?*

"I'd like to make a plan to enable you to do that," Sylvie stated assertively.

When I didn't respond right away, she asked, "What do you think about that?"

"I'm surprised. I mean, I know I am depressed and I have a hard time with food and stuff, but you really think it's *that* bad?"

"Yes, your condition is that serious."

I nodded, still stunned.

"You really need this, Azure. Can you give this to yourself?"

"I can't leave my job for three months."

"There is a medical disability program through the state that is meant for this very purpose."

"But there's a lot going on at work right now and I just can't take that large of a time-out from life. Plus, I feel like I need to be able to do this in the confines of real life. Going to live on a ranch somewhere, yeah, I will probably do well, but this is my life, and it has to work here."

"To be frank, I think it is a serious mistake to not do this as your next step. I think we have exhausted what we can do in our work together."

"Oh!" I exclaimed, shocked at this ultimatum. She could fire me as a client?

She silently held my gaze.

"Well," I started. "I am surprised but I understand your position. But I simply cannot leave my life and my responsibilities for three months." I gulped, thinking fast. "But I really do thank you for everything you've done for me and all our work together." *Is this really the end with Sylvie?*

"I urge you to reconsider. Often people underestimate their employer's level of understanding. Can you have a conversation with them about it?"

"Yeah," I lied.

"I will reach out and check on you soon. And please, don't be a stranger."

"Okay," I answered, confused because she was the one who was breaking this off.

After the awkward goodbye, I clicked the laptop shut.

22

KRAFT MACARONI AND CHEESE

At first it felt like the familiar aching emptiness I had when my mom left, but in the months after Sylvie and I parted ways, I settled into a routine. Early mornings were spent sweating and getting carpet rash from Beachbody workouts in my bedroom. Free time was spent devouring self-help books and talking on the phone with Erin and Tiff. Work even seemed to stabilize a bit, or maybe I had finally acclimated to the level of pressure. I ate cleanly and it seemed like the more green that was in my grocery cart, fridge and plate, the better Sean and I got along. In fact, it seemed like we were friends again. With my focus on being lighter in body and spirit, our life seemed more romantic comedy than intense drama. We laughed a lot, clinked glasses often and his hand spent more time resting on my thigh.

It felt like things were finally getting better, that I was finally past, well, my past. But there was a vague feeling somewhere in me that there was still something huge and lurking beneath the surface. And then an email would arrive like a crested cryptid's back in dark waters:

Still looking for the transfer of the money to my checking account. Until I get it, you will be branded a liar and a thief by me and my family and subject to any actions I may choose against you. You are, and continue to be, the biggest disappointment in my life. What father does not want a jerk like you for a daughter? I have always told you that the only person dumb enough to buy your BS is you.

Love and kisses,
Your father

What did I do that is so wrong? Why am I such a disappointment? I was a clean cut girl, who was on the honor roll, who went to college and did volunteer work. Was it because I was a girl? Was it because I called my treatment what it was?

I remembered the time my brother pulled a knife on my dad during a hike in a rare display of backbone. He had cut Dad's forearm enough to bleed but not require stitches. I had been terrified for what was in store for Jake. But to my amazement, nothing happened! If I so much as gave a look my dad didn't like, he was on me. But when Jake cut Dad, it was as if Dad shrugged it off as 'boys will be boys!' I couldn't reconcile the difference. What wasn't I getting?

How many times will you go back to a dry well? I heard Sylvie's voice ask in my head. *Life doesn't have to be this way. Not every interaction has to be a fight. Life can be peaceful, copacetic.* I wished Dad could see that. There was no explaining that to him, so defeated and resolved I elected not to answer. *What else is there to say?* I was tired of seeing my dad and other dad in everything. More than that, I was tired of being myself because being myself meant I still had to deal with the unrequited love triangle.

The more those feelings came up, the more sit-ups, wall squats, and high knee runs I did, the more spinach I ate, the more I pushed those feelings down. Soon enough, I was back to a single digit size and was getting "good job!" cheers from people at work and from Sean. Had I finally been able to put it all behind me? Had all I needed all along was a strict vegan lifestyle excluding all processed or baked foods? Was this the answer to everything?

When it was time for our annual camping trip with our friends, I felt ready to tackle it. I would work out while we were there and I would bring mostly detox-friendly food... but had to bring Kraft mac and cheese, because camping just isn't camping without it. There were several familiar blue and gold boxes among the mountains of gear and supplies in the living room that would need to somehow fit in the back of our vehicle.

"Babe, we gotta go," Sean said as he walked up behind me to retrieve another load to take to the car. I grabbed an armful of stuff as well and followed Sean out to the truck. As I stood there, hatch open and piled with stuff, the car morphed into a familiar silver '89 Nissan pickup truck and I heard a voice I wished I could forget. It started as a faint echo but moved at lightning speed and was suddenly upon me, or rather, my mom.

~

"What the hell is taking so goddamn long?!" my father exclaimed, but of course not loud enough for the neighbors to hear since we were outside. My mom flinched. It seemed that the constant in his outbursts was an element of surprise.

My petite and slight mom had been killing herself schlepping the camping gear into the back of the truck. She was exhausted but nearly finished and the camper was full to the brim, especially because he insisted on bringing our own firewood to save a dollar. "I'm almost done!" she exclaimed, unable to resist defending herself.

A look of rage came over his face as if to say *that's it!* He grabbed her by the upper arms and pushed her backward until the backs of her legs were against the truck's tail gate, then lifted her up and threw her inside the small remaining space in the back of the truck.

She screamed my dad's name. "No, please, don't! Please doooon't!" in the desperate tone I imagine in which all kidnapping victims plead.

BANG! The tailgate slammed up, narrowly not pinching a large part of her thigh inside. She was frantically looking around, her eyes calling: *Would any neighbor please just walk by?* The tinted glass door came down, like a coffin lid closing her inside.

My dad started chuckling and mumbling "stupid bitch" to himself but loud enough for us kids to hear as we stood there stunned. He pulled out his keys and proceeded to lock the handles on the glass, left then right. Jake and I tried to look as natural as possible; we knew if we didn't succeed, we would be next. He looked over at us and said, "Where the hell have you guys been? Let's go." Perhaps he was unaware that we had witnessed what he had done. We obediently got into the truck but not before I touched my hand to the black glass once he turned to get in on his side. I am not sure if she saw or not.

"Babe? Babe!"

"Yeah?"

"You ready to go?" Sean asked.

I nodded, wondering how long I had been standing there, and assuming Sean must have been annoyed with me for not helping him.

"Sorry, babe!" I said as I grabbed more camping gear to load.

The drive to the campground was long and interspersed with breaks at the amazing sandwich place in Bishop, the exotic meat jerky place on the edge of town, and the gourmet lobster tacos at a gas station in Lee Vining, the tiny town on the edge of Mono Lake.

Growing up, our trips to Memorial Park in San Mateo County, although a much shorter drive, never had fun stops along the way. On the camping trip I can't help but remember most, my dad jerked the wheel left and right at turns and even in small bursts on straightaways and slammed his brakes and floored it at stop signs. Every time, I heard the thuds and clangs of the gear, ice chest, and firewood banging around the truck bed, knowing that my mom was a casualty each time. I wondered what she was doing in there. Was she sitting a certain way to try to keep the stuff propped up? Was she even conscious? Was she even alive? *Please God, just please help her!* I pleaded, poker faced in the front seat with Jake between us. *Please God, when we get there and open the back please just say she'll be okay.* A vision of my dad flashed in my mind of opening up the back and my mom being gone, vanished, as I thought happened when we die.

~

When my dad finally pulled into the parking spot, my brother and I went to the back of the truck to carry gear as always. Surprisingly, I noticed my dad had a weird nervous look on his face before he suggested, "Why don't you guys go check out the campsite and the creek?" We did, even though I knew exactly what he was doing. We barely got to the creek when I heard my dad say, "Get out of there, quit fooling around." I didn't need to see the people walking by to know why. He was always selective with what he did in front of people. I wondered if the campers walking by were oblivious, or if they thought my mom was joking around, or if they knew she wasn't but didn't want to get involved. I suspected even then that most people were in this last category.

As usual, my mom acted as normal as she could during that camping trip. She stayed behind while my dad took Jake and me on walks through the redwood trees, to the amphitheater, creek, and swimming hole. Back at the camp site Jake and I spotted deer, raccoons, scrub jays and banana slugs. We collected acorns, made an inedible and probably poisonous acorn stew as Jake and I imagined the Native Americans had done on that very land many years ago. We picked up and dropped the helicopter seeds from the maple and sycamore trees, watching them corkscrew through the air to the pine-needled earth.

For dinner we ate Kraft macaroni and cheese with hot dogs boiled in the same water the macaroni was boiled in. I hated hot dogs and having them in there tainted the taste of the entire mac and cheese, but beggars can't be choosers and I ate as much as my parents would allow me. At the wooden picnic table that was only lit by a single lantern, I would patiently push a macaroni lengthwise on each prong of my fork and suck all four of them off and let them linger in my mouth until they almost melted, savoring every bit of the cheddar, margarine, and milk. I was always like this with things I wasn't allowed to have. I thought about how much better the prepared mac and cheese was than the packets of cheese powder I would sometimes retrieve from the garage, throwing the crunchy, uncooked macaroni away.

~

Sean and I unloaded the car and set up our tent in this beautiful campground just east of Yosemite. The group of friends got a bunch of spots a short walk from the parking area. It was like a little cul-de-sac of campsites with the stream at our backs. We used the central spot as the communal cooking area and the adjacent site for the beer and boy activities. I sat at the wooden picnic table at the cooking site with the girls while Sean and the guys drank from the keg and shot cans with a BB gun. Erin was already dirty, having gotten there the day before us, but that didn't stop me from hugging her super hard and long. I missed her so much and still couldn't believe she was a whole state away now. I inhaled in a deep breath of the clean, fresh air and took in the beauty of the place. I loved camping. Beyond the perfect set up of sites, we were also surrounded by sequoias, whose bark looked like tall unfrosted carrot cakes.

As always, conversation quickly turned to dieting, and I was undoubtedly the one who steered it that way. Comparing the experience and efficacy of Weight Watchers, Lindora, Medifast, and my most recent obsession, detoxing. I was happy for Erin and Blair and envious of their sustained success.

"Does anyone want to go on a walk with me?" I asked with a level of enthusiasm I'm sure annoyed my fellow campers, who were on the pleasant side of beer. No takers. I wore a puffed out rubbery plastic sweat suit reminiscent of that plastic wrap summer long ago and with my largest dog for company, huffed and puffed down the trail. It was dusk when I got back to the campsite and cooking was already underway. My plan was to drink my lemon and cayenne pepper concoction, to delay the food as long as possible, and to eat as little of it as possible.

Salty water poured out of the gathered elastic bottoms outside of the tent. I shrugged in an almost shiver. Once inside the tent, I Shaun T high kicked out of my saturated pants and flailed as though my shirt were a colony of slugs on my back. For a moment, I even thought about calling for Sean to help, but after a few more attempts I was able to get the shirt and sports bra off and throw them onto the floor where they made the sound of a wet towel. I changed into a sweatshirt, sweatpants and sandals and headed out to the warmth of the fire.

"Azure, aren't you going to eat?" Erin asked.

I told her I would in a minute and when I didn't soon enough she insisted again. I dished up, ravenous at this point. *As freaking usual*, I thought as I shoveled bite after bite into my gullet. *You never change.*

Though I tried to drown them out with stories by the fire, I couldn't stop thinking of that camping trip as a kid. How Mom, Dad and Jake behaved and how it puzzled me. Was I the only one who remembered what happened? Why were we supposed to act like nothing happened all the time? I instinctively looked at the discolored skin on the inside of my forearm, scarred from accidentally touching the lantern that weekend, all those years ago.

On the long car ride home from Yosemite I began to cry, again. It seemed like I had been doing so much better lately, and felt so weak that one memory resurfacing could mess me up so much.

"What's wrong?" Sean asked.

"Going camping brings up memories about my dad."

Sean grunted as he hit the steering wheel with the heel of his hand, "I'm so tired of hearing about your freaking dad!"

I sat there in stunned silence while he continued.

"We were having such a great time. We had a fun and happy weekend and it's like you have to always turn it into something heavy!"

He was right. I did have a tendency to turn everything light into something dark, because what was light and easy felt like a facade I wore and the dark, depressed interior felt like the real me. I wanted him to hold my pain as delicate and fragile as a glass ornament, instead of dropping it with hands up saying "I don't want it."

"This is who I am. What I'm *actually* going through. Do you want me to pretend?"

"No! I just want us to be able to be happy and not so freaking intense all the time."

"I thought you would want to help me through it, since you are my *husband*." I noticed the familiar anger and sarcasm.

Azure, Sean is not your dad and you are no longer a teenager.

I sighed. "It's just that it feels like you think of this as *my issue* and mine alone to deal with," I said. "It feels like your opinion on it is 'not my problem, call me when you're cured.'"

"No, I'm there for you."

"How?"

He was quiet for a moment, so I took a guess at what he was about to say.

"You've stayed with me, yes," I explained, "and I am grateful because I know most people couldn't handle this, but this is an *illness* and we committed to each other in sickness and in health. It's almost as if you were looking for a cardboard cut-out of a wife but not a real person with feelings, let alone issues. If I were battling something that you saw more as a physical condition, I feel like you would be more understanding, but since this is more mental or emotional, it honestly doesn't feel like you consider it as a legitimate illness."

I sighed and noted his continued silence. I pressed on.

"I guess what I am saying is that I feel staying with me isn't the same thing as *really* being there for me and supporting me," I said.

"That's not fair, I've been there for you a lot," he said chopping the air with this hand.

"True, you have been there for me when my grandma died, and lots of times with drama with work and my dad, but when it comes to food and this, I don't know, depression, it honestly doesn't feel like you have really been there for me."

"How so, because I truly do feel I have been there for you. I've gone to Weight Watchers with you, I bought an elliptical machine, I stopped bringing tempting foods into the house. What more can I do?"

"You could ask me how I am doing. You could ask me how you can support me. You could learn about what I am struggling with. Have you even read a single article? Done one Google search?"

"But see, now you are just trying to put this on me and it's bullshit. Like I've told you before, your problem is taking accountability."

"I do take accountability!" I said, noticing the twinge in my stomach. I took a breath. "I mean, I am *trying* to take accountability. I really am trying. For many months, I went to therapy once a week to pay someone a lot of money to take out all my garbage, splay it out in front of me and sift through it, analyze it and critique it. Do you know how hard that is? Well, it is, which is why most people don't do it. And yes, your pointing out my stuff is putting me on the defensive right now, I'm not going to lie, but I really am trying really hard to be open and hear what you are saying. I know I am not healed yet from my eating disorder, and I know that is frustrating to you, and believe me, I wish I could be. Not just for you, by the way, but for me. I have struggled with this my *whole* life. As much as I wish I could promise you I will be healed and give you a timeframe, I cannot. I wish I knew if or when I will be better. It just honestly feels like you minimize my struggle, especially when you imply how easy this should be with your 'flow chart of life' thing. As a former addict, can you imagine what it's like to have a problem with drugs, but having to take them several times a day, every single day? Where it's not about abstaining, but about forming a healthy, respectful and balanced relationship with drugs? Most addicts I'm sure would agree that it would be near impossible, if even possible, and that is what recovery with food is like for someone like me. Let me ask you something else. Can you imagine what it's like to struggle with this addiction and not be able to get compassion from your husband who has himself struggled with addiction? To be judged by him all the time? I can't even tell you how much it disappoints me that you of all people, don't help me. I didn't expect you to be my sponsor or anything, but I look up to you and what you've been through so much and wish I had your mentorship, I guess. I wish you could have some empathy and compassion for how hard this is and not approach this like it is some easy, straight forward thing."

"I get all that, but you say you need a supportive environment but then I'll find wrappers under the bed. Meanwhile I am walking on eggshells, not able to say certain things because it will hurt your feelings and turn everything bad like right now. And I have to keep food in my car so the house can be a supportive environment for you, but then you'll order a burger when we go out. It's like you're not even trying."

"Sean, you are equating the impact this has had on you, where you keep your crackers and cookies, with the impact this has had on me—a life long struggle with failure and judgement and ridicule every step of the way. I know this has had an impact on you and I am sorry but it's like you don't really consider the daily impact this has on me."

"It's not just about the snacks!"

"Then what? What are you not saying? My appearance?"

Sean was quiet.

"I know I look different and believe me I am sorry. Of course, I want to look the way I did when we met.

"You think it doesn't bother me? You think it doesn't bother me when people ask me what's going on with you and I have to figure out what to say?"

Tears stung my eyes, and my chin quivered.

"I am sorry if at the beginning I misrepresented myself and you thought that was my natural size. I told you I had just lost a bunch of weight and you saw the hours on the stair climber, the two hours of sit ups and leg lifts in front of the TV at night, the carrot sticks and chicken bouillon. You knew I was injecting myself every day before the wedding. You couldn't have thought that was normal or sustainable? I'm sorry!

I always knew the way I was with food and exercise and my body wasn't normal but shit didn't hit the fan until after we were married and moved into the house. I'm sorry. I guess you really picked the wrong girl."

Sean shook his head, frustrated.

"I feel like you're not really hearing what I'm saying," he said.

"How so?"

"I know! What about having a baby?"

Caught. I crossed my arms.

"What's the deal? How come you don't want to have a baby?"

"It's not that I don't want to, it's just that I'm not *ready* to."

"Why? Why aren't you ready? Is it because of this food and weight stuff? Because I bet it is."

I looked away.

"It is, right?" He pressed.

"Yeah, okay? Do you blame me? I want to be healed and have my body in a different place before I do that. Maybe I don't want to pass it on to an innocent child.

"But you just said that you didn't know when or even if you ever will be healed. What if you never get there? Are you telling me we just won't have kids?"

"No... I don't think so... I don't know. I just need more time."

"You say that, but then you aren't taking action to make changes. That's my whole point, it won't change unless you choose differently."

"It's not that easy! And that's *my* whole point!"

Sean shook his head, angry and out of words.

I shook my head too, so pissed and alienated and feeling more distant from him a foot away than when he was hundreds of miles away for work. It was as if what had drawn us together when we first met, our troubled pasts, had finally fully reversed polarity and was now repelling us apart with tremendous force.

I turned my head away from him and stared out the window as nature whipped on by as I had done thousands of times with my dad in hundreds of locations. As I calmed down, my thoughts went from expletives to *he just doesn't understand* and then finally the ticking time bomb.

Sean's getting to be about done with you. It's just a matter of time. The only question is, will it be today, next week, next month, a year from now, a few years from now?

I heard Sylvie's voice echo in my head asking *"Do you carry these fears of abandonment into your current relationship?"* And my answer *"It's not a fear if it's a certainty."*

I felt Sean's hand envelop the top of mine.

I turned and looked at him, tears in my eyes. His face was softer, less like a bull with his jaw no longer clenched.

"Babe," he said, "I do want to be there for you. I just want this all to be behind us. I love you."

I sniffled and mumbled "I love you too."

He curled his fingers tighter around my hand.

"You know you're my better half," he said.

I snorted.

"You are, Babe. When we first met, you took a chance on me. You talked me into going back to school, getting a better job, going after promotions. Now things are going so well at work. None of that would have happened without you. I would have just been doing the same old thing, hanging out in the garage after work drinking beer with my friends, comfortable."

I nodded. "I guess."

"You have been there for me a lot and I hear what you are saying that you want me to be there for you the way you would be there for me. I know I suck at emotions. I will try to get better. I thought the things I was doing was being supportive, but I guess you're right, I never even asked you what you needed. I guess, it's just so hard being away from home all week working twelve hours a day, that when I get home, I just want things to be light and easy, you know?"

"I understand."

I hadn't really considered it quite in those terms before.

"You're a good guy Sean. You have no idea how grateful I am for your saying that. I wish I could have figured this all out before I even met you. I wish I never had this in the first place. I am sorry for how this affects you. I guess even though I didn't think a husband was a knight in shining armor, I was expecting you to hold my hand and go through this with me."

"I am," he said, squeezing my hand tighter.

Just say it. Now. Say it.

"There is one more thing," I started.

"What?" Sean asked in a concerned way.

I felt the lump in my throat that had been there most of my life. A lump who's sole job was to hold in this statement, to prevent me from speaking it into existence. I took in a deep breath and let it out, letting the first word ride the wave of the exhale.

"The truth is that I'm afraid if we had a kid, they might be like my dad… Or that I might become like my dad too."

Sean looked horrified. "Why would you think that?"

"Because it is in me. *He* is in me. I am of him… What if it's something genetic and I become like that as a mother? What if it skips a generation and our kid is like that? I couldn't live with myself."

I looked away as though it would make my reality different even though it never worked any of the million times I had done it before.

"Babe!" Sean said reassuringly. "There is *no way* you or our kids will be like your dad. Your dad is like that because of how he handled things in his own life. And they won't be like your mom either. You are nothing like your parents. We won't be treating our kids that way—hurting and abandoning them. You have to have faith that all the work you've done has been for something and not for it to start all the way at the beginning again. Remember? You and me against the world."

"Okay," I answered, trying to be hopeful. "I'll try to do that and not be so intense all the time… and I'll try to be more consistent, not so all-or-nothing."

"And I will try to be better with feelings."

I noticed he said the word "feelings" the way a boy who thinks it has cooties would. I understood that we were *both* compromising to do something that we each felt was foreign to us. And that felt good. I felt less alone.

"It's going to be okay," Sean continued. "We are going to make it through this," he answered, lacing his fingers through mine and pulling the back of my hand to his mouth and kissing it.

"Okay." I said again, smiling this time, and feeling like it actually would be.

23

ONE GRAPE, ONE CHIP, ONE PIECE OF CHOCOLATE

The round conference room tables had the same little white paper cups at each place that are used to give patients at mental hospitals their medications. Each contained one grape, one Dorito chip, and one piece dark chocolate. We, a couple hundred women and perhaps two men, were to wait to eat this shadow of a snack until we were told to do so.

Nervous, I introduced myself to the young woman who sat to my left, Brigid, an executive from Sacramento. She was beautiful with long, cascading, curly chestnut hair and blue starry eyes, which was fitting because she was an astrologer. She had that glowing presence about her, like a goddess, and was just captivating. And she was like me, I deduced by way of her very presence at this retreat. She was easy to talk to, informative, wise, nonjudgmental, and fascinating in her practice of tarot, crystals, essential oils, and many more oracles beyond astrology. She was well-traveled and well-educated in general but especially in soul stuff—past life regression, reiki, the teachings of various gurus, and she'd been a participant at many retreats. Basically, she had her PhD in the

Woo Woo sciences. We were instant friends, both finding the retreat's required journaling difficult, silence just plain difficult, and both sharing mutual hatred and unwillingness to participate in the crazed, silly dancing—body undulation and arms waving as though trying to cast a demon out. Even if our self-consciousness meant we were unevolved in that regard, we were unified in being just fine with that.

When I met Brigid, I was immediately glad that I had happened upon the guru leading this retreat after regaining the weight lost with detoxing. When the leader walked into the room from a side door all chatter in the room immediately silenced. She was a 60-ish woman dressed in clothes that looked like they were purchased in one of those high-end eccentric women's stores in an artist community like Laguna Beach. In her distinctive warm and slightly nasally voice, she asked us what it would be like to be satisfied having just one of something. Wouldn't that be nice, to be able to just have one? Imagine the possibilities, the freedom in the restraint. We compulsive overeaters marveled at this notion. This disease that plagued us was one of bulk and excess. What came to my mind was when I had eaten one entire family size package. Maybe one slice of pizza when I was trying to lose weight, but never just one of anything tiny. *Never, ever chips.* I thought. *One bag, sure, but one single chip? Was this even possible? Is it even a good idea? Won't it just leave me wanting more? There is no way that I will feel satisfied. I'm just going to head straight for the hotel gift shop later in search of a bag of chips to keep the single chip in my stomach company.*

Our leader continued, "When you have just one of something that you are able to fully experience, you are satisfied." She then asked us to fully experience the three morsels before us and reminded us that we don't have to eat each thing one at a time or alone, we could combine them. "Be playful, be curious, be present, have fun!" she encouraged as the exercise commenced.

The salty tangy flavor of the cool ranch Dorito chip tingled on my tongue as it lingered there and I could feel my mouth get watery from it. I felt a twinge in my jaw, the same kind I get when I eat something sour.

Hmmmm, I thought as I noticed the sensation. I was surprised at how quickly the chip softened when I wasn't rendering it to cement between my molars. It almost melted in my mouth. The skin of the green grape buckled only slightly before bursting into two pieces cleaved by my teeth. The flesh had the perfect balance between tartness and sweetness which, combined with the level of crunchiness, made it the perfect grape. Or had all of my green grapes been this good? I didn't know. Had I ever before been fully present to experience them? I was present during binges, wasn't I? I thought so, at least at the beginning. But I could not recall ever bingeing on grapes before. I chuckled thinking about it as it moved its way down my throat. Last was the chocolate. I peeled off the wrapper slowly, the way a woman wants to be undressed by her lover, one shoulder, the other, and the wrapper falling to the floor, or the table in this instance. *Mmmmmmm, you are going to taste so good!* as I gazed upon her shiny dark chocolate skin. I brought a rounded corner to my mouth and bit and while the chunk dissolved on my tongue, I was surprised to observe that the chocolate was so sweet that there was a subtle stinging on my tongue from the sugar. I had never associated chocolate with anything other than pleasure, but comparing my body's level of pleasure from just a moment earlier, my tongue asked me to believe that I actually preferred grapes to chocolate. *Is that possible?* The world of food was entirely different and enhanced when I slowed down.

A short lady with a voice raspy from yelling interrupted the rapture to announce that it was time to wrap up and head to our next session. Brigid and I compared our printed agendas as we filed out of the banquet hall. Sadly, we were not together. Now that I had a friend at the retreat, it was with trepidation that I headed to the next session alone.

As I walked the short path through the retreat center grounds, I thought *I'm going to say goodbye to food when I get home. I'm going to get a balloon and write on it everything food has been to me. 'Food, I don't need you to be my best friend anymore. Food, I don't need you to stand in for Grandma anymore. I don't need you to protect me from Dad. I don't need you to put your arm around me and console me. I don't need for you to bring out my wild, spontaneous, creative side. Thank you for all that you have done, for saving my life, but I don't need you anymore.' Then, I'm going to send that balloon up to the sky.*

I felt my fists clench as I came to a small, rounded shingled structure. Thirty or so other women and I filed inside. The room smelt like stale potpourri and it was clear it was not often used. The plastic chairs with metal legs, the same kind my middle school and Overeaters Anonymous used, were arranged in a large circle. *Can I ever escape these chairs?* There was one man in the room full of women and he stood at its center. He was tall, slender, Nordic looking. *Why did they choose a male instructor?* A beautiful blonde woman, shaped like a yoga instructor, in exorbitantly priced stretchy pants, tank top, and cream knit open sweater caught my eye as she sat across from me. I am sure she felt me studying her, but she was probably used to it. She was stunning. What was she doing here? Her body looked like what I aspired to but would never be. Effortlessly put together, tall and slender, sophisticated and sexy. She reached up and pushed her bangs back behind her ear and I could not help but notice her ginormous rock.

The instructor's Swedish accent broke my gaze. In his charming accent, he let us know that his name was Sven and we would be doing some inner child work. This would be our safe place, our chance to allow our inner child to speak to those who had wounded us. He emphasized that this was a safe and private environment. We could stand up for our inner children by way of journaling, in pairs, or with himself or his helper as they circulated the room. He asked for a brave volunteer. Miss Yoga volunteered. *Of course.*

"What is your name?" the instructor asked.

"Jennifer."

Naturally, I thought as I adjusted in my seat.

She pulled her bumpy cream sweater in at the sides as if to bundle up.

"Who is your wound-er?" only it sounded like "vounder."

"My mom."

Her feet even look nice in those Birkenstocks. How?

"Can you share with us a little bit about the impact this has had on you?" Sven continued.

"She was always very critical of me and very scary to me growing up. She was like a monster, she had a very bad temper. Even all these years later, with a wonderful husband who is so loving and even taking care of our four kids so that I could be here, she still affects me."

Four kids and you look like that? And loaded husband who watches four kids and buys ginormous rocks? God? It's called fairness!

"And how does this affect your eating?"

"It's not so much that I find myself eating bad food, as much as I will overeat on good, healthy foods."

Oh my God, is this even a problem? She's worried about overeating kale chips?

"For this exercise, I will play the role of your mother. I want you to tap into the scared little girl inside you. I want you to notice the same fear, the same timidness, only I also want you to remember that you are not a little girl anymore. You are a strong adult woman. I want you to defend your inner child against these attacks."

Jennifer looked nervous, but said okay.

Suddenly Sven's overly friendly Nordic face became angry and stern looking.

"Jennifer!" he shouted the way parents do. "Look at this mess! Look at you! You are such a bad little girl!"

Jennifer stood there terrified-looking and unsure of what to do.

"I'm sorry, Mom!" she offered.

"You're sorry? Why don't you stop making these mistakes? There is no teaching you! What will people think if they saw you looking messy like this? You are an embarrassment to me!" Sven raised his arms in the air, suddenly transformed to a woman with an apron holding a ladle in her hand and raising it in a threatening way to now five-year-old Jennifer.

Jennifer's eyes started to well up. "Mom, I'm doing the best I can."

Sven broke character for a moment. "Okay, Jennifer, I want you to get

252

strong now. You aren't a little girl anymore. Defend your child. Okay." He put the angry look back on his face. "You are just a dirty little girl who likes boys too much!"

"Stop, Mom," Jennifer said in an unconvincing way.

"More!" Sven yelled not breaking character but letting his coaching blend into it. "More! More Jennifer!"

"Mom! Shut up!" Jennifer commanded with more authority than I thought she was capable of.

"Go on!" Sven said in his coaching voice.

"Mom, I was just a little girl and it was not right to belittle me and scare me! I am not a little girl anymore. You don't scare me anymore!"

"Very good, Jennifer!" Sven exclaimed. He turned his body to the room, motioning for us to applaud. We did and it was genuine. Perfect-looking Jennifer was more like me than I ever would have guessed looking at her perfect body, hair, diamond, life. I had been wrong for judging her and wanting to be her. She was just me in a different body.

"Before we end," Sven turned back to Jennifer, "I want to ask you. How do you feel right now?"

"Powerful," Jennifer replied confidently.

"If you were to choose food right now, who would choose, your inner child or your wise woman?"

"Wise woman," Jennifer said, beaming.

Now it was our turn. We could pair with partners or journal our way through and Sven would walk around and talk to us through this dialogue. The air in the room was thicker after Jennifer and Sven's role play. I felt as though I were coughing and suffocating on its stale thickness. I thought I was just going to take a break, get some fresh air, but my legs kept walking along the paved path. I was headed toward the beach but that was too out in the open for what I needed. I looked to my left off the trail to the chaparral shrubs. I followed the sudden urge to nestle my way into them. I winced as the surprisingly hard tiny branches scraped and poked me. Once in the center of this cave that did not provide much shelter at all, I took a deep inhale and on the exhale, I whispered "why?"

drawing out its sound until the air was gone, just like I had countless times as a teenager. I began to cry. I imagined my dad sitting across from me in silence, just receiving what I had to say. "Why do you hate me so much? Do you have any idea what I would give up to be skinny? Do you have any idea what I would give up for you to just love me?" I was sobbing hysterically, no longer caring if passersby wondered why the bush was shaking and sobbing. "I'd be willing to make way less money. I would trade my education. I would never travel again. I would trade my house. I would trade my…"

I stopped myself. I would *not* trade my marriage to Sean. I would *not* ever trade my future children. I would not trade the turbulent but overall peaceful existence Sean and I had carved out. I would never, ever, ever be willing to go back to my dad's house under any circumstances.

A sudden calm washed over me. If there were things that I wasn't willing to trade in exchange for my dad's love, then that meant, contrary to my belief, that his love wasn't the most important thing to me, that he wasn't the most important person to me anymore. After catching my breath, and wiping my wet cheeks with my fingers, I got up and emerged from the bushes, less cautious of the branches than before. I left my dad and the full strength of his power over me sitting there in the bush.

I almost skipped to the bookstore. I didn't even think about purchasing chips. Rather, I purchased a postcard of an otter on its back joyfully cracking abalone on a rock that sat on its belly. I walked to the beach, retrieved a pen from my bag and began writing.

Sean,

I am learning so much in my retreat. I see how I have been approaching this "food stuff" incorrectly. I almost thought of it in a self-righteous, martyrdom kind of way, like, look what a good person I am taking stuff out on myself instead of others. I see now that this self-destructive behavior is not honorable at all. I also see how it affects not only me but those around me, like you. I know I haven't been easy to be married to. You haven't always understood what I've been struggling with, but I do appreciate your companionship and sticking by me. Thank you. I know I still have stuff to work on but I see that it doesn't have to keep our lives at a stand-still. I love you and I'm ready to move forward.

24

BAKED PICKLES

Finally! I thought on the way home from work, still getting used to the fact that Sean would actually be there. We would make dinner together and watch TV with his arm around me and we'd fall asleep under the same roof, on a weeknight! Years after our graduation promise to move back to San Diego one day, the day had actually arrived when Sean and my jobs both transferred us from Bakersfield. And we had done it by ourselves, as I had eventually transferred the money from Grandma's estate to my dad, since I had given him my word that I would, even though he never did go to a therapist with me. Life felt like it was finally starting for us and there was a lovely fullness in the house with him home.

Overcome with contentedness, I knew an accompanying craving was coming, as I was used to when I got emotional, but what surprised me was the intensity with which I just *had* to have fried pickles with ranch dressing. At a stoplight, I searched for restaurants that carried them and groaned that none of the little red dots on the map were on my way home. *Azure, why don't you just have whatever is at the house? No! Fried pickles! What is this? This stronger than a regular craving, it's like I actually physically need them. It's so intense it's almost as if... Oh my God.*

I was self-conscious at the grocery store that the belt contained a jar of pickles, a jar of yogurt ranch dressing, panko breadcrumbs, and a pregnancy test. *The only thing that would make this even more of a pregnancy caricature is a jar of peanut butter. Ooh, maybe I should get some.* The teenaged boy didn't even notice the obviousness of my selections. As he asked me to enter my phone number, I smirked. All those times I had purchased binge food and clean food, practically asking for two receipts to pretend the junk was for someone else—*not a bad idea*—and all that time the clerks had never even noticed. They had just been doing their jobs and waiting for their next break, just like everybody else. I had thought everyone was staring at me, judging me, but that wasn't happening at all.

When I pulled into the garage, I pulled the pregnancy test and instructions out of the box and into my pocket. I threw the box away in the outside garbage can, making sure it went underneath other things just as I had done so many times with food wrappers. Only this time instead of concealing out of shame, I was concealing out of the desire to plan an elaborate surprise.

When I walked into the house, Sean stopped me at the island in the kitchen and kissed me with such purpose it reminded me of our wedding (though that was at a very different type of island). We hugged and I took in his smell from his short sleeve flannel shirt, which made me realize just how much I had missed him during those years he was gone and we were so disconnected and not able to hear how much each other were hurting.

"How was your day? How are you doing?" Sean asked as he walked around the counter and sat in a barstool.

"Pretty good. Thank you for asking. How about you?"

This exchange made me chuckle a bit. After I had gotten back from my retreat, Sean and I had both been making a concerted effort to see things from the other's perspective. Even though it seemed a little contrived and unnatural, I really appreciated him asking since I knew how much that was outside of his comfort zone. And though he didn't say it,

I think he was enjoying my tailoring of the communication to him being a thinker and not a feeler, as a coach I had been working with pointed out to me. He liked things short and sweet and to the point and I liked to bathe in the details, subtlety and innuendos of any life drama. This work I had been doing made me see where the golden rule had gone wrong. I had been treating Sean as *I* had wanted to be treated and not necessarily how *he* wanted to be treated, and vice versa. He wasn't like me and that was okay, in fact preferable because clearly, I could barely handle one of me.

After preheating the oven, I retrieved a baking dish. I opened the jar, picked out twelve pickle coins, and laid them flat in the grey metal dish. I opened the bag of gluten-free panko, pinched some between my fingers, and sprinkled them over the pickles. I placed the pan inside the oven and walked through the master bedroom to the bathroom. I wondered if I had ever peed for a ten full seconds, let alone when trying to line up a device between my legs. I capped what I figured was a wasted pregnancy test, and put it in the drawer beside the sink.

I went back out to the kitchen, opened the oven door, and smelled the hot pickles. I pulled them out and poured some yogurt ranch into a little dish and asked Sean about his day. Still too hot I pinched one with my fingers and winced as I dipped it in ranch and brought it to my mouth and exhaled sharply trying to expel the heat as I chewed.

"What are you eating?" Sean asked.

"Baked pickles."

"Good idea," Sean said as he helped himself to one. I didn't mind this time.

I finished my plate, washed my dish and snuggled up next to Sean and watched TV. Trixie and Ruby pressed their little bodies into both of us. I was so grateful that I had finally been willing to pull my hand back from the painful stimulus and let myself love Sean more than the fantasy of love from my dad.

I had half forgotten about the pregnancy test, when I opened the drawer to retrieve toothpaste before bed and saw "pregnant" staring back at me.

~

Sean was flabbergasted a few weeks later when I surprised him at the piano bar we had frequented in the Gaslamp Quarter when we were dating. We were both thrilled. Despite our differences, Sean and I did have the most important thing in common for this endeavor: a dogged determination to do whatever it took to do things differently than our own upbringings so that our baby would have the very best chance of being emotionally healthy and not falling into the trap of the addictive process. We figured, if the hole isn't there to begin with, then maybe our child wouldn't feel the need to fill it.

Beyond my excitement for the future, I loved being pregnant. I never felt better. And it wasn't just because Sean spent sweet moments touching and talking to my belly. I loved the relaxed sense of peace I felt in my body. I loved how I no longer hated my body because it was impossible to distinguish between where my body ended and my baby began. I loved the firmness of my belly beneath my cupped hands that grasped it countless times a day. I loved how clear it was when I was hungry, what I was hungry for, how in-tune I was with my body, how natural it felt, how natural *I* felt, and how I never felt more like a woman in my entire life.

I couldn't wait to meet my baby and when I did, I was astounded. It was like the top blew off a geyser and a volume of love spewed out of me so vast that my body was minuscule in comparison. *My body, minuscule! Who would have thought!*

Aveline, true to the meaning of her name, was a child who was longed for. Her little fingers with the tiniest fingernails I've ever seen wrapped around my index finger as she lay on my chest, skin pressed on mine. She looked like me but small and perfect and brand new and the most beautiful thing I have ever seen. It never occurred to me that she might look like me. I always assumed Sean's dark hair and eyes would color the light features she'd get from me. And at first, it seemed like she had, since she was born with a full head of dark hair. But as I came to study every inch of her, I saw more and more familiar features. Her nose was unquestionably my mother-in-law's, her smile and feet with beautiful straight toes were definitely from Sean along with the forward-growing nature of her hair. Her face, eyes, hands, fingers, legs, the smile crease under her tummy, they all were familiar to me. All of those features that I now shared with her, the most beautiful girl in the world to me. I kissed the top of her head and breathed in that wonderful new baby smell. I couldn't help but wonder as I pondered her exquisite nature that if she is the most beautiful thing I have ever seen, and she looks like me, then doesn't that mean I consider myself beautiful as well?

My days, weeks, months following Aveline's birth consisted of nursing in the rocker in my bedroom or the couch in the living room. Life was so busy that I barely noticed that my dad didn't call or email when she was born. Aveline woke easily and every attempt to set her down was thwarted. *There goes my maternity leave spin biking plan!* Instead, I held and studied her. As she slept so peacefully it struck me—the difference between us. She looked like me, but knew nothing but love. Would she be who I might have been without the pain, the consumption by pain, the addictive behavior to stave off pain? Growing up I had wanted to be a boy so badly, wanted to have the respect and power it meant in my family, and yet now I wouldn't trade being a woman for anything. My body had the power to grow life, to give life, to sustain life through nourishment my body created, the source of this all-powerful love, a love that trumped all others I had ever experienced before. Aveline's smiles made me feel like I could fly. When she was in pain, I practically buckled over in pain myself. And even though I was so glad to give Aveline this endless love, there was a tiny part of me that was a little sad to no longer be ignorant to it, knowing that I had never and will never receive that kind of love myself. *There must be something so wrong with Dad, to not have this, to actually seem to enjoy inflicting pain upon his child. And, Mom, how much of her must be cut off to be able to walk away from her children with such ease.*

As Aveline grew, the twinkled eye way she and Sean gazed at each other made me know there truly is something about fathers and daughters. My desire for the same had never been my defect, it didn't make me dirty, it had been natural all along. I had never been crazy or wrong about food either, as the way Aveline was comforted by breast milk best illustrated that food is love, by its very design.

Eventually I did hear from my dad, by way of my brother. Jake told me that Dad said to stop by with Aveline when I was in town. My initial response was to laugh. It was so very my dad. But the humor was quickly replaced by agitation. *That's it? Really? After the last thing he said to me was that Sean and I would only be good parents if we put our kids up for adoption? After everything else he put me through? That's all he has to say? And he's not even saying it himself?*

Despite my reservations, I emailed my dad that I was willing to FaceTime so he could meet Aveline over the phone and we could see how it goes from there.

"Let me know what FaceTime is and I'll tell you if I'm interested," my dad responded.

You'll tell me if you're interested in meeting your granddaughter, depending on what the terms are?

I rolled my eyes, let out a sigh, then clicked the arrow icon to move to the next email.

25

FAKE FOODS

When it came right down to it, no number of "it's going to happen soon" prepared me for the night Trixie began violently seizing. Sean and I placed our hands gently on her body and told her through our tears that it would be okay, it would all be over soon. My Trixie. My sweet Trixie. My companion, my first baby, who was there with me from living with my dad to the squalor of the outdoor kitchen place in La Jolla to the OB place where she didn't bark at Sean when he came over for the first time, Trixie who licked my newborn daughter's toes, was gone. I felt tremendous guilt that her absence seemed so much larger than her presence which I had so clearly taken for granted, especially after becoming a mom. I wouldn't have known I was capable of such sorrow had I not felt it before when Grandma died.

I wept and wept. The sunny San Diego sky seemed inexplicably darker than it really was, like I was wearing sunglasses. I was angry and resentful at people who still had their pets and was just angry at the fact that death is a part of life. My stomach was sour and acidic and not hungry. My sleep was anxiety- and nightmare-ridden and devastatingly sad. I woke in a cold sweat half the time and the other half wondering if it had all been a bad dream and then realizing it hadn't. In some, I relived the moment of Trixie's violent and frightening seizures, body jerking, teeth reeling and biting involuntarily. In others, echoes of her yelping reverberated in my mind. In others I woke gasping, having been holding my breath as the movie played in my mind of her chest ceasing to bob up and down. In others I remembered the beautiful energy that seemed to rise up from her body like millions of little invisible blossoms and me trying to breathe them in, to take her into me, to make her even more of myself than she already was. It had been real, hadn't it? It seemed real. Still, as consuming and devastating as it was, the grief for Trixie was pure, as my love for her had been. I would soon come to yearn for that sweet, uncomplicated grief in that we're-not-in-Kansas-anymore kind of way.

Weeks later, when casually leaving the office on the way to the gym, I clicked my phone's home button and pulled up my texts. "Dad's dead. Found him on the floor," the text read. I stopped mid-step. Hands shaking, I clicked the sender's name, Jake, and pressed to call. He answered in tears. I asked him what had happened. He told me through sobs that he had come over after work and found Dad dead. He had tried CPR but to no avail. So stunned that I was practically stoic, I managed "Jake, I'm so sorry... not just because you found him, which I can't even imagine, but because I know you and he had a very different relationship than he and I did. I am truly sorry for your loss."

I heard him nod. "I just wish I could have said goodbye."

"I know," I tried to console.

"I just thought there'd be more time. It was so sudden."

"I know." I agreed. Any fantasy of my dad asking for me on his death-bed to settle our differences was officially just that—a fantasy.

"Oh, hey Azure? Nick is calling me back, he's figuring out flying down here."

"Okay, call me back right after," I said and as I clicked the red button it clicked in my mind. *Call Nick back? He called our cousin? I had just gotten the text, when had he called Nick?*

Just then my phone rang. It was my aunt, saying how sorry she was, that Jake had called them, that she understood this must be complicated for me.

Are you kidding me? I am his daughter, and I find out via text message and after everybody else? I know Dad and I weren't on great terms, but not because I didn't want to, desperately *want to be.*

A day later, the knowing nod the Snow White oak trees gave me made descending the moss covered steps toward the front door only slightly more surreal than it already was. A knot balled tightly in my stomach. My body wanted no part of this place. I took a deep breath of the worm-rich earthy smell that I had missed and reminded myself that he wasn't there anymore. The house looked the same but a little dilapidated, as if it were re-becoming part of the elements. I didn't want to throw rocks at the house as Jenny had in Forest Gump, but I did want to go Fargo on that big, unmoving table where I was tortured literally and figuratively, sending it through a god damn wood chipper.

The squeaky brass handle screamed when I turned it to make my way inside. The house was as I remembered but also different. The first thing that struck me was the smell that told me that sometime between the last time I'd seen him and his death, my scary dad had become an old person. He had also become a very sick person as evidenced by an oxygen concentrator and tubing and cannula made by the company I worked for.

"Jake, did Dad know that he was using product made by my company?" I asked stunned.

"Yeah, he bragged about it to anyone who would listen."

Except me. I would have listened.

My father had also been living in unspeakable conditions, having been confined to the upstairs due to his being on oxygen and there were now boxes and trash bags about in our attempt at making it more house than hamster cage. *I wish I had known. No one, not even him, should live like this.* Sifting through Dad's belongings was exhausting, strenuous and a constant rotation between infuriating, disturbing, and confusing. There were both hand written and all caps typed manifestos about me, his "spoiled, ungrateful, disrespectful, lousy daughter," stashed about along with his last wishes to be remembered "for being a great parent, a super dad" and of course the will stating that he had "intentionally made no provisions for Azure Moyna (daughter), or her descendants." His final hurt. His final rejection, made to sting even more by the fact that sizable amounts of money were left to cousins and second cousins who saw him for a couple hours a year and on his best behavior, people he had never once called a name or physically hurt. He wanted this to hurt me, he wanted to single me out. Though I had expected it, it was still so devastating to be so blatantly disowned after already suffering a lifetime of his hurt and rejection.

"This is our property," I remembered Dad telling Jake and me as children on a walk of the land which spanned three large houses and multiple empty lots. *"This is your birthright,"* he had told us. *"I don't pay you to work on the rental properties because you will be inheriting one of them,"* he had said. *Liar!*

Just like all fights with my dad, there had to be a signature knockout punch, that even when I knew was coming, always seemed to hurt way more than I anticipated: the baton pass. My dad would pass the baton of mistreatment to my brother and cousin to hurt me by way of executing the multi-million dollar estate in which I was to receive not even a single dollar. All those times I did everything I could think of to prevent Dad from tainting Jake's gentle nature into anything like his, Dad had held the trump card all along.

"What did I do to deserve all this hurt? All this betrayal?" I wailed in my rental car. "He didn't see! He never felt wrong, never felt sorry, never regretted a thing!" I caught my breath and myself. I thought of how disgusted and disappointed Grandma would be with my dad, my cousin and my brother. "But I never prostituted myself to him, and this was probably going to happen all along no matter what I did," I told myself. I could tell my body agreed.

Still, searing hot anger coursed through my veins. My blood boiled until my anger would be replaced with disturbed nausea when I would come across things like the dozen masks Dad had made of his own face, or mason jars filled with wish bones or his own teeth with gold and silver fillings, or the pair of dead lizards that he had hung from the screen on the kitchen window. And then that disturbed nausea would soften into a confused and hopeful sadness when I would find the subtlest of signs that *maybe* he cared. A picture of three year old me in the bathtub hung in the bathroom, a picture of me on the cover of the college catalogue sat beside the desk, a card I had given him a decade ago sat propped up on his dresser. Confusing, infuriating, disturbing, confusing, infuriating, disturbing, a perfect microcosm of my relationship with him. Through the chaos, three truths emerged: my dad loathed me, my dad was deeply disturbed and mentally ill, and somewhere in him he seemed to care about me on some level, I think, I hoped, I'd officially never really know for sure.

My mom, brother, cousin Nick and I went to see my dad before he was cremated. He was in a corner sectioned off by cheap tan plastic accordion wall partition. He was on a table, partially covered by a sheet and dressed in the house clothes he'd been found dead in, "grubbies" he called them. I had assumed the funeral home would be given a suit or at least office type attire by my brother and cousin and hadn't thought to ask them. The dignity my dad had been stripped of on top of dying alone in squalor was so sad to me, even though I knew I had wished him dead more than once.

He looked like himself, which made me both tense and grateful. Grateful because Jake said Dad looked like he had been crying when my brother found him, which made me feel sorry for him. I had never seen or even heard of him crying, even when my mom left or when my grandma or uncle died. He looked hollow, which was not entirely unlike how he looked in life, and yet he still looked like he had the potential to make one final reanimation, like the villain in a scary movie. My breath became fast and shallow. *He can't hurt you anymore. He can't hurt you anymore* I repeated over and over like a mantra until my breathing slowed and his Mona Lisa mouth seemed to change from scowl to neutral. Was it possible for it to keep changing, for his deep anger wrinkles between his eyebrows to fade and for new smile wrinkles on his cheeks to form, for his face to even fill out more for having had enjoyed himself more in life, for him to fully morph into my other dad? How was it possible to so desperately miss a man I had never met, a man who sipped air tea with me, who cheered me on at swim meets, who saw me off to prom, who danced with me at my wedding, who held my daughter when she was born? How was it possible to miss the way he smiled, the way his eyes lit up when he saw me, his advice, his friendship, his voice, his laugh, his hugs, when I had never known those things?

His body remained unchanged. It was official—my dad would never become my other dad or any iteration between who he was and the man he could have been. It was the death of both of them. We'd never have Paris. Sometimes stories don't have happy endings. I lamented, aching for the man I wished he was, the person I had always felt he had the potential to become, the version of him that had belonged to me entirely, and whose love was entirely mine.

Would I miss him? The real him? I don't know. There weren't great memories, times were either bad or waiting for them to become bad. Moments like driving in the car to San Luis Obispo or faking it as best we could in front of family in Seattle or family friends on camping trips were the closest thing to good times I had. I sobbed and then out of habit of being in his presence, became aware of my body. My body. My body. My body. My shrine of disappointment, heartbreak, every pound an offering. Every morsel eaten when not hungry a personification of my despair, rage, and resentment, of my longing for his love. Everything I ate trying to make something nourishing and delectable out of foul, rotten, spoiled, and putrid ingredients. Every bit I stuffed trying to fill the gaping hole inside me the size of a 185-pound man. *This* 185-pound man. Yearning for a love as light and rich as mousse au chocolat but having to settle for scorched, nauseating, noxious, sour, and caustic cardboard, totally inedible and yet I had been trying to live off of it for years. And hadn't I had enough of inedible things? Fake things? Bland, fat-free, sugar-free, "I hate this but I want to lose weight" crap? I had a whole lifetime of fake food.

Was it possible to heal? Could my life, my body be capable of bridging despair and joy? When you're in love and you are loved back you feel weightless. When you love someone and they don't love you back, that's when you feel like a lead weight sinking to the bottom of the ocean, even and perhaps especially, when you have been the one to make your body that way.

Dad, where do I even start? I peered down at him. *I'm sorry we never figured it out. I tried so many times. And you hurt me every single time. You know that right? When you died and you saw your life flash before your eyes you saw the degradation, the humiliation, the manipulation, the deceit, the terror by your own hand, right?* His face remained unchanged. *How could you treat people like that? How could you treat me, your daughter, like that? How could you premeditatedly attempt to annihilate my very sense of self so you could control me, toy with me, play God with me, only to reject me when you were done with me like a piece of trash? Why did you hate me so much? All I ever wanted was for you to accept me, be proud of me, love me. Why could you never give me the teeniest morsel of love? Why is the nicest thing you've ever said to me that you don't worry about me? Nick said you told him you loved me. I never heard you use the word "love" in any context let alone to describe your feelings about me. How come you could tell him but not me, if it's even true? Jake said you bragged to everyone who would listen about my working for the company that made your oxygen products. Why couldn't you tell me? Was it stubbornness or was it just part of your game? That you got to look like the nice, caring father to other people, and further invalidate me and what really happened at the same time?* I glared at him. *I want you to know something: you didn't break me, despite all your efforts. And I have chosen to live a happy, functional life. And you can't take credit for any of it, since you not only did not help us but actually tried to prevent it financially and otherwise.* I scowled down at his unchanged face that for once was not engaging back with me. Then I remembered the disturbing things from his house. I sighed.

Whatever was wrong with you, I wish it had been more visible, more clearly distinguishable from you like cancer or even schizophrenia. Did I ever even meet the real you, or was all I knew some kind of disease? I'm sorry for whatever pain you experienced in your life that led you to treat me like that. I wish you could have seen how much we are actually alike, both kids whose fathers hurt us. I wish I could have once reached that part of you. Maybe then we could have been friends.

My eyes moved to his hands, clasped and resting on his chest. Too overcome with curiosity, I lifted his right hand, cold and clammy and held it. So many times I had imagined how those hands might have felt. So many times I imaged them rough and calloused, when in fact they were to my amazement, soft.

Dad, I just wish you could have owned up to how you treated me, at least given me that, apologized to me one time.

And then it dawned on me. Our relationship now was whatever I wanted it to be. Any version of him, born by me, that belonged to me entirely, didn't have to die, at least not yet. He could apologize now, he could give me what I needed. With hands still clasped, I closed my eyes and heard his voice inside my head.

I'm so sorry for everything. Every name call, every poke, every laugh at your despair, every degradation, every expectation of you being your brother's mother, every hour I made you sit there and take it, every scrutinized meal, outfit, workout and weigh in, every humiliation, every denial of abuse when you confronted me with it, all of it. You're right, it was premeditated, you're right, you were targeted, and you're also right, I was a very sick person who never sought help. I'm so sorry. You deserved so much more. You deserved to feel that you were smart, beautiful, tenacious, loved, cherished, and special, because you are. You were never wrong for your body any more than you were wrong for being more creative than mathematical. I was the one who was wrong for making you feel wrong. I was wrong for wanting to control and destroy you. I was a delusional hypocrite who thought that my bullying you for your weight would save you from being bullied for your weight. I know I single-handedly taught you disordered eating. I'm sorry for not being able to trust that your body knew best, to have been so audacious to think that I knew better than nature. I hope you can see that I couldn't trust anything in life. If I could go back and change everything I would. I would treat you with love and respect and adoration. I know all that is good about you is in spite of me, not because of me, and I am proud of the woman you have become. You are braver than anyone in this family for holding me accountable, for getting help, for doing the emotional work, for changing the family's trajectory. From the highest version of myself, I am proud of you.

I paused, opened my eyes, returned his hand to his chest, wiped away my tears and said aloud, "I forgive you, Dad," then turned around and walked away. I walked away from him and the place from whence I came and toward my present, my future, my own family: Aveline who is blissfully unaware of her lineage, and Sean, who counter to statistics was not abusive like my dad. I may not have been successful in transforming my dad into my other dad, but I *had* married someone like my other dad—imperfect sure, but someone who was stable and caring and committed to evolving with me. Even though the love triangle between my dad, my other dad, and me didn't end the way I had wanted, perhaps this ending was even better than what I could have chosen for myself. Perhaps like all dead things, it could fertilize and allow something new and beautiful to blossom.

26
FULLNESS

The light on Rock Mountain is peach and apricot outside my kitchen windows. The view is fitting because it feels like it's the dawn of my new life, six months after my dad's death. I sip a little decaf and take in the last few moments of silence before—"Mom-mom!"

"Yes, baby I'm coming!"

I race to the bedroom.

Aveline's golden hair, the same color as mine, makes a nest on her face. "Hi, baby!" I coo to her gently and lovingly. I kneel over and kiss her. Her little arms wrap around me and pull me in and I jump in the bed. She giggles and marvels at her own strength that could pull my entire body. "I love you," I whisper to her.

"No, no, no, no, I love *you*!" she replies with joy.

"No, no, no, no, I love *you*!" And on and on. After a few rounds I asked her what she wants to wear.

"Um, um, um," Aveline says in the way toddlers do. "A pink shirt and purple shorts!"

I retrieve them from the closet. "What would you like to have for breakfast?" I ask her as I pull her shirt over her head.

"Um, um, um, um, yogurt!" she calls enthusiastically.

I guffaw and finish getting her dressed and in the car. I hand Avie her breakfast to eat on the way to nursery school. We sing songs and tell jokes and she asks for crayons, toys and food that I do not have in the car. I unfailingly get frustrated when her repetitive requests grow in volume and urgency each repetition. I tell her that Mom-mom likes to hear her requests one time and to be given time to get it for her. Like with all things in life, when it comes to parenting, I am still a work in progress. Part of me is compassionate towards my parents now that I know first-hand the stresses of parenting. I can't imagine tackling it with one's own un-dealt-with child abuse and undiagnosed and untreated mental illness. I shudder at the thought of how I might be as a parent had I never sought help. I am grateful for the work I've done. I am grateful for the multiple therapists, hypnotherapists, coaches and spiritual practitioners who have been part of my healing. And ironically, I am even grateful for my eating disorder for leading me to do the work in the first place.

I park outside of Aveline's school, extract her from her car seat, and walk to the door, which has a flier advertising the Daddy–Daughter Dance being held tomorrow. I smile because I know Aveline has such a different father than I did and Sean will dance with her and look silly and not care. Lucky girl. I hold Aveline's little fleshy hand as we walk inside before she breaks free and sprints toward the windowed classroom door down the hall. I open it and she starts to bound inside, but she whips around and throws her arms around my legs just above the knee and looks up at me. I put my hands on her back to hug her and bend over and kiss the top of her banged head. "I love you. I'll see you later," I tell her. Instead of running off with her friends, she clings there like a locked-jaw Chihuahua until her pre-school teacher is able to effortlessly lure her away as the magical child-speaking fairy she is. I am (again) astounded by her abilities.

I drive the short distance to the office. I open my laptop and delete all the emails I can, then deal with the ones I can't. My heart rate increases when I come to those containing the latest fires I need to put out. I consciously try to calm myself down. I then attend a meeting, then another, and another, trying to answer the urgent emails during and between them as best as I can. My job is still stressful, and that stress still makes me think about anesthetizing myself with double cheese burgers more often than I'd like, but I *act* on it much, much less often and I can't even tell you the last time I've had a bonafide binge. I used to think that recovery from "the food stuff" would be the absence of a single impulse to use food in a non-fuel way, but it's not. Well grooved addictive thought patterns remain there like freeways offering the shortest and least conscious route to the destination of comfort. Recovery from compulsive eating doesn't mean a perfect track record of never finding yourself on the freeway, but taking the nearest exit when you do. The scenic route may not be direct or easy and it might even feel like you're heading the opposite direction from comfort but you are going where you need to go, and more importantly you are actually present for the journey.

So while my job is still a source of stress, I handle it better, taking it in stride. I know I am good at my job and even still, no longer think it defines me or my worth. I am excited for the future. I've written my story and hope to publish it. I plan to transition to more freelance work so I can write more and spend more time with Aveline and maybe even have a second child.

During the day, as my stress level fluctuates, I still have to slow down and ask myself if I'm actually hungry. From time to time I still have to remind myself that there will be another meal, that food isn't as scarce as it once was. I still sometimes get momentarily tempted by diets. On occasion, I still have to stop the automatic thoughts that pop in my mind when my eyes meet their twins in the mirror, but I course-correct. I am still overweight, but I no longer think that made my dad right about me. I know he was wrong. My size never made me unlovable. Nothing actually made me unlovable, because I am not unlovable at all. And I never was.

The afternoon flies by. I am able to put most of the day's fires out. And I know the rest will be there Monday. I drive to the school to pick Avie up.

"Mom-mom! Mom-mom!" Aveline calls as she runs around the counter to find me and throw her arms around my legs.

"Hi, baby!" I tell her, eyes lighting up to see her.

"She had a great day," the teacher tells me.

I take Aveline to the nearby trampoline park and jump with her for a solid hour, sweating profusely and laughing our butts off. This is my new favorite exercise and I do it as often as possible.

On the drive home, Aveline sings songs and I think about life, think about how accepting that my dad would never become my other dad, allowed me to finally accept myself. I remember how in college I learned that every seven years, all of the cells in your body are recycled. *Is it a coincidence that it's been seven years since that night I choked on regurgitated jalapeño corn casserole? Or that another seven years earlier I escaped my dad's house? No. Change isn't just possible, we are biologically wired to do so.*

They say time heals all wounds but it takes more than time, just as gathering of ingredients and passing of time does not magically cook food. Only deliberate actions alchemize ingredients into something else, something better.

I am a whole two of me removed from that house. And I have *done* the work, cried my million tears, come to accept and love who I am. I'm not a delicately prepared, micro-portioned, Michelin star meal. And I no longer desire to be. I am something that took what life dished out for me and turned it into something else entirely. I used to think of myself as a hot mess, but I now know that I am like a casserole, mixing unrefined and unlikely ingredients into something hearty, gritty, plentiful, familiar and most of all real.

As I drive up the street parallel to ours and see our house across the mini-canyon, I notice the embankment glowing lavender from the blooming ice plant. I smile, realizing that the house doesn't look entirely *unlike* the Hearst Castle guest house Sean and I declared as our dream house years ago.

Sean catches running Avie when we walk in and he launches her up in the air. She squeals and says "again, again!" He kisses me hello. It's nice to have him home, as he still travels quite a bit for work, but much, much less than he used to.

"Avie said the funniest thing today," I tell Sean.

"What's that?" he asks.

She said, "Mom-mom, I think I got fired!"

Sean and I burst into laughter and question where the heck she heard that.

Sean tells me about work, even vents a little. I am happy to be there for him and proud of him every time he opens up emotionally. We are in the best place we have ever been in our marriage and it is based on being us, the real, flawed us. And it feels really good to pretend no more. That isn't to say we never have disagreements. We had one last week. Parenting a child has a tendency to illuminate any feelings of inequity. But now, we listen to each other more, remain calm, diffuse the tension and solve the problem. Most of the time. We aren't perfect at that either. Hey, practice makes progress, not perfection.

We open the Styrofoam containers Sean picked up and divvy up sushi and udon soup onto dishes and bowls. We all sit on the couch and watch a movie together. Avie rests her head on the same fleshy part where my chest and shoulder meet that my dad liked to poke so much. How different this feels. Sean rests his hand on my knee. I love my family.

I shoot off texts with travel details and "can't wait to see you!" as I have plans to get together with Connie, Tiff, Erin and Brigid in the coming months. I am no longer waiting for life to start because I am finally living it. I look over and see that Avie and Sean have fallen asleep. I carry Aveline to bed and shake Sean and tell him to go to bed too.

Snuggled up under the covers, I reach over and touch Sean's back, the same back that was beside me on that jalapeño corn casserole night long ago. What a different place we are in. We made it. We are on the other side. Relationships can survive depression, addiction, and the aftermath of abuse. I think back to when Sean and I first met and wish I had been able to be more forthright with him about the extent of my struggles. I suppose the toughest kind of inauthentic person to be is the kind who doesn't even realize they are inauthentic. I am so grateful that with time, patience, tolerance and compassion, two very different people can come together and learn how to be, together.

I gaze at Avie sleeping between us, her little face soft and peaceful and angelic. *I love you!* I kiss her on the forehead. As I roll over to go to sleep, I think to myself, *my life is so different now—so happy, so calm, so peaceful, so... normal.* I smile contentedly at the thought. *And full.*

ACKNOWLEDGEMENTS

Aveline, my love, my muse, my purpose, I am honored to be your mom.

Sean, my husband, thank you for sticking with me through thick and thin (or perhaps better stated, thank you for sticking with me whether I have been thick or thin).

Grandma, you taught me that it only takes one person seeing a child's potential to get them through the darkest and most challenging of circumstances. I miss you every day.

My family and created family, thank you so much for encouraging courageous truth telling. In alphabetical order, I'd like to especially thank:

- Arsineh
- Ashley
- Bernie
- Celine
- Chris
- Cole
- Connor
- Deb

- Edna
- Elise
- Gary
- Glen
- Jean
- Jen
- Liz
- Mike

- Rebecca
- Shelly
- Sherri
- Shannon
- Shannon
- Stephanie

The professionals who helped me on my journey, which were far more numerous than the story's "Sylvie," thank you for sharing your healing wisdom with me. In alphabetical order I'd like to thank:

- Andrew Lindeman, Licensed Therapist
- Britt Felix Lopez, Coach
- Geneen Roth
- Lisa Carpenter of Emerald Quest Coaching
- Lorene Ibbetson
- Mandy Sciacchitano, Coach
- Marc David and the Institute for the Psychology of Eating
- Natalie Baack, Coach
- Shelly Tannehill, Astrologer, Coach
- Teresa Campos, Coach

Teachers who encouraged my writing, you aren't told enough the difference you make.

Editors Mary DeDanan, Debby Englander and the staff at Linda Langton Agency, thank you for your valuable editorial feedback. The book would not be what it is today without it.

Artists Anastasia MacGillivray, Miladinka Milic, Ashley Claure and Catherine Williams, thank you for the photography, cover design, painting and formatting work for this book, respectively.

Youtubers Bethany Atazadeh, Jenna Moreci, Meg LaTorre, and Tom Corson-Knowels, thank you for teaching the public, myself included, how to navigate self-publishing.

Food and Body, you have been my greatest spiritual teachers. Thank you.

And, lastly, I'd like to extend my sincere gratitude to you readers. You are society's implementers of change. Thank you.